Immigrant Performance in the Labour Market

IMISCOE

International Migration, Integration and Social Cohesion in Europe

The IMISCOE Research Network unites researchers from, at present, 28 institutes specialising in studies of international migration, integration and social cohesion in Europe. What began in 2004 as a Network of Excellence sponsored by the Sixth Framework Programme of the European Commission has become, as of April 2009, an independent self-funding endeavour. From the start, IMISCOE has promoted integrated, multidisciplinary and globally comparative research led by scholars from various branches of the economic and social sciences, the humanities and law. The Network furthers existing studies and pioneers new scholarship on migration and migrant integration. Encouraging innovative lines of inquiry key to European policymaking and governance is also a priority.

The IMISCOE-Amsterdam University Press Series makes the Network's findings and results available to researchers, policymakers and practitioners, the media and other interested stakeholders. High-quality manuscripts authored by Network members and cooperating partners are evaluated by external peer reviews and the IMISCOE Editorial Committee. The Committee comprises the following members:

More information and how to join the Network can be found at www.imiscoe.org.

Immigrant Performance in the Labour Market

Bonding and Bridging Social Capital

Bram Lancee

IMISCOE Research

AMSTERDAM UNIVERSITY PRESS

Cover illustration: No Title (from the series Digital Mapping) 2011, oil and spray-paint on canvas, 60 x 30 cm
Artist: Aquil Copier (1973) lives and works in Amsterdam.
www.aquilcopier.nl

Cover design: Studio Jan de Boer BNO, Amsterdam
Layout: The DocWorkers, Almere

ISBN   978 90 8964 357 5
e-ISBN   978 90 4851 495 3 (pdf)
e-ISBN   978 90 4851 661 2 (ePub)
NUR   741 / 763

Table of contents

List of figures and tables

Figures

Tables

Acknowledgements

This book is the result of a migration experience through various academic institutions. It is based on the doctoral research that I carried out at the European University Institute (EUI) in Florence. The manuscript was revised at the University of Amsterdam where I was a postdoc, completed at the Social Science Research Center Berlin (WZB) where I am a Humboldt Research Fellow and the finishing touches were made at Nuffield College, University of Oxford where I am currently a visiting scholar.

I would like to acknowledge the people who were of key importance to the process of writing this book. First, a great many thanks to all my friends and colleagues at the EUI who made doing research such a rewarding experience. Beyond doubt, being at the EUI formed me as an academic. I express gratitude to my supervisor, Martin Kohli (EUI), for his advice and support. I am also truly grateful to Jaap Dronkers (EUI/ Maastricht University), whose enthusiasm and feedback always inspired me. Chapter seven is based on a co-authored paper with Anne Hartung (CEPS/INSTEAD). I thank her for the work we carried out together. Appreciation goes to my colleague and co-author Sergi Pardos-Prado (University of Oxford), in whose office I am writing these words. I have very much enjoyed all our discussions, be they about work or otherwise. I am also indebted to Jonas Radl (Universidad Nacional de Educación a Distancia) for continuing to share his Stata wizardry with me. In the sociology department of the University of Amsterdam, my colleagues offered me an inspiring and productive environment. My colleagues at the WZB proved very welcoming as well as patient with my German. My gratitude also goes to Karina Hof, my editor who converted all of my 'Duchisms' into proper English. Last but not least, I thank my family and friends from the Netherlands for their more-than-enthusiastic support of my endeavors. And I thank Theresa for everything, she was always there for me.

Bram Lancee
Oxford, January 2012

1 Introduction and research questions

One of the main challenges that Western countries are faced with is how to deal with the increasing share of immigrants and their descendants. The incorporation of immigrants into the host society is of utmost importance to social cohesion. In almost all Western societies, the discussion on the consequences of immigration is a key topic on both the public and political agenda. Also among policymakers, the incorporation of immigrants in terms of employment, income and occupational status has been of major concern. The economic incorporation of immigrants in their host society is therefore of great interest to scholars studying the consequences of immigration.

It is well known that immigrants perform worse on the labour market than native residents (see e.g. Heath & Cheung 2007; Borjas 1994). This is also the case in the countries studied in this book. In the Netherlands, for example, in 2008, 10 per cent of the non-Western immigrants were unemployed, compared to 4 per cent of the native population (Statistics Netherlands 2008: 98). In Germany, in 2007, of those with a migration background, slightly under 15 per cent were unemployed, compared to just under 8 per cent for native Germans (Statistisches Bundesamt 2009: 236).

These differences remain when taking into account socio-economic background. Even when controlling for their (host country-specific) human capital and language proficiency, immigrants generally have a lower employment rate, income and occupational status than the native population (Borjas 1994; Heath & Chueng 2007; Heath & Yu 2005), both in Germany (Granato & Kalter 2001) and in the Netherlands (Dronkers & Wanner 2006; Tesser & Dronkers 2007; Van Tubergen & Maas 2006). This also holds for the second generation (for a review, see Heath, Rothon & Kilpi 2008).

One of the approaches to explain the labour market outcomes of immigrants is to use social capital theory. Social capital implies that people well equipped with social resources – in the sense of their social network and the resources of others they can call upon – succeed better in attaining their goals (Flap & Völker 2004: 6). In other words, one's social network can be used as capital. Researchers have suggested that possessing social capital contributes to economic outcomes such as access to the labour market (Aguilera 2002; Granovetter 1995), wages (Aguilera & Massey 2003;

Aguilera 2003; Boxman, De Graaf & Flap 1991) and occupational status (Lin, Ensel & Vaughn 1981; Lin 1999; Franzen & Hangartner 2006).

Especially for immigrants, social networks are important to make headway on the labour market. In Germany, for example, almost 50 per cent of the immigrants find their job through networks; this percentage is even higher for the young and the low-educated (for German native residents, this percentage is around 30; see Drever & Hoffmeister 2008). The use of networks may be an efficient strategy for job-seeking in the face of potential discrimination (Mouw 2002). Furthermore, social capital provides access to host country-specific human capital and job opportunities.

However, other research suggests that, although immigrants rely heavily on their social network for finding a job, this results in lower-quality jobs (Kazemipur 2006; Falcon & Melendez 2001; Elliott 2001) and lower wages (Green, Tigges & Diaz 1999). By 1987, Wilson (1987) had argued in *The truly disadvantaged* that living in an isolated ghetto has two negative consequences for urban blacks: the loss of role models and exclusion from job networks. Stainbach (2008) finds in the United States that using interethnic contacts reduces the ethnic matching of employees, but he does not find any difference in wages with regard to the different types of contacts used. Reviewing the empirical literature on social capital, Mouw (2003, 2006) concludes that the major part of the effect of social capital on finding a job reflects the tendency for similar people to become friends. According to McPherson, Smith-Lovin and Cook (2001: 420), ethnic homophily is the biggest divide in social networks.

A possible approach to better understand these diverging findings is to examine the different forms of social capital. Recent discussions on social capital distinguish between 'bonding' and 'bridging' (Gitell & Vidal 1998; Putnam 2000; Woolcock & Narayan 2000; Leonard & Onyx 2003; Schuller 2007; Szreter & Woolcock 2004). Loosely defined, bonding refers to within-group connections, while bridging social capital refers to between-group connections. It has been argued that returns depend on the different forms of social capital that people possess (Beugelsdijk & Smulders 2003; Putnam 2000; Portes 2000). It is often assumed that, whereas bonding social capital is to 'get by', bridging social capital is to 'get ahead' (Narayan 1999; Putnam 2000). The dilemma is perhaps more accurately described by Flap and Völker (2004: 15): 'A relevant question regarding social capital is to what extent do ties remain within social groups, or to what extent are they also crosscutting and connect the resource-rich with the resource-poor?' In other words, to better understand the returns of social capital, it is necessary to tease apart its different forms.

Distinguishing between different forms of social capital seems especially important for immigrants. First, because social capital – especially bridging – is expected to yield positive returns for immigrants. As Haug (2007) points out, since most employers are natives, it is particularly useful for immigrants to have contacts with natives. Building bridges to the native population is therefore an effective strategy to gain access to host country-specific resources and to circumvent discrimination. Researchers find indeed that interethnic relations can be associated with better labour market outcomes (Ode & Veenman 2003; Haug 2007; Kalter 2006; Kanas, Van Tubergen & Van der Lippe 2009; Lancee & Hartung 2012).

Second, the 'lack' of returns may not be that straightforward with respect to bonding. Ethnic minorities are repeatedly characterised as having a tight social network (Fernandeze-Kelly 1995). This can have advantages as well as disadvantages. On the one hand, networks of immigrants are often characterised as being isolated and therefore hindering economic integration (Portes & Sensenbrenner 1993; Portes 1998, 1995b). That is, being embedded into ethnic networks may impede successful upward mobility due to social obligations, pressure to conformity or downward levelling norms. On the other hand, immigrants' social networks are often said to provide security, high solidarity and opportunities, for example with respect to the ethnic economy (Zhou 1992; Waldinger 1994; Menjivar 2000; Waldinger 2005; Patacchini & Zenou 2008). For instance, family-based and ethnic-based networks are found to be contributing to the performance of immigrants on the labour market (Waldinger 1994; Kloosterman, Van der Leun & Rath 1999; Sanders & Nee 1996; Sanders, Nee & Sernau 2002; Nee & Sanders 2001b; Greve & Salaff 2005).

Research questions

Whereas social capital researchers nowadays agree on a division of the concept in bonding and bridging, these dimensions have not yet been conceptualised systematically (Patulny & Svendsen 2007; Schuller 2007). The objective of this book is to conceptualise bonding and bridging social capital for immigrants and, subsequently, to analyse their impact on the labour market outcomes for the main ethnic minority groups in the Netherlands and in Germany.

This study enriches the academic debate in a twofold manner. A first contribution is theoretical. I develop a conceptual framework for the analysis of bonding and bridging social capital of immigrants. Furthermore, I identify the causal mechanisms that link bonding and bridging social capital to the labour market performance of immigrants. I also contribute to the field by making a cross-national comparison. By including both the Netherlands and Germany, I link the macro-context with the individual-level results. This allows me to control for the possible influence of macro-level differences on the relation between immigrants' social capital and labour market outcomes.

The second contribution is empirical. I contribute to the field by measuring the different forms of social capital more precisely and simultaneously.

To analyse the economic returns of social capital, I use several different outcome variables. As a way of methodological triangulation, I apply different estimation methods.

The research question central to the book is thus: To what extent can bonding and bridging social capital explain the labour market outcomes of immigrants in Germany and the Netherlands? To answer this question, I formulate a variety of sub-questions:

1 How can immigrants' bonding and bridging social capital be conceptualised (chapter 2)?
2 To what extent do the macro-contexts differ in the Netherlands and Germany, and how does this impact the relationship between immigrants' social capital and labour market outcomes (chapter 3)?
3 What are the expected economic returns of immigrants' bonding and bridging social capital (chapter 4)?
4 How can bonding and bridging social capital be measured for immigrants in Germany and the Netherlands (chapters 5, 6 and 7)?

Structure of the book

The book is outlined as follows. Chapter 2 deals with social capital theory. It starts by discussing the elements that form the concept of social capital and explains the approach that I take. Subsequently, taking these elements, the concepts of bonding and bridging social capital are discussed. Chapter 3 describes the macro-contexts for both the Netherlands and Germany. It provides an overview of the macro-context with respect to migration history, migration and integration policy and the labour market. I also discuss here what extent these factors are expected to influence the relationship between immigrants' social capital and labour market performance. In chapter 4, the outcome variables as well as the individual-level hypotheses are discussed. The chapter starts with the concept of labour market outcomes. Secondly, the hypotheses of bonding and bridging social capital are developed, bringing forward five arguments that link immigrants' social capital to their labour market performance. Lastly, chapter 4 discusses the role of human capital and the differences between men and women with respect to social capital. Chapters 5, 6 and 7 contain the empirical results. Chapter 5 presents the results for the Netherlands, chapter 6 for Germany. In chapter 7, using event history analysis, the differential effect of bonding and bridging social capital is analysed for German natives and Turkish immigrants in Germany. In conclusion, chapter 8 brings together the ideas outlined in the theoretical framework and the empirical results.

2 Social capital theory

Introduction

One of the main insights in contemporary social science is that 'no man is an island' (Flap 2002). People are embedded in the social networks that they form and these networks affect their lives. A social network can be considered a social resource, which can produce returns in order to improve the conditions of living. Consequently, people can use their network to better attain their goals. In other words, one's social network can be treated as capital. One of the first to define social capital was Bourdieu (1986: 248). He described social capital as follows:

> The aggregate of the actual and potential resources which are linked to the possession of a durable network of more or less institutionalised relationships of mutual acquaintance and recognition – or in other words, to membership in a group – which provides each of its members with the backing of the collectively-owned capital, a 'credential' which entitles them to credit, in the various senses of the word.

Social capital implies that people well equipped with social resources – in the sense of their social network and the resources of others they can call upon – better succeed in attaining their goals. Second, people will invest in relationships in view of the prospective value of the resources made available by these relations (Flap & Völker 2004: 6). Lin (2001b) defines social capital as 'investment and use of embedded resources in social relations for expected returns' or 'resources that can be accessed or mobilised through ties in the networks' (Lin 2008). Van der Gaag and Snijders (2004: 200) define individual social capital as 'the collection of resources owned by the members of an individual's personal social network, which may become available to the individual as a result of the history of these relationships'.

There is no commonly accepted definition of social capital. A solution to conceptualise it is to discuss the elements that are generally considered to form social capital. In this chapter, I discuss these elements, taking the definition of Van der Gaag and Snijders (2004) as a starting point. These

elements are visualised in Figure 2.1.[1] In the next sections, I first differentiate between cognitive and structural social capital. Second, I discuss
the differences between the use of and access to resources. Third, I differentiate between individual and collective social capital. Using these elements, I conceptualise bonding and bridging social capital for immigrants
in the following two sections.

Cognitive and structural social capital

Social capital can be split into structural and cognitive components (Van
Deth 2008). The structural component refers to the 'wires' in the network:
the extent and intensity of associational links or activity (Poortinga 2006).
As opposed to cognitive social capital, structural social capital involves a
behavioural component. Within structural social capital, one can differentiate between the type of ties and the institutional embeddedness of ties.
That is, structural social capital consists of 1) a collection of ties characterised by the relation between the people connected and 2) the possible institutional embeddedness of these ties. The basic idea of the latter is that
when ties are embedded in institutions, it is more likely that resources will
be exchanged (Putnam 1993; Veenstra 2002; Völker & Flap 1995).

The cognitive component refers to the 'nodes' in the network: the attitudes and values such as perceptions of support, reciprocity and trust that
contribute to the exchange of resources (Poortinga 2006). The most frequently used indicator of cognitive social capital is trust.[2] Trust involves
confidence or faith in the reliability of people, systems or principles
(Veenstra 2002). Often, trust and solidarity are seen as the single component of social capital (Putnam 1993; Fukuyama 1995; Coleman 1990;
Gambetta 1988; Portes & Sensenbrenner 1993). For example, Brisson and
Usher (2005, 2007) operationalise bonding social capital as a scale of trust
and social cohesion on the neighbourhood level. According to Portes and
Sensenbrenner (1993), bounded solidarity and enforceable trust are the
main components of social capital in immigrant communities. In a slightly
different approach, I label the level of solidarity and trust in the nodes of a
network *cognitive* social capital.

Access versus use

Within social capital research, there is a distinction between access to and
the actual use of resources (as discussed by Lin 2001b). In this book, I
consider social capital as *access* to resources. The reason for this is twofold. First, it may be argued that it is not only the resources one actually
uses that are essential, but also the ones that are *potentially* available. An
example is the ability to borrow a large sum of money from a friend: it is
likely that one never borrowed a large sum before, but its potential access

is itself a valuable resource to possess; it is hence part of one's social capital.

However, one can argue that it is the *use* of social capital that results in improved labour market outcomes rather than its access. That is, when analysing the link between having social relations and finding a job, one wants to know whether it is the relations that actually caused it. Measurement of actual use thus seems to be a suitable technique. In this book, I am interested in explaining to what extent a person's social capital can be related to better labour market outcomes, rather than merely explaining whether he or she found a job through the social network (see e.g. Mouw 2003). The latter is a different question: although an individual could have found a job through channels other than social capital (for example, through a regular job application), this does not mean that social capital was not effective. The very fact that an individual applied for a job can be the result of his or her social capital. Furthermore, a person can be hired *because* he or she has a certain level of social capital. For example, Völker and Flap (2004) find that social capital also enhances performance on the job. Mouw (2003: 891) concludes:

> … the benefit of contacts cannot be measured by analyzing the difference in wages for jobs found with and without contacts, because well-connected workers raise their reservation wages so that the wages of all accepted job offers are higher, regardless of whether they were found via contacts.

Hence, it is not the use of relations as such that matter, but the resources that are accessible through one's social network. Moreover, according to Lin and Ao (2008), people often receive useful job information in routine exchanges, rather than in explicit job referrals. Measurement of use by reporting the use of job contacts only may therefore overlook an important part of social capital. This argumentation directly relates to the relevance of cognitive social capital. Following the argument outlined above, it is access to resources that matters. As a logical conclusion, one should not limit measurement to structural elements of social capital.

Moreover, when measuring activated social capital only, one potentially underestimates its effect. For example, Drever and Hoffmeister (2008) investigate to what extent immigrants in Germany found jobs through their social networks. Analysing the returns to social capital in such a manner overlooks the fact that social networks can be effective in other ways as well, such as receiving help with job applications, providing references or negotiating wages. Besides, when analysing the returns of social capital in terms of *finding* employment, one cannot answer the question using activated capital of this kind. Since all people considered already found a job, this would be selecting on the dependent variable.

Figure 2.1   *Different elements of individual social capital*

Individual social capital: the collection of resources owned by the members of an individual's personal social network, which may become available to the individual as a result of the history of these relationships		
Structural: The wires in the network		Congnitive: The nodes in the network
Type of tie	Embeddedness of tie in institution	Attitudes and values

Source: Author

This book thereby analyses whether having access to a number of resources available in one's network can account for a better position on the labour market. In other words, besides the direct effect (such as job referrals), I also aim to include the indirect effect of social capital (such as help with applications).

The second reason for considering social capital as access to resources is practical: measurement of use requires special measurement techniques due to its retrospective nature (see also Van der Gaag 2005: 16-18; Lin 1999), among other things. Because of this, the actual use of social capital is hardly ever included in regular surveys. To properly measure it, one would have to collect new data.

Collective versus individual-level social capital

It is debated whether social capital is a concept that operates at the individual or collective level (Snijders 1999; Kadushin 2004). Some scholars discuss social capital as collectively produced and benefiting the community (Coleman 1990; Putnam 1993, 2000). Others (Bourdieu 1986; Flap 2002; Lin 2001b) have focused on social capital as a pool of resources, which may be helpful for the individual's goal attainment. There is also empirical (multilevel) research that accounts for both the collective and individual levels in social capital (Kim, Subramanian & Kawachi 2006; Poortinga 2006).

When taking the collective approach, it has to be specified what constitutes the 'collective'. A collective or group can be defined by its degree of network closure. In a network with total closure, all individuals are connected with one another (Coleman 1988). A family, for example, is characterised by a high degree of network closure. One could also define the collective by similarity in socio-economic characteristics such as ethnicity, the neighbourhood or, following Putnam (1993; see also Beugelsdijk & Van Schaik 2003), regions or an entire nation. A group is then defined by its similarity and not by the relations people have, per se. The idea is that those who are similar have a higher degree of network closure than those that are not.[3] Thus, additional questions arise, such as: Are all Turks in a country to be seen as a group whose members profit from each other's social network(s)? Do all immigrants in a city form a community? Is a group simply defined by the borders of a nation?

In addition to the difficulties of defining a group, one has to justify that the group *as an entity* profits from the available social resources. For example, when two groups overlap, some people belong to both groups (see Figure 2.2). By belonging to multiple groups, the network becomes larger and more resources are potentially available. Hence, by definition, the amount of social capital increases. If the amount of social capital increases when networks overlap (i.e. bridging social capital), how does this translate into the amount of *collective* social capital? Does the amount of social capital increase equally for those in one group as for those in two groups? This is unlikely. Since people in both networks have ties that provide access to more valuable resources, it is reasonable to assume that the amount of social capital is higher for them than for those in one network. As Lin (2001b: 69) puts it: '[t]he closer individuals are to a bridge in a network the better social capital they will access for instrumental action'. Hence, a group as an entity does not profit equally from overlapping networks.

This implies that different levels of social capital exist within a group. A relevant question is then: What makes the 'collective' in social capital? How is social capital defined on a collective level when different amounts of social capital are present within the group? A solution could be that when estimating social capital on a collective level, one adds up all the

Figure 2.2 *Two partially overlapping social networks*

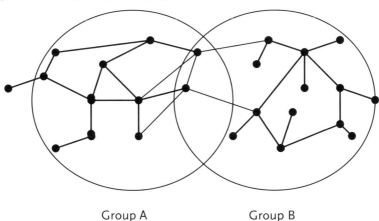

Group A   Group B

Source: Author

social capital of the individuals belonging to the collective. This implies, however, that collective social capital is not more (or less) than the sum of its individual parts.

As noted above, Van der Gaag and Snijders (2004: 200) define *individual* social capital as: '[t]he collection of resources owned by the members of an individual's personal social network, which may become available to the individual as a result of the history of these relationships'. However, this is not the complete picture. One can think of social capital that is not represented by the sum of people's individual social capital. In Figure 2.2, group A contains an individual without ties. Although this person does not have ties, it is very well possible that he or she profits from the social capital available in the group. For example, the group can be a neighbourhood with a high level of trust and well-organised neighbourhood committees. Even without ties, he or she still profits from living in a safe neighbourhood with effective institutions. In other words, there is social capital available to this person that is not represented by his or her individual social capital. This can only be collective since, although belonging to the group, the individual is not part of the social network.

As a result, I define the collective part of social capital as the collection of resources that may become available to *all* members of the group.[4] Since one can belong to a group without having relations to its members, I omit the definition part that specifies 'as a result of the history of these relationships'. The 'all' is essential: if resources are not available to all members, they cannot be a part of collective social capital. In other words, the resources available to member 1 of group A should be also available to member 2 of group A. If they are not, these resources form part of one's individual social capital or those of a sub-group within group A.

Therefore, even when defining one's *individual* capital, a collective part should be added to the definition. An individual's social capital consists of 'the collection of resources owned by the members of an individual's personal social network, which may become available to the individual as a result of the history of these relationships' *plus* 'the collection of resources which may become available to all members of the group(s) one belongs to'.

The choice of a 'collective'

The unit of analysis in this research project is the individual. This implies that in the empirical study, I concentrate on the effects of individual social capital, rather than on the returns of collective social capital. However, since I also identify collective social capital, it has to be decided upon what constitutes the 'collective'.

One way to describe the collective is by using the concept of 'collective identity'. The term 'collective identity' refers 'to those social identities that are based on large and potentially important group differences, e.g. those defined by gender, social class, age, or ethnicity' (Kohli 2000: 117). Collective identity is used to differentiate one group from the other; the ethnic category is one through which people are differentiated. Ethnic identities can be described as 'a subset of identity categories in which eligibility for membership is determined by attributes associated with, or believed to be associated with descent' (Chandra 2006: 398). According to Gonzen, Gerber, Morawska, Pozzetta and Vecoli (1992: 4-5): ethnicity is not a collective fiction, but rather a process of construction of invention which incorporates, adapts and amplifies pre-existing communal solidarities, cultural memories and historical memories. That is, it is grounded in real life context and social experience. People have an ethnic identity, or express 'ethnic solidarity' (Alberts 2005; Grenier & Stepick 1992; Portes & Sensenbrenner 1993; Portes 1995a), which links them to people of the same ethnic category to some extent. According to Portes (1995a: 256), ethnic solidarity among immigrants consists of two elements:

> 1) A common cultural memory brought from the home country and which compromises the customs, mores, and language through which immigrants define themselves and communicate with others, and 2) An emergent sentiment of 'we-ness' prompted by the experience of being lumped together, defined in derogatory terms, and subjected to the same discrimination by the host society.

In this book, the collective is defined as the 'ethnic group'. The argument is that due to their ethnic identity or solidarity, people have on average more ties and/or trust with somebody from the same ethnic origin.

Immigrants are often characterised as having a distinct 'ethnic' social network. Examples include the networks of ethnic entrepreneurs or 'enclave' economies (Kloosterman & Rath 2001; Kloosterman, Van der Leun & Rath 1999; Sanders & Nee 1987), the interrelatedness of ethnic organisations, civic or otherwise (Fennema & Tillie 1999, 2001; Fennema 2004) and closely knit immigrant families that generate social capital (Bankston & Zhou 2002; Zhou & Bankston 1998; Sanders & Nee 1996). These ethnic networks make the exchange of resources among immigrants more likely; there could thus be an aggregate effect between different groups, independent of individual effects (this is also the argument of Putnam 1993).

In other words, an ethnic community possesses collective social capital. For example, Phalet and Heath (2006) refer to ethnic social capital as the social capital of an ethnic community in a city; their proxy for measurement is 'ethnic background'. Equally, I take the ethnic group as the collective. In the empirical analyses (based on quantitative individual level data) I include a dummy for ethnic background, but I do not refer to this as collective social capital. Rather, in the empirical analyses, I test by including interaction terms of whether the effect of individual social capital is different for the ethnic groups included.

To sum up, social capital can be referred to as the collection of resources owned by the members of a social network, which may become available as a result of the history of these relationships. It consists of a structural and a cognitive element. The structural element refers to the wires in the network: the type and institutional embeddedness of ties. The cognitive element refers to the attitudes and values such as perceptions of support, reciprocity and trust that contribute to the exchange of resources. Furthermore, social capital operates on the individual level, i.e. the resources available in the social network of the individual, and on the collective level, which is represented by the resources available in the ethnic community. Whereas the collective part is the same for all members of the ethnic community, the individual part differs per person. This book focuses on individual-level social capital.

Bonding social capital

Bonding social capital implies having dense ties and thick trust. The underlying principle is that of network closure: in a network with closure, members have ties with all members (Coleman 1988). Individual bonding social capital is defined as the collection of resources owned by the members of an individual's close and dense social network, which may become available to the individual as a result of the history of these relationships. Collective bonding social capital is defined as the collection of resources owned by an ethnic community which may become available to all members of the community.

Structural bonding social capital

The clearest case of a network with a high degree of closure is probably the family. In his seminal article 'Social capital in the creation of human capital', Coleman (1988) emphasises the role of the family as a source of social capital. His central argument is that of network closure. With respect to immigrants, as Sanders and Nee (1996: 233) point out: '[a]s a social organisation, the family's chief advantages are not simply tangible products, such as unpaid labour, but also involve the mutual obligation and trust characteristic of small groups'. In their forms-of-capital model for immigrant incorporation into the labour market, Nee and Sanders (2001b) emphasise the pivotal role of the family. Their general argument is that:

> The mode of incorporation is largely a function of the social, human-cultural capital of immigrant families and how these resources

are used by individuals within and apart from the existing structure of ethnic networks and institution. (Nee & Sanders 2001b: 388)

According to their forms-of-capital model, the family is central to the process of incorporation of immigrants in the labour market. They see the family as the primary basis of trust and collective action. Nee and Sanders (2001b: 389) emphasise how 'social ties associated with common ethnicity are unlikely to replicate the household communism and solidarity of the family household or to be as strong as the social ties within extended family networks'. Within the family, social capital is distributed and effectively used (Coleman 1988; Bubolz 2001; Nauck 2001); for example with respect to family businesses (Alesina & Giuliano 2007; Sanders & Nee 1996). Sanders, Nee and Sernau (2002) find a positive correlation between family and ethnically based networks and finding employment for Asian immigrants in the Los Angeles area.

Whereas one may argue whether or not the family network is indeed *the* pivotal element in immigrants' labour market incorporation, the forms-of-capital model emphasises that for immigrants, family networks are of high importance. Nee and Sanders (2001b) refer to the family as both nuclear and extended (see also Menjivar 1997). As Georgas (2006: 4) points out, the nuclear family (mother, father and children) may reflect to a certain degree Western societies' values about family. In most nations, more extensive relations of kinship (paternal and maternal grandparents, aunts, uncles and cousins) are considered family. Moreover, family is not restricted to biological relations (Georgas 2006; Parkin & Stone 2004). Family can thus have a different connotation across different cultures or ethnic groups. Some items in the surveys used in this book refer to 'family' without further specification. In the measurement, one must therefore keep in mind that the perception of 'family' may differ across the various ethnic groups. What is measured is therefore what the respondent refers to as family. In this book, I refer to the 'family' as both nuclear and extended.

Not only do family ties contribute to a network with a high degree of closure. One could classify all ties with co-ethnics as contributing to a dense network with closure (for a review of studies on social relations and closure in ethnic communities, see Sanders 2002). Portes and Sensenbrenner (1993) identify two sources of social capital. 'Bounded solidarity' involves a sense of group solidarity that manifests as a reaction to real or perceived threats of a group, and 'enforceable trust', the monitoring and sanctioning capacity of a group. Parkin (in Sanders 2002: 330) describes 'solidaristic closure', which '... involves social relations with underpinnings of ethnic solidarity that generate and channel opportunities to a cross-section of the group'. Sanders (2002: 348) concludes: '[r]esearch leaves little doubt as to the importance of social capital derived through ethnic networks in promoting economic action'. Besides the family, it seems that the ethnic community is an important source of social capital for immigrants because it contributes to network closure.

However, as Sanders and Nee (1996, 1987) argue, a limitation of solidarity based on ethnic ties, per se, is that it might be difficult to enforce. The reason is that when opportunities are available outside the ethnic community, one is less dependent on ethnic resources; therefore the mechanism that maintains bounded solidarity and enforceable trust within the ethnic group is weaker. Within the family, solidarity is likely to be less vulnerable. As Sanders and Nee (1996: 233) point out: '[c]ooperation in the family stems not simply from self-interest, but from a moral order in which the accumulation of obligations among members builds a solidarity best described as "household communism"'.

There is ample research suggesting that ethnic networks function as a means to make headway on the labour market, since these networks rely on ethnic solidarity and enforceable trust (Waldinger 1995; Portes & Sensenbrenner 1993; Portes 1995b). Furthermore, there is some evidence that, for immigrants, the main source of information on jobs is through relatives and friends, particularly those who belong to the same ethnic origin (Zhou 1992; Menjivar 2000; Waldinger 1994; Pichler 1997). According to the 'enclave' economy hypothesis, those immigrant communities who build enclave economies can – with little assimilation – even achieve economic parity (Wilson & Portes 1980).

As a result, I include family as well as co-ethnic ties in individual structural bonding social capital. Therefore, ties that form bonding structural capital are defined as 'ties that closely connect people and increase the degree of network closure'. On the individual level, this is operationalised as the strength of family and co-ethnic ties, on the collective level as all ties within the ethnic community.

Cognitive bonding social capital

In terms of cognitive social capital, the relations in a network can be characterised by their degree of solidarity and trust (Portes & Sensenbrenner 1993; Szreter & Woolcock 2004). Solidarity networks consist of people who mutually support each other because they share a similar social identity. This support is likely to be limited to insiders (Onyx & Bullen 2000). Portes and Sensenbrenner (1993) identify two sources of social capital. 'Bounded solidarity' involves a sense of group solidarity that manifests itself as a reaction to real or perceived threats of a group and as 'enforceable trust', the monitoring and sanctioning capacity to a group. Bounded solidarity refers to a sense of 'we-ness' in the group, based on outward confrontation.

Trust involves confidence or faith in the reliability of people, systems or principles (Veenstra 2002). Trust is often seen as the main component of social capital (see e.g. Fukuyama 1995; Coleman 1990; Putnam 1993). Within trust, one can differentiate between thick (i.e. specific) and thin (i.e. generalised) trust. Thick trust is associated with strong ties, solidarity, frequent and primary contacts, whereas thin trust refers to instrumental solidarity, loose ties and trust in institutions (Hughes, Bellamy & Black 1999; Newton 1997). The two kinds of trust promote access to different kinds of resources (Patulny & Svendsen 2007). Bonding social capital is associated with thick trust.

The advantage of thick trust – as opposed to thin trust – is that it is more likely that resources will be exchanged (or, in the terms of Portes and Sensenbrenner (1993), enforced). Coleman (1988) relates this to network closure: the combination of closure and thick trust increases the likelihood of resource exchange. Such networks consist of people who mutually support each other because they share a similar social identity. This support is likely to be limited to insiders (Onyx & Bullen 2000). For immigrants, this is likely to be beneficial. For example, Zhou and Bankston (1994) find that Vietnamese immigrants in New Orleans with strong adherence to family values tend to have disproportionately high educational degrees, have more definite university plans and score higher in terms of academic orientation. Zhou and Bankston (1994: 821) conclude that 'strong positive immigrant cultural orientations can function as a form of social capital that promotes value conformity and constructive forms of behaviour'. Moreover, they conclude that conformity to the expectations of the family and the ethnic community provides individuals with resources of support and direction. Hence, thick trust in a social structure contributes to the exchange of resources within this structure. Subsequently, cognitive bonding social capital can be described as the attitudes and values (such as trust and solidarity) that contribute to the exchange of resources among the members of an individual's close and dense network. For the collective level, this refers to the 'attitudes and values (such as trust and solidarity) that contribute to the exchange of resources among the members of an ethnic community'.

Bridging social capital

Bridging social capital is defined by ties that span structural holes and thin trust. On the individual level, this refers to the collection of resources owned by the members of an individual's wide social network, which may become available to the individual as a result of the history of these relationships. Collective bridging social capital refers to the collection of resources not owned by the ethnic community or its individual members, which may become available to all members of the community.[5]

Structural bridging social capital

Structural bridging social capital refers to the collection of ties that form an individual's 'wide' social network. A wide social network is a network that contains structural holes (Burt 1992, 2001). According to Burt (2001: 31):

> [t]he structural hole argument is that social capital is created by a network in which people can broker connections between otherwise disconnected segments. Structural holes separate non-redundant sources of information, sources that are more additive than overlapping.

Structural holes are gaps in networks that provide opportunities to broker the flow of information between people or groups; they therefore create an advantage for the individual whose relationships span the holes. A bridge is a tie that spans a structural hole (Burt 2002). The advantage of bridging ties is that unique information and opportunities come into reach (Putnam 2000: 22). According to Burt (2004), those positioned near a structural hole in a network structure have a higher likelihood of having 'good ideas': people connected across groups are more often confronted with alternative ways of thinking, which gives them more options to select from.

In most empirical studies, no conclusive network information is available; consequently, structural holes cannot be directly observed (see also Marsden 1990). Because only a part of ego's social network is measured, it is not possible to determine exactly which ties of ego span structural holes. They therefore need to be measured with a proxy. Structural holes consist of gaps across relevant socio-economic categories such as class, ethnic group and age (Portes 1998; Narayan 1999). Ties that cut across these socio-economic categories can be taken as a proxy for ties that span structural holes. For example, if ego reports having interethnic ties, this indicates the capacity to span a structural hole between the otherwise disconnected elements of the category 'ethnic group'.

Wuthnow (2002) differentiates two types of bridging ties: identity and status. Identity bridging refers to ties that span culturally defined differences, such as ethnic identity and national origin. Arguably, for immigrants, bridging the ethnic divide and connecting to native residents is the most important form of identity bridging. Interethnic ties are especially important for immigrants, since they are a link out of the ethnic community and consequently create a wider network containing valuable resources and job opportunities (Granovetter 1973; Heath & Yu 2005). For example, Aguilera (2003) finds that friendship networks that are more ethnically diverse positively affect how many hours Mexican immigrants in the US work. Interethnic ties par excellence are interethnic marriages (Bijl, Zorlu, Van Rijn, Jenissen & Blom 2005: 69-74) and friendships with natives

(Haug 2003). The second type of bridging tie concerns status: those ties that span vertical arrangements of power, wealth and prestige.[6] Status bridging suggests possibilities for those with less influence to acquire influence and other resources through their connections with people of higher status. Having status bridging ties may be beneficial for getting jobs or moving up economically (Wuthnow 2002; Granovetter 1973). Since immigrants often have or are perceived to have a lower 'status' than natives, it is likely that interethnic ties contribute to status bridging. In chapter 4, I argue *how* interethnic ties are expected to affect the labour market outcomes of immigrants.

According to Granovetter's (1973) 'strength of weak ties hypothesis', it is usually weak ties that serve as bridges, since strong ties do not provide new information. The strength of a relationship refers to its degree of intensity, frequency, intimacy, reciprocity or acknowledged obligations. The stronger the relationships, the more likely the sharing and exchange of resources (Lin 2001b: 66). However, Burt (2001; see also Lin 1999) points out that it is not necessarily tie strength, per se, but spanning a structural hole that encloses new information. Once a hole is bridged, opportunities to access valuable information increase. In other words, building bridges is the spanning of structural holes, either through strong or weak ties. In the measurement of structural bridging social capital, I therefore define spanning structural holes as having interethnic ties, rather than as having weak ties. This implies that one can have strong ties that are ethnic bridges, such as interethnic marriages. As a result, I include strong interethnic ties, such as having a native-born partner, and weaker ties, such as having native-born friends or acquaintances.[7]

On the individual level, structural bridging can be described as the ties in an individual's social network that cut across the ethnic divide and as that span structural holes. On the collective level, this implies all ties that an ethnic community connects with those not in the community, i.e. interethnic ties.

Bridging institutions are those institutions that contribute to spanning structural holes by establishing crosscutting ties. Some see *all* institutions as facilitators of crosscutting ties, which implies that in measurement the average number of memberships of an individual is sufficient (e.g. Putnam 2000). However, several scholars argue that one should also take into account the diversity of the background of the people involved, the so-called 'heterogeneity argument' (Sabatini 2005: 42-44; Grootaert 2002). I will follow the heterogeneity argument.

For example, Jabobs, Phalet and Swyngedouw (2004; see also Bretell 2005) identify ethnic social capital that is embedded in ethnic associations, as opposed to cross-cultural social capital: embedded in mixed and more mainstream organisations. Stolle (2001) finds that ethnic diversity in voluntary associations (such as sports clubs or self-help groups) in Germany,

Sweden and the US is associated with higher levels of generalised trust.[8] Wuthnow (2002) finds that membership in religious organisations correlates with having high-status friends. In other words, it seems that institutions have two functions: 1) they facilitate building status-bridging ties and 2) when organisations are mixed or more mainstream, they contribute to building interethnic ties. In the empirical analyses, I include being a member of organisations in which most members are native residents of the country.

Cognitive bridging social capital

Cognitive bridging social capital is characterised by thin trust, which 'tends to be associated with the organic solidarity or gesellschaft of looser, more amorphous, secondary relations' (Newton 1997: 578). Thin trust is also associated with confidence in institutions or in the government (Nooteboom 2007). Thin trust is often related to values of modern society.

Uunk (2003) analyses the 'modern' attitudes of the four main immigrant groups in the Netherlands. He differentiates between 1) the gender-specific division of roles, 2) the role of women in society, 3) central family issues such as marriage and children, 4) authority relations, 5) moral issues and 6) religion. For immigrants in the Netherlands, Uunk finds a relation between modern attitudes and the extent of interethnic contacts. Ode and Veenman (2003) also include outward orientation in their analysis, which includes both opinions on interethnic contacts and use of the host society's language. They find that both modernisation and outward orientation positively contribute to the economic integration of immigrants in the Netherlands.

Cognitive bridging social capital can be described as thin trust, that is, the attitudes and values such as modernisation and outward orientation that contribute to the exchange of resources in one's wide social network.

Conclusion

The elements of bonding and bridging social capital are summarised in Figure 2.3. Bonding social capital refers to the collection of resources owned by the members of an individual's close and dense social network, which may become available to the individual as a result of the history of these relationships. A close and dense network has a high degree of closure, i.e. a high degree of interconnectivity among its members. A higher degree of closure implies a higher likelihood that resources will be exchanged. Structural bonding is operationalised as family and co-ethnic ties. The key concept for cognitive bonding social capital is thick trust. It refers to the attitudes and values that contribute to exchange of resource in

Figure 2.3 *The elements of immigrants' bonding and bridging social capital*

Social capital		Bonding	Bridging
Individual	Structural	Network closure • Family ties • Co-ethnic ties	Structural holes • Interethnic ties • Access to institutions that contain mainly native residents
	Cognitive	Thick trust • Family values • Solidarity/reciprocity	Thin trust • Outward orientation • Modernisation values
Collective	Structural	Network closure in an ethnic community Access to ethnic institutions in an ethnic community	'Structural holes' in an ethnic community
	Cognitive	Thick trust in ethnic community	Thin trust in an ethnic community

Source: Author

one's close and dense network. This is operationalised as the importance of and attitudes on solidarity and reciprocity within the family. The collective level refers to the ethnic community. On the collective level, the resources to be potentially exchanged are available for all members of the community.

Bridging social capital refers to the collection of resources owned by the members of an individual's wide social network, which may become available to the individual as a result of the history of these relationships. A wide social network is one that contains structural holes. When a structural hole is spanned, unique and valuable resources can be accessed. A bridge is operationalised as an interethnic tie. For cognitive bridging, the key concept is thin trust, which refers to the attitudes and values that contribute to the exchange of resources in an individual's wide social network.

Notes

1   When empirically searching for the elements within social capital, Onyx and Bullen (2000: 36-37) come to similar conclusions. They construct the following factors: 'A) refers to participation within local community organizations and events, B) refers to agency or proactivity in a social context, C) refers to feelings of trust and safety. Factors D, E and F are concerned with participation and connection within a variety of contexts, within the neighbourhood (D), among family and friends (Factor E), and within the workplace (Factor H).'

2   For a discussion on social capital and trust, see Fukuyama (1995, 2001) or Gambetta (1988).

3   In many studies, it is not possible to determine the degree of network closure. When doing empirical research, it therefore seems reasonable to theoretically discuss the degree of closure and use similarity on socio-economic criteria as a proxy.

4   Note that 'may become available' refers to the differentiation between the access and use of resources, rather than to a question of available for 'whom'; if accessible, the resources are available to all members of the group.

5   Note that on the collective level it is the resources that are not owned by the community: they are all resources available through between-group connections, available to all community members. The resources owned by the community are defined as collective bonding social capital.

6   Since bridging is a horizontal metaphor, the ties between people with a different authority or social-economic status (i.e. vertical ties) are sometimes also referred to as linking social capital (Woolcock & Narayan 2000; World Bank 2001: 128).

7   Granovetter (1973) defines the strength of a tie as a combination of the amount of time spent investing in it, emotional intensity, intimacy and reciprocity. Whether friendships are considered to be weak or a strong ties depends on the reference category. If compared to acquaintances or fleeting relations, friendships are clearly the stronger ties. If compared to family members, friendships are considered weak ties.

8   However, more heterogeneity does not always mean that more cross-cutting ties are built: Alesina and La Ferra (2000) find that in neighbourhoods with ethnic diversity, participation in social activities is much lower.

3 Immigrants in Germany and the Netherlands

Introduction

Migration background and its terminology

The concept of migration background categorises people with respect to their migration experience. It not only refers to those who have migrated themselves, but also to foreign people who are residents in the destination country and to all their descendants (Statistisches Bundesamt 2009).

In the field of migration research, there are several ways to label people with a migration background and people without one. Within the former category, those who have migrated themselves are generally labelled 'first-generation immigrants'. There is less consensus about how to label their descendants: the children of immigrants and their subsequent generations. They are referred to as second- or third-generation migrants; some refer to them as ethnic minorities or as native-born with non-native heritage (i.e. non-Dutch or non-Germany heritage in these cases). Strictly speaking, the term 'native' refers to someone born in the country of residence. From this perspective, a second-generation migrant should also be labelled 'native'. The question is why someone would be classified as an immigrant (second-generation or otherwise) if he or she was born in the country and holds its citizenship? Those who have no migration background are often classified as native, as the majority group or as the indigenous population.

Within this discussion, there are differences in the statistical categorisation of people. Identifying criteria may differ, including characteristics such as place of birth, parents' place of birth and the individual's age at immigration. Often, the categorisation does not depend on substantial considerations, but on what is available in the data. Particularly when comparing countries with different immigration regimes, it usually impossible to harmonise classification. For example, while Germany often categorises according to nationality, the most common criteria in the Netherlands is place of birth and parents' place of birth. This is also the case in the survey data used for my empirical analyses: in the case of the Netherlands, people are categorised based on their country of birth and that of their parents, while in the German case they are categorised by country of birth and nationality.

In this book, 'first-generation immigrant' refers to people who were born abroad and migrated to another country older than age six and whose parents were born abroad as well. Their citizenship may be that of the country of origin or that of the country of destination. I refer to their descendents as 'second-generation minorities' or, simply, as the 'second generation'. The second generation thus comprises people who were born in the country of current residence with at least one parent born abroad, as well as people who were born abroad and migrated to another country at the age of six or younger with at least one parent born abroad. In Germany, people holding a non-German nationality who were born in Germany or migrated to Germany at the age of six or younger are also considered second-generation ethnic minorities.

To differentiate between people with a migration background and those without one, I use the term 'immigrant' or 'ethnic minority' versus 'native'. By classifying all people with a migration background this way, I am grouping first and second generations together under one heading. Even though the second generation in most cases did not migrate themselves, I apply the label 'immigrant' when referring to both them and the first generation. Where relevant, the two generations are referred to separately. This implies that in this book, the term 'native' does not include the second generation. 'Native Dutch' refers to someone who was born in the Netherlands, possesses Dutch nationality and whose both parents were born in the Netherlands. 'Native German' follows the same criteria for Germany. Finally, to differentiate among different countries of origin, I use the term 'ethnic group'.

Migration history and background of the ethnic groups

The Netherlands

The way ethnic minorities are identified in the Netherlands is determined by the country's migration history. In the Netherlands, adherence to an ethnic minority is classified by an individual's country of birth and his or her parents' country of birth, rather than by nationality. This approach was pursued as a way to differentiate the native Dutch from people from Suriname and the Netherlands Antilles, as those two countries were part of the Kingdom of the Netherlands and its natives were hence also Dutch citizens.

The ethnic minorities discussed by politicians and most scholars comprise the immigrant communities who settled in the Netherlands after World War II, the result of colonial history and the guest worker agreements (Guiraudon, Phalet & Ter Wal 2005). Minorities were perceived by the government as having a different background, language, culture and religion; this was the primary reason for the difficulties they faced.

Immigrants were therefore only classified as ethnic minorities if their economic situation was worse than that of the native Dutch (Guiraudon,
Phalet & Ter Wal 2005). With respect to policy that was to be developed,
ethnic minorities were thus not only defined by their ethnic background,
but also by their socio-economic position and the responsibility the Dutch
state felt towards them.

In Table 3.1, the twenty largest ethnic groups in the Netherlands are
listed, classified by their country of birth and that of their parents. For
comparison, in Table 3.2, the most frequently occurring nationalities are
listed. The main differences between the tables lie in Dutch colonial history. Based on country of birth, the two biggest ethnic minority groups in
the Netherlands are Germans and Indonesians (see Table 3.1). A classification of ethnic minorities based on socio-economic status, however, has kept
Germans and Indonesians classified as 'Western Immigrants' and therefore
not traditionally included in policies towards ethnic minorities (Guiraudon,
Phalet & Ter Wal 2005).

For this reason, most studies focus on the four largest immigrant groups
and their descendants who are deemed socio-economically disadvantaged:
Turks, Moroccans, Surinamese and Antilleans (see also Bijl et al. 2005).
Suriname and the Netherlands Antilles were former Dutch colonies, while
Moroccans and Turks came to the Netherlands in the 1960s providing
mainly unskilled labour. From the 1960s until the 1990s, these four groups
dominated immigration. In the 1990s, Dutch immigration patterns changed
due to refugees arriving from other countries.

The first immigrants from Turkey arrived in the 1960s to supply the
shortage of low-skilled labour. A labour agreement between Turkey and
the Netherlands institutionalised the flow of workers. From then until the
early 1970s, immigration increased rapidly; at the end of 1973, the agreement expired and Turkish immigrants were no longer allowed to enter the
Netherlands as workers (Ter Wal 2007; Bevelander & Veenman 2006,
2004). Due to family reunification and formation, the migration flow did
not, however, decrease in the 1980s.

Morocco's first migrants arrived in the Netherlands in the 1960s as well.
Mostly men with a poor educational background, predominantly recruited
through the agency of the Moroccan government, came to perform mainly
unskilled labour. Many were from the Rif, a poor region and one of the
country's more traditional parts. Most of the workers arrived assuming they
would return to Morocco as soon as they had saved enough money to start
a business of their own. When the labour agreement with Morocco was
stopped in 1973, the migration flow was expected to decrease. However,
due to family reunification, the number of Moroccans actually increased in
the years after 1973. Family reunification peaked in the mid-1980s; at this
point, marriage migration started as future partners began moving to the
Netherlands.

Table 3.1   *Largest ethnic groups in the Netherlands as of 1 January 2007, by country of birth*

	First + second generations		First generation[1]		Second generation[2]	
	N	%[3]	N	%[3]	N	%[3]
Indonesia	389,940	2.38	126,048	0.77	263,892	1.61
Germany	381,186	2.33	101,221	0.62	279,965	1.71
Turkey	368,600	2.25	195,113	1.19	173,487	1.06
Suriname	333,504	2.04	186,025	1.14	147,479	0.90
Morocco	329,493	2.01	167,893	1.03	161,600	0.99
Netherlands Antilles and Aruba	129,965	0.79	78,907	0.48	51,058	0.31
Belgium	112,224	0.69	36,126	0.22	76,098	0.47
Former Yugoslavia	76,465	0.47	52,857	0.32	23,608	0.14
United Kingdom	75,686	0.46	42,604	0.26	33,082	0.20
Poland	51,339	0.31	34,831	0.21	16,508	0.10
Former Soviet Union	47,450	0.29	35,962	0.22	11,488	0.07
China	45,298	0.28	31,236	0.19	14,062	0.09
Iraq	43,891	0.27	34,729	0.21	9,162	0.06
Afghanistan	37,230	0.23	31,330	0.19	5,900	0.04
Italy	36,495	0.22	17,163	0.10	19,332	0.12
France	33,845	0.21	17,095	0.10	16,750	0.10
United States	31,154	0.19	18,957	0.12	12,197	0.07
Spain	31,066	0.19	16,897	0.10	14,169	0.09
Iran	28,969	0.18	23,526	0.14	5,443	0.03
Cape Verde	20,181	0.12	11,444	0.07	8,737	0.05
Other						
Total	3,170,406	19.38	1,601,194	9.79	1,569,212	9.59
Native Dutch	13,187,586	80.62				
Total population	16,357,992	100				

[1] Refers to those born abroad with at least one parent who was born abroad.
[2] Refers to those born in the Netherlands with at least one parent who was born abroad.
[3] All % expressed as a share of the total population.
Source: Statistics Netherlands (2007)

Being a former colony, Suriname has a long migration history in the Netherlands. The first immigrants consisted mainly of elite and middle-class Surinamese, arriving to study or to seek good schooling for their children. In the early 1970s, low-skilled Surinamese also moved to the Netherlands. Suriname's independence in 1975 caused a boom in which over 50,000 people moved to the Netherlands, having anticipated more difficult entry into the former mother country. At the end of 1980, the Dutch government introduced visa requirements to enter the Netherlands from Suriname. This was anticipated by many Surinamese, leading to a second wave of some 30,000 Surinamese arriving in the Netherlands in 1979 and

Table 3.2 *Most common nationalities in the Netherlands as of 1 January 2007*

	N	%
Turkish	96,779	0.59
Without/unknown	89,268	0.55
Moroccan	80,518	0.49
German	60,201	0.37
British	40,335	0.25
Belgian	25,999	0.16
Polish	19,645	0.12
Italian	18,627	0.11
Spanish	16,468	0.10
Chinese	15,266	0.09
French	14,697	0.09
United States	14,641	0.09
Portuguese	12,234	0.07
Indonesian	11,389	0.07
Surinamese	7,561	0.05
Greek	6,627	0.04
Japanese	5,736	0.04
Thai	5,504	0.03
Indian	5,381	0.03
Other	135,056	0.83
Dutch	15,676,060	95.83
Total	16,357,992	100.00

Source: Statistics Netherlands (2007)

1980. Due to economic and political reasons, immigration increased again in the 1990s (Bevelander & Veenman 2004; Vermeulen 2005a). At the beginning of 2007, the Netherlands counted as part of its population 333,504 Surinamese, 44 per cent of whom are considered second generation (see Table 3.1).

The Kingdom of the Netherlands today comprises four countries: the Netherlands, Aruba,[1] St. Maarten and Curaçao. Until 2010, the Netherlands Antilles consisted of five islands in the Caribbean Sea: Bonaire, Saba, the southern half of the island of Saint Martin (i.e. Sint Maarten), Saint Eustatius and Curaçao. Since 2010, St. Maarten and Curaçao have been separate countries from the Kingdom of the Netherlands, while Saba, Saint Eustatius and Bonaire are special municipalities of the Netherlands. I refer to immigrants from these five islands as 'Antilleans'.

The first immigration wave from the Antilles started in the 1960s, when Dutch companies recruited workers, mainly unskilled though later also skilled. After 1973 and again after 1985, the migration of unskilled workers increased rapidly. In the early 1990s, due to high unemployment in the Antilles, many young people moved to the Netherlands. This created quite a contrast: whereas the second generation had managed to bridge the

educational gap with the native Dutch, the young new immigrants were se-
verely disadvantaged in terms of educational attainment, language proficiency (Bevelander & Veenman 2004) and labour market position.

Germany

As in the Netherlands, migration history in Germany determines which categories are used to classify people as an ethnic minority. For a long time,
Germany had defined immigrants and their descendants by nationality,
though more recently came to adopt the concept of migration background.
Differences concerning incorporation regimes are discussed in more detail
in the 'Immigration and integration policy' section. Meanwhile, here I
briefly discuss the migration history of Germany and its ethnic minority
groups.
    Since the criterion to differentiate 'native' Germans from other ethnic
groups was that of nationality, census data on country of birth is not available in Germany (Statistisches Bundesamt 2009). Until 2000, nationality
was primarily based on the principle of ius sanguinis. Since nationality
was based on ancestry and not on place of birth, the second generation
could also be distinguished from native Germans by their nationality. Table
3.3 lists the most common nationalities in Germany.
    However, in 2000, the naturalisation law changed drastically and, be-
sides ius sanguinis, also included ius soli, the place-of-birth principle. To
identify those with a migration background, classification of people based
on nationality was no longer sufficient. Hence, the German Office of
Statistics adopted the principle of migration background and now incorporates this principle in its micro-census. The concept of migration background does not identify people's country of birth, per se,[2] but differentiates them according to their migration experience. The idea is that the concept of migration background not only refers to those who have migrated
themselves, but also to foreign people who are residents in Germany and
all their descendants (Statistisches Bundesamt 2009). People with a migration background are considered

> all people who migrated after 1949 to the current territory of the
> German Republic, as well as all foreigners born in Germany and all
> those German-born in Germany with at least one parent who mi-
> grated, or with one parent who is born as a foreigner in Germany.
> (Statistisches Bundesamt 2009: 6, author's translation)

Those with a migration background can be split up into those with and
without migration experience. Of the 15.4 million people with a migration
background, 10.5 million have migration experience themselves; the rest
were born in Germany. In both categories, there are people who do and do

not hold German nationality. In 2007, there were 15.4 million people with a migration background, 18.7 per cent of the population. Of those, 7.3 million (8.9 per cent of the population) do not have the German nationality. In Figure 3.1 an overview of the categories and their figures for 2007 is presented.

With respect to migration flows, Germany has for much of its history been a 'sending', rather than 'receiving', country. This changed only shortly after World War II. However, this is not to say that immigration did not exist before that. For example, in 1910, there were 1.3 million foreigners registered in Germany, nearly half of them from Austria. In 1925, this number was one million, with more than one quarter comprising Poles as the dominant group (Kalter & Granato 2007; Münz 2002).

Post-war migration to Germany can roughly be split into five waves. Directly after World War II, millions of refugees and expellees from former German territory arrived in Germany. Due to the right of political asylum and the citizenship law in Germany, *Aussiedler* – as people with German ancestry living in Eastern European states were known – could claim citizenship upon arrival. They came mainly from former German territories in Eastern Europe and from the Soviet Union and its sphere of influence. Up

Figure 3.1 *People with a migration background in Germany*

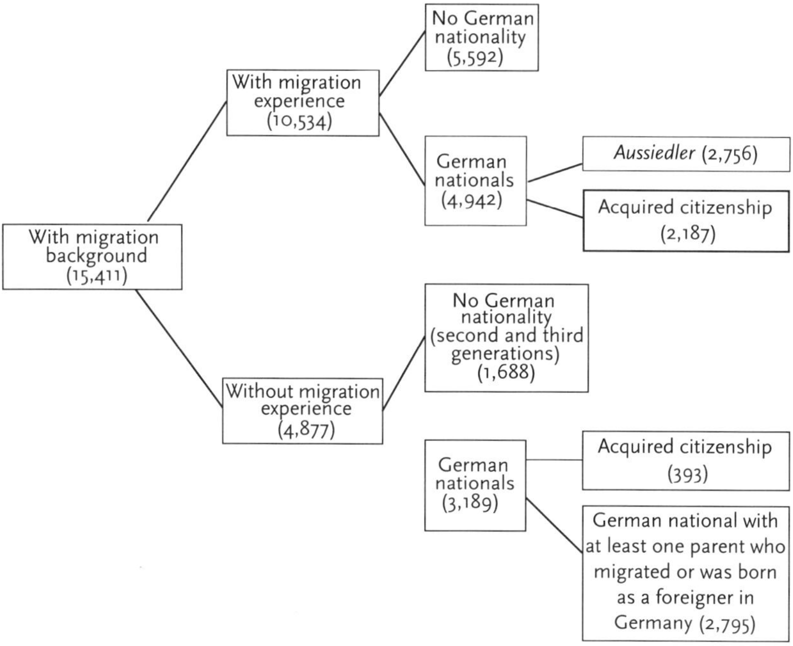

Note: Numbers in thousands
Source: Micro Census 2007, Statistisches Bundesamt 2009

until construction of the Berlin Wall in 1961, citizens of the German Democratic Republic (GDR) were the most significant immigrant group in the Federal Republic of Germany (FRG) (Kalter & Granato 2007); GDR citizens were also seen as FRG citizens by the West German state.

This first wave was followed by about fifteen years that were dominated by the immigration of guest workers. In the FRG, recruitment of guest workers started in the 1950s. Due to the accelerating economy, Germany faced a shortage in the labour force and started an active recruitment policy (Ireland 2004). Germany established guest worker agreements with Italy (1955), Greece and Spain (1960), Turkey (1961), Morocco (1963), Portugal (1964), Tunisia (1965) and Yugoslavia (1968). The recruitment policy officially ended in the wake of the oil crisis in 1973.

The abolishment of the guest worker programmes marks the transition to the third wave. After 1973, migration in Germany mainly consisted of family reunification and asylum seekers from politically unstable countries. Between 1975 and 1981, family reunification accounted for 50 to 70 per cent of the influx (Velling 1993; Kalter & Granato 2007). In the GDR, borders were closed to migrant workers until the early 1980s, when the country began 'importing' workers from other socialist states, mainly Poland, Cuba, Mozambique and Vietnam (Cyrus & Vogel 2007).

The fourth wave is marked with a shift from the classic labour migration to new arrivals seeking asylum and 'ethnic' Germans (people with German ancestry living in Eastern European states, the so-called *Aussiedler*). When in 1989 more than 377,000 *Aussiedler* arrived, more restrictive measures were proposed (Kalter & Granato 2007).

These restrictions (both for *Aussiedler* as well as for asylum seekers) were implemented in 1993, which marks the beginning of the fifth phase. In this, the current phase, immigration to Germany dominantly consists of new labour migrants from Poland, the Czech Republic and other Eastern European states (Kalter & Granato 2007).

Leaving aside the immigrants with German citizenship, Germany's main immigrant groups today are Turks, Italians, followed by Poles, former Yugoslavians and Greeks (see Table 3.3). One must be careful, though, when interpreting Table 3.3, as only nationalities are listed. Ethnic Germans therefore all end up under the German nationality category. Furthermore, it is not possible to identify the second generation accurately. Naturalised Germans as well as those recently born of immigrant parents are therefore not identified. The naturalised first generation is also unidentifiable.

The German micro-census provides some insight into the size of the ethnic groups living in Germany. The micro-census consists of a 1 per cent sample of households. Kalter and Granato (2007) describe the immigrant population with the micro-census and calculate that roughly one out of six migrants can be designated as belonging to the second generation. Since

Table 3.3 *Most common nationalities in Germany as of 31 December 2007*

	%	Absolute numbers
Turkish	2.08	1,713,551
Italian	0.64	528,318
Polish	0.47	384,808
Serbian Montenegrin	0.40	330,608
Greek	0.36	294,891
Croatian	0.27	225,309
Russian	0.23	187,835
Austrian	0.21	175,875
Bosnia and Herzegovinian	0.19	158,158
Dutch	0.16	128,192
Ukrainian	0.15	126,960
Portuguese	0.14	114,552
French	0.13	106,549
Spanish	0.13	106,301
US	0.12	99,891
UK	0.12	97,070
Other nationality	3.02	2,476,527
German	91.18	74,962,442
Total	100	82,217,837

Source: Central Register of Foreigners (www.destatis.de)

they arrived earlier, the guest worker immigrants represent a somewhat higher fraction. Furthermore, the report 'People with a migration background' (Statistisches Bundesamt 2009) provides some information on the current and the former nationalities of those naturalised. Table 3.4 lists people with a migration background (i.e. the left box in Figure 3.1), split up by nationality, showing the largest groups only.

Germany and the Netherlands compared

The migration history of the Netherlands and Germany is thus rather different. Whereas migration to Germany has been dominated by immigration of ethnic Germans and asylum seekers, as well as of guest workers and their descendants, immigration to the Netherlands has been dominated by influxes from former colonies and guest workers and their descendants. Furthermore, the classification of people was different, although nowadays the countries have become more similar in this respect. In the Netherlands, people are classified by country of birth and their parents' country of birth. In Germany, up until 2000, nationality was the main criterion; since then, place of birth is also taken into account.

Besides the differences in 'types' of ethnic minorities, another difference concerns the ethnic groups themselves. Aside from Western European immigrants, these countries have only one large ethnic group in common: Turks. As Van Tubergen (2004) shows, the specific combination of origin

Table 3.4   *People with a migration background in Germany, by current or former*
nationality (if current nationality is German)

			Absolute numbers*	Relative numbers
	Of which:	Of which:		
Europe			8,499	55.15
	EU-27		3,686	23.92
		Greece	384	2.49
		Italy	761	4.94
		Poland	638	4.14
		Romania	240	1.56
	Further Europe		4,813	31.23
		Bosnia Herzegovina	283	1.84
		Croatia	373	2.42
		Russian Federation	561	3.64
		Serbia	391	2.54
		Turkey	2,527	16.40
		Ukraine	215	1.40
Africa			480	3.11
America			346	2.25
Asia, Australia, Oceania			1,501	9.74
		Kazakhstan	215	1.40
Not specified			4,586	29.76
Total			15,411	100

* X 1,000
Source: Micro Census 2007, Statistisches Bundesamt (2009: 132)

and destination country has an impact on the economic incorporation of
immigrants. With respect to returns to social capital, differences between
Germany and the Netherlands could therefore be attributed to composition
effects.

Besides the various ethnic groups, there may also be differences in population size or concentration. For example, levels of residential segregation generally seem to be lower in Germany than the Netherlands (Musterd
2005; Koopmans 2010). Furthermore, there may be differences in educational levels. For example, Van Suntum and Schlotböller (2002) show that
educational attainment of non-Western immigrants in the Netherlands is
lower than that of natives, but this difference is larger in Germany. On the
other hand, Doomernik (1998) finds that educational levels are lower for
immigrants in the Netherlands than in Germany.

In the empirical analyses, I will try to control for compositional differences by including the ethnic groups and educational attainment as control
variables in the models. There are, however, differences that cannot be

controlled for, such as the fact that there are simply different ethnic groups in the two countries.

Immigration regime and integration policy

The Netherlands

In the Netherlands, policy specifically targeted towards immigrants started in 1960s with bilateral agreements to admit temporary workers to the Netherlands. Entzinger (2001: 322-334) classifies the policy aimed towards the integration of immigrants chronologically. The next sections briefly describe these policy eras (based on Entzinger 2001).

The first period (1950-1961) is characterised by 'avoidance'. In this post-war decade, since birth rates were high and the country was recovering from war, emigration was encouraged. At the same time, immigrants started arriving in the Netherlands, mainly from the colonies. These people integrated smoothly, as they were mostly Dutch citizens and could speak Dutch. Furthermore, an expanding labour market and a strong assimilative policy characterised the era. This did not hold for arriving Moluccans, who were exiled from Indonesia. Since they were supposed to return as soon as the political situation would allow them to, public policy promoted the opposite of assimilation. For example, they were initially held in separate camps and were not allowed to take up employment.

The second period (1961-1980) is characterised by Entzinger (2001) as one of 'ambivalence'. The first year with an immigration surplus was 1961. Unskilled migrant workers arrived and were supposed to fill temporary gaps at the bottom of the labour market. The policy response was no longer that of assimilation but of preserving of one's own culture. Although people were expected to return to their places of origin, the Dutch welfare state generally treated immigrants just like its other citizens. Until the mid-1970s, labour migration was only minimally regulated. Often, regulation took place even after arrival. From 1975 onwards, not the employee but the employer had to demonstrate the need for foreign workers. Although immigration was now restricted, family reunification became a significant source of migration (Doomernik & Jandl 2008). Since employers could request foreign workers, immigration was not actually fully restricted.

Due to a rising number of immigrants, their concentration in urban centres and a changing labour market, the problems of the ambivalent policy became visible. In the period 1980-1994, a conscious ethnic minorities policy was developed, realising that most immigrants were to stay for good. Under this policy, people were seen as members of an ethnic group rather than as individuals. The basic assumption of the policy was that in the wake of immigration, the Netherlands had become a multi-ethnic society

in which majority and minority should live harmoniously, with equal opportunities for everyone. In practice, this meant integration with preserva-
tion of own identity. Three basic elements formed the policy. First, emanci-
pation in a multicultural society, which was the successor of the former
period's emphasis on cultural identity. Second, equality before the law. In
this spirit, foreign residents should neither be forced to take up Dutch citizenship nor be at a disadvantage because of their own. Third, the promotion of equal opportunity. This resulted in a range of measures, such as
granting minorities equal access to housing and education.

   From 1994 onwards, integration policy changed, emphasising multiculturalism less and integration more. Citizenship became more important, not
only legally but also in terms of the cultural meaning attached to it. The
new integration policy was no longer limited to ethnic minority communities, in particular, but to the society as a whole. The philosophy was that
the ethnic minority concept should be an integral aspect of public policy in
all fields. In each policy area, it had to be insured that minorities benefit
sufficiently. The group approach shifted in this period to a more individual
approach. Also, the state now more heavily emphasised the need to learn
the Dutch language and other social skills to function in society.
Furthermore, entry to the Netherlands was made much stricter by the new
asylum law of 2001.

Germany

Despite the substantial immigrant population, only with the Immigration
Act of 2005 did Germany officially acknowledge that immigration is taking place and is something that should be properly organised (Cyrus &
Vogel 2007). Up until then, the German state's stance was simply that it
was not an immigration country (*kein Einwanderungsland*). Although other
countries also held this position, according to Joppke (1999: 62), 'the only
country that has not become tired of repeating it and evaluating it to the
first principle of public policy and self-definition is Germany'. Guest worker immigration was supposed to be temporary. This, however, does not
mean that no policy existed.

   German immigration policy up until the 1990s is often described as exclusionary (Sainsbury 2006; Green 2004). On the one hand, immigration
was open to all 'ethnic' Germans, who could claim citizenship upon arrival. Easy access was also granted to refugees. On the other hand, immigration was very restricted for all others, since nationality was defined in
terms of ethnic descent. In practice, this meant that citizenship was granted
to *Aussiedler* practically directly upon arrival, whereas other non-ethnic
German immigrants were only eligible for citizenship under specific conditions. These conditions included fifteen years of residence, no prior convic-
tions and the ability to earn one's own livelihood (Takle 2007;

Zimmerman, Bonin, Fahr & Hinte 2007). Besides entering Germany as an *Aussiedler* or a refugee, one could enter under a guest worker programme and receive a residence permit or for family reunification (albeit with very limited possibility of acquiring citizenship) (Zimmerman et al. 2007).

In the 1990s, the German immigration policy changed from being exclusionary and ethnic-based to one that was more inclusive for immigrants with a residence permit (Münz 2002; Takle 2007). The citizenship law of 2000 changed access to citizenship drastically: in addition to the principle of descent, the principle of birthplace was introduced. Children of foreign-born parents thus automatically qualify for German citizenship if at least one parent was born in Germany or has been a legal citizen for at least eight years. Prior to their 23rd birthday, they must opt for either German citizenship or that of their parents (Zimmerman et al. 2007: 14-15). In contrast, people who have German citizenship on the basis of German descent can keep their second nationality (Sainsbury 2006). Having to give up their nationality has prevented some from applying for German citizenship, since they do not want to give up their other nationality or its attached privileges. For example, Turks lose their right to inherit land in Turkey if they give up their citizenship (Faist 2007). In 2004, Germany adopted the German immigration act, which made it easier for high-skilled workers to emigrate to Germany, although the labour market remains relatively closed-off for low-skilled workers (Zimmerman et al. 2007).

The German welfare state grants immigrants and their descendents the same social rights as German nationals: 'The welfare state is nationality blind, only residence in the territory and labour force participation matters' (Joppke 1999: 190). Since entitlement to social benefits is determined by labour market participation, labour migrants have rights similar to the native residents (Sainsbury 2006). However, these rights are acquired by participation in the labour market, thus being dependent on the contributions made. Furthermore, long-term dependence on social assistance can disqualify immigrants from acquiring citizenship or a permanent residence permit (Koopmans, Statham, Giugni & Passey 2005). Newly entering family members are also at a disadvantage. For example, to obtain a permanent resident permit in Germany one must have made five years of social insurance contributions. Yet, an arriving spouse is banned from employment for two years (it was four years before the rule amendment in 2000) (Morris 2002). By contrast, *Aussiedler* are granted German citizenship with full social rights and recognised refugees enjoy far more favourable rights than other immigrants.

Besides social assistance, it is difficult to get insight in policies established explicitly to promote integration. Until 1997, there was no legal framework that set integration of immigrants and their descendants as a key task (Liebig 2007). Liebig (2007: 25) notes:

As a consequence, policy action has resorted to other areas, such as employment promotion, youth support and welfare assistance. When this was insufficient, federal and non-governmental actors stepped in. This has resulted in a large variety of governmental and non-governmental actors at all levels, shared responsibilities, and a plethora of co-financed and project-based activities.

In other words, the approach was not uniform, but many policy initiatives and responsibilities were divided among different ministries.

Since the change of the citizenship law and the immigration act of 2005, Germany is developing an explicit integration policy that is in many respects similar to that of the Netherlands. The integration of newcomers with the objective to stay is a policy objective, as is granting more secure residence rights and integration courses (Bade, Bommes & Münz 2004). The policy actively targets immigrants in helping them self-integrate on the labour market and in society at large. It provides language training for all new arriving immigrants, provides specific programmes to support the education of immigrants and their children and offers career advice (Liebig 2007; Die Beauftragte der Bundesregierung für Migration Flüchtlinge und Integration 2007).

Germany and the Netherlands compared

To compare Germany and the Netherlands with respect to their immigration and integration policy, one can use the notion of an immigration policy regime (Soysal 1994). Two elements are central to this concept (Sainsbury 2006). First, the immigration policy regime regulates immigrants' inclusion or exclusion from society. It consists of rules and norms that govern immigrants' opportunities to become citizens, to acquire residence and work permits and to participate in economic, cultural and political life. The second component of the immigration regime is the form of immigration, i.e. the 'entry' categories associated with various forms of immigration, such as labour migration, asylum seekers or as *Aussiedler* (Morris 2002). The categories involve specific rights and access to social benefits (Sainsbury 2006).

The immigration regime in Germany has been described mostly as exclusionary with respect to access to citizenship or residence permits (Faist 1995; Sainsbury 2006; Green 2004; Koopmans 2010). The Netherlands is often described as being more inclusive and multicultural with respect to naturalisation, residence, housing and voting rights (Thränhardt 2000; Entzinger 2001; Koopmans et al. 2005).

A useful tool to compare Germany's and the Netherlands' immigration and integration policy is the Migration Integration Policy Index (MIPEX). MIPEX (Niessen, Huddleston & Citron 2007) compares the EU-25 member states plus Norway, Switzerland and Canada across a range of im-migration and integration measures to provide a comparison of legal equal-ity of immigrants. Countries score high when immigrants can more easily obtain equal rights to native residents. Germany scores consistently 'aver-age'; the Netherlands scores mostly 'favourably'. Of the 30 countries in-cluded, the Netherlands is ranked fourth with a score of 68; Germany ranks fourteenth with a score of 53 (which is also the EU-25 average). Germany is ranked lower in all dimensions except family reunion. For example, whereas Germany belongs to the group with the lowest naturalisation rates, the Netherlands belongs with the highest rates (Koopmans 2010). In Table 3.5, the scores relative to the best practice are presented for the six dimen-sions that the MIPEX consists of (based on 140 indicators in total). Germany scores considerably lower on access to nationality, anti-discrimi-nation political participation and labour market access.

Historically, ethnic minorities policy has been very different in Germany and the Netherlands. While the Netherlands formulated an explicit policy towards migrants (based in the 1980s and 1990s on the idea of multicultur-alism and, later, converging more towards an assimilation-type policy), Germany long denied its being an immigration country and therefore did not develop an official explicit policy until the end of the 1990s. A main difference is that the Netherlands' integration policy has been targeted to-wards specific ethnic groups, whereas Germany's was aimed towards indi-viduals. Besides in the MIPEX scores, this is also reflected in the index of cultural rights granted to immigrants, where the Netherlands scores highest and Germany, only moderately (Koopmans et al. 2005).

Current differences in policy towards immigrants may, however, not be as significant as would be expected from the history. For example, Vermeulen (2008) compares the unemployment policy for immigrants in Amsterdam and Berlin and concludes that the similarities are bigger than the differences. In any case, the current integration policies of both coun-tries are more similar now than before 2000 (Avci 2008); both countries display restricted access for new arrivals, language training and support for education and labour market entry. With respect to new entry on the labour

Table 3.5   *MIPEX scores for Germany and the Netherlands as % of best practice in 2007*

	Germany	The Netherlands
Anti-discrimination	50	81
Family reunion	61	59
Long-term residence	53	66
Political participation	66	80
Access to nationality	38	51
Labour market access	50	70

Source: Niessen, Hudleston and Citron (2007)

market, the countries are also similar: both have a closed market for low-skilled labour and a restricted open market for high-skilled workers.

The labour market

The Netherlands

In the Netherlands, labour market participation and earnings of immigrants are lower than those of native residents; unemployment rates are higher for immigrants than for natives. In general, this also holds when controlled for socio-economic background (Dagevos 2001; Van Tubergen & Maas 2006; Tesser & Dronkers 2007).

In Table 3.6, the 2008 employment rate in the Netherlands is presented for the ethnic groups, separated for men and women and different levels of education. The share of natives between ages fifteen and 65 who have paid employment for at least twelve hours per week is 77 per cent for men and 59 per cent for women, while that of non-Western immigrant men and women is 62 per cent and 45 per cent, respectively (Statistics Netherlands 2008: 90). This also differs per ethnic group: for Moroccans it is 50 per cent; for Surinamese it is 63 per cent (see Table 3.6). Participation also differs highly between men and women, the first and second generations and among the different educational levels (see Table 3.6).

With respect to unemployment, the differences between natives and ethnic minorities are similar to those for participation. According to Statistics Netherlands (2008: 98), in 2008 the unemployment rate (of the active labour force) for natives was 4 per cent; that of Turks 9 per cent; Moroccans 11 per cent; Surinamese 8 per cent; Antilleans/Arubans 10 per cent. Among the ethnic minorities, women are more often unemployed than men; there is no difference between the first and second generations.

Germany

As Kalter and Granato (2007: 271) state: 'No matter what indicator one chooses, almost all empirical studies arrive at the general conclusion that

Table 3.6 *Employment rate in the Netherlands for population aged 15-65, by ethnic group (in %)*

	Native Dutch	Turks	Moroccans	Surinamese	Dutch Antilleans/Arubans
Total	68	51	50	63	59
Men	77	63	62	65	68
Women	59	38	36	59	54
First generation	-	53	51	67	59
Second generation	-	46	46	55	61

Source: Statistics Netherlands (2008: 90)

Table 3.7 *Employment rate in Germany for population aged 25-65, by migration background and gender (in %)*

	Without migration background	With migration background		
		With migration experience		Without migration experience*
		Foreigners	Holders of German nationality	
			Naturalised	Aussiedler	
Total	75.8	58.3	69.5	73.8	71.9
Men	81.8	69.3	78.7	80.1	78.1
Women	69.8	47.2	60.1	67.2	64.1

* No separate data available for those without migration experience
Source: Micro Census 2007, Statistisches Bundesamt 2009; author's own calculations

nearly all of the distinguishable immigrant groups are less successful than the indigenous population.' Among native Germans, the 2007 employment rate – referring to persons in employment as a percentage of the population between ages 25 and 65 – was just above 80 per cent for men and just under 70 per cent for women. For foreigners with migration experience, this was just below 70 per cent for men and just above 45 per cent for women. Those with migration experience and German nationality have higher employment rates: the *Aussiedler* come close to those of the German native population (see Table 3.7). The employment rate is especially low for Turkish women (just below 30 per cent in 2004) and Turkish men (just above 55 per cent; see Liebig 2007: 21-22). For the other ethnic groups, no separate data were available.

The variations look similar for unemployment. In 2006, 16.6 per cent of foreign nationals were unemployed, compared to 12 per cent for the entire population (OECD Statistics 2006). In 2004, this figure was 18.3 per cent for immigrant men and 10.3 per cent for native German men. Among women, it was 15.2 per cent for immigrants and 9.6 per cent for natives (Liebig 2007). The rate of social assistance recipients among foreign nationals is, at 9.4 per cent, much higher among immigrants than German nationals (2.9 per cent) (Cyrus & Vogel 2007). However, one must keep in mind that the statistics are somewhat distorted due to 2000's naturalisation of foreign nationals; this group may have left the less successful behind in the category of immigrants.

Germany and the Netherlands compared

When one compares labour market outcomes, there are clear differences between the Netherlands and Germany (see also Koopmans 2003). The

Table 3.8 *Employment rate and relative employment of native-born and foreign-born population aged 15-64 in Germany and the Netherlands*

	Native-born (%)	Born in non-EU-15 country (%)	Relative employment level of persons born in non-EU-15 country
Germany	68.5	59.4	.87
Netherlands	75.1	57.8	.77

Note: Figures are averages for the years 1999-2004
Source: Koopmans (2010)

Table 3.9 *Unemployment rate and relative employment of native-born and foreign-born in Germany and the Netherlands*

	Men			Women		
	Native-born	Foreign-born	Foreign/native	Native-born	Foreign-born	Foreign/native
Germany	9.3	16.4	1.76	9.2	14.7	1.6
Netherlands	2.99	9.44	3.15	3.9	9.5	2.4

Note: Unemployment rates averaged over the years 2000, 2003, 2004 and 2006
Source: OECD (2009); author's own calculations

unemployment rate – namely that of the foreign-born divided by that of the native residents – is much lower in Germany (with 1.8 for men and 1.6 for women) than the Netherlands (3.15 for men and 2.4 for women; see Table 3.9). The level of unemployment is considerably higher in Germany than in the Netherlands both for foreign-born and native residents. However, the difference between the two groups' unemployment rates is much greater in the Netherlands.

Similar conclusions can be drawn for the employment rate (Table 3.9). The relative employment level of persons born in a non-EU-15 country as compared to the native-born is .87 in Germany and .77 in the Netherlands (for 1999-2004, see also Koopmans 2010: 13). In other words, whereas in Germany the employment rate of the foreign-born is about 13 per cent lower than that of native residents, in the Netherlands it is 23 per cent lower. There are also differences concerning social benefits: whereas 23 per cent of the people on welfare in Germany in 1997 were foreigners, in the Netherlands one year later, ethnic minorities comprised 47 per cent of all people on welfare[3] (Koopmans 2003: 164; Voges, Frick & Büchel 1998).

Few studies compare the labour market outcomes of ethnic minorities in Germany and the Netherlands. Euwals, Dagevos, Gijsberts and Roodenburg (2006) find that the gap between Turks and natives is larger in the Netherlands than in Germany with respect to employment rates and tenure rate. In contrast, the disparity in job prestige score is larger in Germany than in the Netherlands.

Several explanations may account for these differences in outcomes. One may be that the composition of the ethnic minority population differs, for example, regarding educational attainment. The aforementioned figures are for the macro-level, not taking into account whether or not migrants are – on average – better educated in Germany than in the Netherlands.

However, there may also be institutional explanations. The first refers to the structure of the labour market. One of the factors affecting economic performance is the flexibility of the labour market. In this respect, employment protection legislation is an important indicator (Kogan 2007b). When compared to other European countries, both Germany and the Netherlands have roughly the same score on the strictness of employment protection legislation. However, Germany scores higher than the Netherlands (Kogan 2007b: 67; OECD 2004). This disparity can mainly be ascribed to Germany's greater regulation of temporary employment, something that could especially decrease opportunities for immigrants who benefit from a flexible and easy-access labour market. This may particularly hold true for unskilled labour, whereby many jobs are temporary. The MIPEX scores for the 'labour market access' area underline this difference. As seen in Table 3.10, the Netherlands scores more favourably than Germany, particularly with respect to security of employment and integration measures.

The specific composition of the labour market may matter as well. Kogan (2007b) analyses the impact of the size of labour market segments on the economic performance of immigrants in Europe. Kogan finds that in countries with a stronger demand for low-skilled labour, immigrants have fewer problems finding employment. Germany and the Netherlands are relatively similar in this respect, although the proportion of low-skilled jobs on the market is lower in the latter than the former. Given this difference, one would expect employment rates for immigrants to be higher in Germany than the Netherlands, which is indeed the case (see Table 3.8).

Besides the composition and structure of the labour market, the welfare regime of a country affects immigrant incorporation (Kogan 2007b; Reitz 2002, 1998; Koopmans 2010). Germany is classified as the prototype of a conservative welfare state regime (Esping-Andersen 1990; Arts & Gelissen 2002; Scruggs 2006). While the Netherlands is often classified as a

Table 3.10   *Labour market access MIPEX scores for Germany and the Netherlands in 2007*

	Germany	Netherlands
Eligibility	33	33
Labour market integration measures	50	100
Security of employment	75	100
Rights associated	50	50
Total labour market access	50	70

Source: Niessen, Hudleston and Citron (2007)

conservative welfare state, it is sometimes also described as being at least partly socio-democratic (for an overview, see Arts & Gelissen 2002: 149). Given the few differences, one would not expect the welfare state regime to have a large influence on the variation in social capital returns of Germany and the Netherlands.

Koopmans (2010: 2) argues – and concludes – that 'in a welfare state context, multiculturalism may not be beneficial for immigrants at all, because it may lead to dependence on welfare-state arrangements and thereby to social and economic marginalisation'. Koopmans (2010) compares the Netherlands with seven other countries (including Germany) to find that those with a generous welfare state and a multicultural integration policy display less favourable immigrant labour market outcomes than those with less generous welfare state regimes and/or an assimilationist integration policy. In other words, the differences in labour market performance of immigrants in Germany and the Netherlands may be due to differences in welfare state benefits and integration policy.

Social capital in Germany and the Netherlands

Besides ethnic groups, the labour market and integration policy, the social capital that people possess should also be considered when analysing macro-differences (or similarities). For example, there is some evidence that levels of individual social capital differ per welfare state regime (Kääriäinen & Lehtonen 2006; Van der Meer, Scheepers & Grotenhuis 2009; Van Oorschot & Finsveen 2009). Furthermore, the social stratification in a country determines levels of individuals' social capital (Pichler & Wallace 2009).

Whether this is due to differences in social stratification, partly different welfare state regimes or some other explanations, there may be some variation in levels of social capital in Germany and the Netherlands. Pichler and Wallace (2007) compare levels of formal social capital (civic participation) and informal social capital (frequency and strength of contact with friends and colleagues) across Europe to find that, together with the Scandinavian countries, the Netherlands has the highest levels of all forms of social capital. Germany scores moderately on all forms of social capital. It should be noted, however, that these findings refer to levels in the general population, not being migrant-specific.

Immigrants' social capital in Germany and the Netherlands

How do macro-differences affect the relation between immigrants' social capital and their position on the labour market? The main difference between Germany and the Netherlands concerns the composition of the ethnic minority population. The groups are different both with respect to types (former colony, labour migrants, *Aussiedler*) and origin countries. It is unclear to what extent economic returns of social capital differ among different ethnic groups. With respect to bridging, one could argue that the group with the greatest 'distance' (however defined) to the native population benefits most by establishing connections with them. By including interactions in the empirical analyses, I check whether such differences exist between ethnic groups.

However, there may be some macro-differences. Generally, ethnic residential concentration is higher in the Netherlands than in Germany (Musterd 2005). Ethnic groups with a larger population or higher concentration in the host country could gain more from their bonding social capital, since this implies more opportunities in the ethnic economy (Waldinger 2005). Furthermore, ethnic groups in the Netherlands are more organised (Vermeulen 2005b). One would therefore expect immigrants' bonding social capital to be more effective in the Netherlands than in Germany.

Policy targeted towards ethnic minorities might also affect returns to social capital. It is clear from the literature that both immigration policy and welfare state regime have a bearing on the economic integration of immigrants (Kogan 2007b; Reitz 1998, 2002; Koopmans 2010). In this respect, the conditions for successful immigrant incorporation seem to be more favourable in Germany than the Netherlands. The question is whether these differences in integration policy affect the relation between immigrants' social capital and their economic position. One could argue that since there was no clearly defined, migrant-specific policy for a long time, the German government never approached people as 'immigrants'. In the Netherlands, the government did do so, emphasising their cultural differences. These differences could have compelled immigrants' bonding social capital to become more developed in the Netherlands, and bridging social capital to become more developed in Germany (compare the argument in Koopmans 2010: 8-9). Again, this is a comparison of levels. The question is wether these differences also imply that bonding or bridging social capital is more or less effective in Germany or the Netherlands.

Previous research suggests that differences in the structure of the labour market influence immigrant incorporation (Reitz 1998, 2002; Kogan 2007b). Kogan discusses the labour market structure and lists the following factors that influence immigrant incorporation: the proportion of low-skilled positions in the labour market, immigrant niches, entrepreneurship and labour market rigidity. Kogan finds that in countries with a stronger demand for unskilled and semi-skilled labour, unprivileged immigrants are less disadvantaged when entering employment. Germany has a slightly larger labour market for unskilled and semi-skilled jobs than the Netherlands. It could therefore be that job-seeking immigrants in the Netherlands gain more from possessing (bonding and bridging) social capital, since there are potentially fewer jobs available for them than for immigrants in Germany.

Furthermore, in countries with a more flexible labour market, male immigrants are less disadvantaged (Kogan 2007b). In particular, labour market rigidity could have an impact on the relation between social capital and labour market outcomes. The German labour market is stricter than the Dutch one. One could argue that in a stricter regime, it is more beneficial to have contacts with natives; therefore, in Germany, bridging social capital is more effective for finding employment and making headway on the labour market.

The last issue discussed in this chapter referred to differences between Germany and the Netherlands in social capital. There are some indications that social capital differs between those countries. These differences – to the extent that they exist – are in *levels* of social capital; they evidently do not imply that the same differences exist with respect to *returns* on the labour market. Furthermore, none of the studies differentiates between immigrants and native residents. Previous research has not answered whether these differences in social capital also hold for immigrants or if they also imply different returns.

It could be, however, that the macro-context caters to, or facilitates, some *forms* of social capital more than others. If this is true for the stock of social capital, it might also be true for its effects. Following this line of argumentation (and apart from individual-level or ethnic group-specific arguments), it seems likely that in both Germany and the Netherlands, bridging social capital improves labour market outcomes since it fits the macro-regime better. Conversely, bonding does so to a lesser extent because it is less well facilitated by the macro-context. To test this hypothesis, however, a comparative design with more variation in types of countries is necessary. This may also hold for the *amount* of social capital: if more social capital also implies a larger effect size, one would expect returns to be higher for the Netherlands than Germany (since higher levels of social capital were found in the former; see Pichler and Wallace 2009). Like the research described above on the welfare state regime, these determinants describe the macro-differences in the amount of social capital, not in its returns.

Differences and similarities in the macro-context

Expectations with respect to macro-level influences are not clear-cut. Partly, this is due to the case selection: the Netherlands and Germany are similar to a large extent, but there are also clear differences. Secondly, there are no clear expectations because it is not clear from the literature if and how the micro-level relationship between immigrants' social capital and labour market outcomes is affected by the macro-context. Third, it has to be noted that the comparison can only be made qualitatively. The data-sets used are different; thus models cannot be estimated simultaneously. If results are different, this can be due to the differences between the surveys.

Bearing these caveats in mind, one can draw two possible conclusions when comparing Germany and the Netherlands. Similar findings suggest that: 1) the mechanism between immigrants' social capital and labour mar-ket outcomes is not being modified by the differences in the national con-text and/or 2) for the macro-level determinants that do matter, Germany and the Netherlands are the same, or the differences are not sufficiently big. If the results are different, there are also two possible conclusions: 1) macro-level differences do matter for the relationship between immigrants' social capital and their labour market outcomes or 2) the differences be-tween Germany and the Netherlands can be attributed to compositional dif-ferences, for example, the different ethnic groups or the differences in measurement.

Notes

1   Until 1986, Aruba was part of the Netherlands Antilles.
2   According to the German Statistical Office (Statistisches Bundesamt 2009: 309), be-cause of limited data availability, it is not possible to classify the population by coun-try of birth. The concept of migration background distinguishes between being born in Germany or not, but it does not account for other countries of birth.
3   Note, however, that this is not a ratio and that the percentage of immigrants in the Netherlands is higher than in Germany.

4 Immigrants' social capital and labour market outcomes

Introduction

An important distinction in the research on immigrants and their position on the labour market is between 'economic integration' and what I will call 'labour market outcomes'. Often, economic integration is defined as the degree of equality between immigrant and native residents (Bommes & Kolb 2004; Van Tubergen 2004). Integration as the degree of equality is understood as the performance of immigrants on a given indicator, compared with the performance of the native population on the same indicator. Except for the analyses in chapter 7, I do not compare immigrants with natives. Although without any doubt, comparing the immigrant to the native population is of high importance, a drawback here is that one cannot take into account migrant-specific information. In other words, one would need to have the same indicators for the native as well as for the migrant populations. This is hardly possible in the case of bridging social capital.

Another way of assessing the position of immigrants in the host society is to explain the performance of immigrants with certain economic indicators. That is, one is in the first place concerned with explaining the economic performance of immigrants, not so much with how immigrants do as compared to the native population. This is the approach taken in this book, which I will refer to as explaining labour market outcomes. An advantage here is that one can easily include migrant-specific information. Naturally, the disadvantage is that one cannot compare the native population. One can therefore not draw any conclusions with respect to migrants 'catching up' (or not) with the native residents. That is, if social capital is found to be effective for immigrants, it does not necessarily mean that their position will become 'more equal' to that of the native residents; social capital may very well be equally effective for native residents. This certainly is a limitation of the approach taken. Unfortunately, most information on bridging social capital is available only for immigrants. However, in chapter 7, Turkish immigrants and native residents are compared. Although this comparison covers a very small part of the entire debate on integration and the role of social capital therein, it does provide some empirical evidence on how to compare the effect of social capital between Turkish immigrants and German native residents.

When selecting indicators that measure labour market outcomes, the most common point of departure is labour force status. This is usually done 'stepwise' (see e.g. Van Tubergen 2004; Büchel & Frick 2005). The first step is to determine the labour force status, distinguishing between people who are active and inactive on the market. The active labour force comprises the employed, the self-employed and people who are unemployed and looking for a job. The inactive labour force comprises all other people, such as domestic workers, students, people in military service and retirees. Second, the active labour force consists of three categories: not employed, employed and self-employed. The first set of analyses in chapters 5 and 6 aim at explaining the effect of bonding and bridging social capital on the likelihood of immigrants being employed. Third, for the employed and self-employed, income and occupational status are analysed. This is visualised in Figure 4.1

Labour market outcomes

Perhaps the most important difference in the labour market is the one between having employment of some kind and having no employment whatsoever. Therefore, the first dependent variable in this book is being employed versus not being employed (including the unemployed, those who are seeking work and those who are inactive on the labour market). The advantage of an analysis that contrasts those with employment and those without it is avoiding the blurry boundary of being inactive on the labour market versus being unemployed. That is, since one estimates the likelihood of being employed (as opposed to not being employed), there is

Figure 4.1   *The dependent variable: Labour market outcomes*

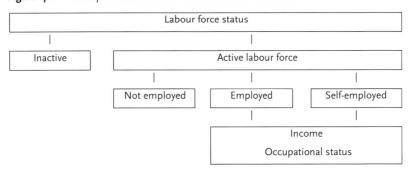

Source: Author

no need to distinguish between those unemployed not registered as unemployed yet seeking work and those not being or seeking to be employed. The disadvantage of this analysis is that the reference category is rough: although the sample has age boundaries, and those in military service or pension are excluded, the sample also contains those not intending to find employment, such as parents with young children. Still, one can argue that this is exactly what one aims to do: predict what forms of social capital increase the likelihood of finding paid employment, regardless of one's situation. In the empirical analyses, the dependent variable is operationalised as the likelihood of being employed. This is analysed separately for men and women. To better account for unemployment dynamics, in chapter 7, I focus explicitly on the unemployed. For those active on the labour market and currently registered as unemployed, I apply event history analysis to see the effect of possessing social capital on the duration of unemployment and the transition to work.

For those who are employed, the second indicator for labour market outcomes I use is that of occupational status. This is an important measure in research on stratification (Grusky 2001; Sorensen 2001; Morgan, Grusky & Fields 2006). Whereas income measures the 'ability to pay', occupational status represents one's rung on the societal ladder. Occupational status summarises the power, income and required educational achievement associated with the various positions in the occupational structure. According to Lin (1999: 467), 'status attainment can be understood as a process by which individuals mobilise and invest resources for returns in socioeconomic standings'. Resources can be personal, but also social: they can be accessed through one's direct and indirect ties.

Occupational status is a suitable indicator of the economic integration in society for several reasons. First, occupational status reflects the outcome of educational attainment and the skills necessary to perform in a job. Second, occupational status reflects the income associated with this job. It may therefore reflect one's financial position even better than income itself, which is a measurement at one given moment in time. Although a less precise instrument for one's financial position in the short term, occupational status provides a more reliable indicator for it in the long term. Especially in cross-sectional research, which is a mere snapshot in time, this argument gains significance. Another advantage is that the ISEI score is specifically designed for international comparison.

Positions of occupations in the stratified system can be measured in at least three ways: prestige ratings, class categories and socio-economic status scores. For the measurement of occupational status, I make use of the International Index of Socio-Economic Status (ISEI), developed by Ganzeboom, De Graaf and Treiman (1992; Ganzeboom & Treiman 2003). The ISEI scale is a continuous scale of occupations derived from the International Standard Classification of Occupations, and data on education and income of about 74,000 full-time employed men in sixteen countries. The scale consists of the weighted sum of the average education and income of occupational groups and is internationally comparable.

The advantage of a continuous approach, as opposed to a class or categorical approach (Erickson & Goldthorpe 2002; Goldthorpe 1992, 1987), is that it allows for an unlimited distinction between occupational groups. A class approach can only identify relatively few distinct categories. That is, whereas the approach based on class assumes that people can be clearly separated into different categories *and* that the people within them are rather similar, a continuous approach allows for unlimited distinction between occupational groups. A second advantage of a continuous approach is that it is more suitable for empirical analysis of quantitative data (Ganzeboom, De Graaf & Treiman 1992). Especially when aiming to analyse social stratification as a 'dependent variable', a continuous approach yields better interpretable models. This being said, there are numerous arguments that support adopting the analytical framework of a categorical approach as well.

Last, the ISEI scale can be contrasted with measures of occupational prestige (Treiman 1977). Scales that measure occupational prestige are continuous as well, but are conceptualised differently, being based on the 'general desirability of occupations' (Goldthorpe & Hope 1972). Prestige scales thus involve evaluative judgements, whereas the socio-economic indices consist of the weighted sum of the average education and income of occupational groups.

A disadvantage of the ISEI scale is that the validation of the original scale was conducted on a dataset containing men only. Professions in which mainly women work are thus based on relatively few observations. Furthermore, the occupations typically filled by women get a higher occupational status because the entire estimate is based on men's salary only (and women earn less than men). Ganzeboom, De Graaf and Treiman (1992) note that this is a drawback, though argue that it does not imply the ISEI score cannot be used for women. It means that the occupational status for characteristically female occupations has been estimated based on the education and incomes of the relatively few men in these jobs. In a later paper, Ganzeboom and Treiman (1996) argue that validating the scale on males only provides more conceptual clarity. A scale including women would be strongly affected because women earn less than men do. Furthermore, the gender distribution differs in an unknown way by country. Therefore, they argue: '[c]onceptually, what we have done is to treat the relationships between education, occupation and income for men as specifying the scale on which the status attainment of both men and women can be measured' (Ganzeboom & Treiman 1996: 218).

The third dependent variable I use is income. Within income a frequently made distinction is that between equivalised household income and personal income. Equivalised household income accounts for economies of scale in a household (Karoly & Burtless 1995; Bosch-Domenech 1991). One can argue that this is what matters for most people rather than personal income. Household income is adjusted for the household size. This implies that income is divided by the square root of the household size. Hence, when there is only one member in the household, it is divided by one; when there are two members, by 1.4; when there are four members, by two (Karoly & Burtless 1995). However, in this study, that may be a disadvantage. Bonding social capital is operationalised as closure in the family network. In other words, people with high bonding social capital have a strong family network and also value their family more highly (in terms of trust, solidarity). It is likely that people scoring high on bonding social capital also have a larger family (or in this case, household). Since there are likely to be more children in the household, the equivalised household income is lower. Thus, it is likely that people who possess much bonding social capital have a lower *equivalised* income, purely due to the fact that they also are likely to have more children. Therefore, personal income is used as a dependent variable. Since personal income does not take into account household size, this is not a problem.

There is also ample research indicating the differences in, and importance of, self-employment versus salaried employment for immigrants (Constant & Schachmurove 2003; Sanders & Nee 1996; Kloosterman & Rath 2001). Constant and Schachmurove (2003) analyse the wage differentials of immigrants and native Germans. They find that self-employed native Germans have a higher income, but only those on the upper side of the income distribution. For immigrants, this does not seem the case, finding Germany's immigrants who are self-employed earn 22 per cent more than the salaried immigrants. Since being self-employed is a strategy immigrants use to get around barriers such as discrimination (e.g. on the labour market), some research also takes being self-employed as a dependent variable or examines the making of ethnic entrepreneurs (Kloosterman & Rath 2001). There are many reasons to analyse entrepreneurship separately, but in this book, I choose to focus on income and occupational status. That is, I aim to explain the effect of social capital on immigrants' income and occupational status, regardless of whether this is gained through self-employment or not. Since migrants who are self-employed earn more, I do include self-employment as a control variable. By doing so, I account for the differences between self-employment and salaried employment, all the while focusing on their result: income and occupational status.

Hypotheses referring to bridging

The bridging argument

The bridging argument is the most abstract argument. It explains why a bridging tie may be profitable to ego in terms of network connections. A bridging tie is one that spans a structural hole. A structural hole is a gap in a network. Hence, a bridging tie connects with people that were not in one's network before. In other words, possessing bridging social capital implies having access to unique information by connecting to other networks. These bridges create opportunities for upward mobility on the labour market (Granovetter 1995; De Graaf & Flap 1988). That is, spanning structural holes in one's network results in more valuable information and better opportunities: those with more crosscutting ties have better chances on the labour market.

In chapter 2, bridging ties are defined as interethnic contacts. For immigrants, interethnic ties are important, since they are a link out of the ethnic community, which thereby open a wider network containing more valuable resources and job opportunities (Heath & Yu 2005; Uunk 2002). For example, analysing the labour market outcomes for Puerto Rican and Mexican immigrants in the US, Aguilera (2002, 2005) finds that having interethnic friends is positively correlated to hourly earnings and participation on the labour market.

Why bridging the *ethnic* divide is important and expected to be benefit migrants is discussed in more detailed in 'The resource argument' and 'The "compensating discrimination" argument' sections. These arguments explain why bridging the 'ethnic divide' for immigrants signifies spanning a structural hole, hence yielding positive returns on the labour market.

The resource argument

The idea of social capital being *capital* – in the sense that investments yield positive returns – is based on the assumption that social relations connect people to valuable resources. In other words, the idea of bridging social capital as profitable is not only because of network diversification, but also because of making connections to a *resource-rich* group (such as the native population). The statement that bonding social capital is to 'get by' while bridging social capital is to 'get ahead' (Narayan 1999; Putnam 2000) is predominantly argued from the perspective of a *resource-poor* group (compare left panel of Figure 4.2). In that case, since it implies building connections in a resource-poor environment, bonding is said to be ineffective. Bridging is effective since it implies accessing a resource-rich environment. Therefore, bonding social capital often has a negative connotation and bridging, a positive one. Were one to take the perspective of the resource-rich group and build connections the other way around (which is

Figure 4.2   *Bonding and bridging in resource-rich and resource-poor groups*

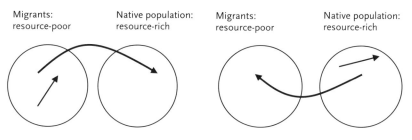

Bonding and bridging for migrants   Bonding and bridging for native population

Source: Author

visualised in the right panel of Figure 4.2), bridging is not likely that profitable. In other words, it is tapping into a resource-rich network that yields positive returns, rather than 'bridging' as such. In this book, I label the idea of bridging social capital tapping into resource-rich networks the 'resource argument'.

It is too crude to simply classify the migrant population as resource-poor and the native population as resource-rich. The distinction between the two is based on access to host country and labour market-specific resources that natives have and migrants have less of. Migrants who build connections to the native population thus gain access to host country-specific resources. It is well established in the literature that for successful integration in the labour market of the host society, migrants need host country-specific skills (Friedberg 2000; Duleep & Regets 1999; Zeng & Xie 2004; Borjas 1994). This is summarised in the title of Friedberg's article 'You can't take it with you? Immigrant assimilation and the portability of human capital'. The argument for a need for host country-specific capital is predominantly made with respect to skills, such as education and language proficiency (Chiswick & Miller 2002). However, this argument is also at the core of bridging social capital: by building interethnic contacts, immigrants realise access to resources that they typically have little of themselves and that are much needed for good performance on the labour market. Furthermore, as Haug (2003: 719) points out, it is host country-specific social capital in particular that is beneficial for labour market outcomes: 'Since [...] in Germany most employers are Germans, it is useful for immigrants to have contacts to Germans.'

The resource argument has two elements: first, bridging social capital builds host country-specific (social) capital. This helps make headway on the labour market in concrete ways, for example, by getting help with applications, translating job adverts and writing cover letters. Second, it provides direct access to job opportunities: since most employers are native residents, it is useful to have contacts with natives. The latter point refers to the fact that in terms of employment opportunities – when compared to the migrant population – the native population is resource-rich.

Hence, the second main argument that bridging social capital is expected to have a positive effect is because migrants realise access to host country-specific resources through building contacts with the native population. The native population can provide knowledge on the functioning of the labour market and links to job opportunities, which in turn facilitates finding jobs and/or better jobs.

The 'compensating discrimination' argument

Another reason bridging social capital, seen as bridging the *ethnic* divide, is expected to be beneficial to immigrants is the discrimination that migrants face. There are two main reasons migrants generally perform less well on the labour market than native residents. The first concerns the supply-side of the labour market: migrants generally have less host country-specific human capital and less experience on the host society's labour market (Kogan 2004; Kalter & Granato 2002; Becker 1964). It is mainly host country-specific human capital that is needed (Borjas 1994; Friedberg 2000).[1] Since bridging social capital is host country-specific capital, almost by definition, it is expected to be beneficial to migrants. Yet, the 'compensating discrimination' argument relates to the demand-side of the labour market.

The second main reason migrants face difficulties on the labour market concerns the demand-side: employers can be (for whatever reasons) less inclined to hire an immigrant than a native (Kalter 2006; Lindbeck & Snower 1988; Heath & Chueng 2007). Discrimination on the labour market tends to occur for two reasons: taste discrimination (employers have subjective preferences reflecting tastes, possibly resulting in prejudices against immigrants) and statistical discrimination (employers have incomplete information and have to deal with uncertainty, hence basing their decisions on easy identifiable characteristics, such as ethnicity).

This book does not deal with the extent of discrimination on the labour market; it neither tries to measure nor to explain it. Yet, one of the reasons that bridging social capital is of importance to immigrants is rooted in the causes of labour market discrimination. Some forms of discrimination (such as taste discrimination) are thought to originate from the idea that people generally identify more with people who are like themselves. According to contact theory, if 'we have more contact with people unlike us, we overcome initial barriers of ignorance and hesitation and come to trust them more' (Pettigrew 1998; Allport 1979). For example, people who live in ethnically diverse neighbourhoods have more interethnic trust (Lancee & Dronkers 2011).

One can therefore argue that those immigrants who succeed in building bridging social capital circumvent, if not compensate for, the potential negative effects of discrimination since they succeed in being trusted more by natives. In other words, immigrants building bridging social capital are successful in overcoming initial barriers of ignorance and hesitation between themselves and natives.

This could be the case in two ways. First, by building bridging social capital one may set oneself apart from other immigrants. By connecting to the native population, one perhaps shows that one is a 'positive', 'good', 'able' or 'integrated' immigrant. This 'positive stigmatisation' may overcome the barriers produced by taste discrimination. As Burt (2004: 349) concludes in his article on structural holes: 'People connected across groups are more familiar with alternative ways of thinking and behaving.' There is no reason to assume that this is a process that only takes places on the ego (hence immigrant) side of the relationship. It is reasonable to expect that employers some how connected to immigrants will have a more positive opinion about them and are therefore more likely to employ or promote them. One can argue that building bridging social capital is an individual property and therefore does not compensate for the negative image of the entire group. However, it is likely that those immigrants possessing bridging social capital also deflect – if not prevent – potential negative attitudes of employers, current or prospective.

One could further argue that this is not a true *network* effect, since the argument is based on a positive attitude or propensity to integrate. However, this is exactly the argumentation behind cognitive bridging social capital: when attitudes are more congruent with those of the host society, the likelihood of being discriminated against is smaller. Hence, immigrants with such an attitude have an advantage over those who do not. This most likely is also the case with structural bridging social capital: those who build connections with the native population are perceived as 'good' immigrants, thus overcoming the initial ignorance and hesitation at the root of discrimination and disadvantages on the labour market.

The second argument is that immigrants connected to natives may reduce the uncertainty of employers and thus the likelihood of statistical discrimination. One of the theories explaining statistical discrimination is that employers face an investment decision based on uncertainty. Employers therefore base their decisions on facile characteristics, such as ethnic origin. Since immigrants are different from natives, there is more uncertainty, which increases the 'costs' for employing immigrants. Arguably, this uncertainty is reduced when an immigrant builds connections to the native population. In other words, immigrants building a social network with many interethnic contacts manage to reduce the uncertainty employers face, something that is argued to cause statistical discrimination. Naturally, one can argue that the arguments of compensating discrimination with positive stigmatisation and reducing employer uncertainty only hold when employers are included in the social network of the immigrants. However, bridging social capital proves important not only when accessing the labour market, but also when already on it (with respect to income attainment or obtaining a better occupational position).

The second reason bridging social capital may compensate the negative effects of discrimination is that unconventional channels become activated to make headway on the labour market. In other words, by building a social network that connects to the native population, one relies less on formal channels, which are perhaps more sensitive to discrimination. Indeed, Drever and Hoffmeister (2008) show for Germany that immigrants make more frequent use of informal methods to find employment than natives do. Also, according to Mouw (2002), the presence of discrimination is precisely the reason immigrants' social networks may be an efficient means to do job searches.

The 'compensating discrimination' argument thus implies that migrants who build bridges to the native population have an advantage: they may be able to overcome natives' barriers of ignorance and hesitation and have natives trust them more. This advantage is different from the argument of network diversification and different from the argument of accessing a resource-rich network. Whereas the first two arguments explain returns from the point of ego, the compensating discrimination argument hypothesises a potential positive effect on the 'other' side of the bridge. It implies that disadvantages originating from discrimination are compensated or circumvented by possessing bridging social capital.

A true test of such a 'discrimination hypothesis' requires information on the attitude of employers towards immigrants. To disentangle the effects of network diversification and advantages due to compensating negative effects of discrimination one needs a design that can differentiate these effects. This is neither possible with the data nor necessary for the purpose of this book. The arguments presented here explain why bridging social capital is expected to yield positive returns for the individual; it is not the objective to test which argument within the concept of bridging social capital has most validity.

To summarise, three arguments were discussed that explain why bridging social capital is beneficial for the labour market outcomes of immigrants. First, by bridging, one diversifies the social network, resulting in more opportunities. Second, bridging the ethnic divide implies accessing a resource-rich network of those being in control of the labour market. Third, building interethnic contacts may compensate and circumvent the disadvantages that immigrants face due to discrimination.

There is some research that confirms the idea of bridging social capital. For example, analysing the labour market outcomes for Puerto Rican and Mexican immigrants in the US, Aguilera (2003, 2005) finds that non-family social capital (organisational involvement and having interethnic friends) is positively related to hourly earnings, the likelihood of being employed and the number of hours worked. Kanas and Van Tubergen (2009) use the Dutch SPVA data to examine the effect of origin and host country schooling on employment; they find little support for the effect of contacts with natives on employment. Furthermore, earlier research shows that a tie with a higher status improves the chances of finding a better job (Lin, Ensel & Vaughn 1981; De Graaf & Flap 1988).

With respect to cognitive bridging social capital, Ode and Veenman (2003) also make use of the Dutch Social Position and Use of Utilities Immigrants Survey (SPVA) data to analyse the relation between informal participation, modernisation and out-group orientation and occupational level for immigrants in the Netherlands. They find a significant positive effect for modernisation.

It is therefore expected that structural bridging social capital positively impacts the labour market outcomes of immigrants. There is no reason to assume that this relation is different for employment likelihood, income or occupational status (compare with Lin & Ao 2008). In other words, bridging social capital helps people find jobs or better jobs more quickly by leading to information on vacancies, help with applications, etc. Furthermore, bridging may also help negotiate better wages or link job candidates to better positions. This is formulated in a general hypothesis.

H1   There is a positive relationship between the level of immigrants' bridging social capital and labour market outcomes (i.e. the likelihood of employment, occupational status and income).

Hypotheses referring to bonding

For bonding social capital, the effects are less clear-cut. Two possible lines of argumentation can be followed, one hypothesising positive returns, the other hypothesising no (or even negative) returns (compare Nannestad, Svendsen & Svendsen 2008 who identify 'BO+ and BO-'; Portes 2000). As Portes (1998: 21) notes:

At the individual level, the processes alluded to by the concept of social capital cut both ways. Social ties can bring about greater control over wayward behaviour and provide privileged access to resources; they can also restrict individual freedoms, and bar outsiders from gaining access to the same resources through particularistic preferences.

The fact that, for immigrants, bonding social capital has two sides is also illustrated by Heath and Yu (2005). According to them, ethnic minorities lack bridging social capital due to isolation and consequently lack access to employment opportunities. On the other hand, they add, geographically concentrated ethnic minorities may develop high levels of bonding capital, which can provide a basis for a successful local economy. Heath and Yu (2005: 218-219) suggest that '[b]onding social capital may thus compensate, wholly or in part, for lack of bridging social capital'. Therefore, for the concept of bonding social capital, two competing arguments are developed: the isolation argument and the closure argument.

The isolation argument

The isolation argument runs counter to the argument of bridging social capital. Although bridging ties create opportunities, high closure in one's network does not because the same information is being circulated within the network. This is the argument rooted in the statement that whereas bonding is to 'get by', bridging is to 'get ahead' (Putnam 2000). This could be true for immigrants, since immigrant communities can be isolated from the native population, which is in control of the most valuable resources. When embedded into ethnic networks only, successful upward mobility may be impeded due to social obligations, pressure to conformity or 'downward levelling norms' (Portes 1998). Such mobility traps can lead to ethnic segmentation or 'downward assimilation' (Portes 1995). Being embedded into ethnic networks may prevent contacts with the host society and thus hamper integration (Haug 2007: 100). Furthermore, social capital, especially that of the bonding type, can be a burden since it may imply giving without receiving (Portes 2000). Especially in the case of the family network, this may be of importance.

The isolation argument may have a second element to it. As explained above, one of the two main reasons that immigrants are disadvantaged on the labour market is that they, on average, possess less human capital than natives do. Furthermore, host country-specific human capital, especially, proves useful on the labour market (Friedberg 2000; Borjas 1994). Since bonding social capital is not necessarily host country-specific, it is likely to be less effective than bridging social capital (which is country-specific).

The closure argument

The countering argument for bonding social capital is the closure argument, as put forward by Coleman (1988, 1990). That is, closure in a network provides more reliable communication channels and protection from exploitation by the members of the network; it is thus a capital with positive returns. One could argue that immigrants, in particular, need reliable communication channels and sincere network support, since they are more vulnerable than the native population. Nee and Sanders (2001b: 389-390) observe how: '… especially for immigrants who do not possess substantial financial capital, the family (nuclear and extended) constitutes the most important capital asset'. They continue:

> The social capital embodied in family relationships promotes cooperation needed in realizing both economic and non-economic values. Coleman's (1988) analysis of social capital, for example, illustrates how relations within the family account for differences in school performance. The social connections that individual members invest in and accumulate provide information and access to resources available to all members of the family. (Nee & Sanders 2001b: 390)

For immigrants, the family network is of special importance. Immigrants cannot rely as much on host country institutions as can natives. The family network therefore functions as a safety net. In an example from Elliott (2001) we see how Latinos are more likely than natives to enter jobs through what he calls 'insider referrals': the matching of people and jobs through ethnic social networks. A strong family network is likely to contribute to insider referrals, both because family members can function as referrers and because a strong family network can link to the ethnic community and, hence, to more potential referrers. In other words, bonding social capital is likely to provide access to the ethnic economy (Light & Gold 2000; Waldinger 2005).

Lin (2004) states that for those who face disadvantages on the labour market, 'chain' length may impact job-seeking; these people must reach farther – i.e. form longer chains – to access better social resources. It appears that in over 50 per cent of all Lin's cases, the first link in the chain is that of ego to a family member. It is therefore likely that a strong family network results in better-quality chains, linking to labour market opportunities. Lin argues that disadvantaged groups, such as immigrants, are especially likely to benefit from a strong first link, since they will need longer chains to reach valuable social resources.

Another reason family-based networks can be expected to benefit immigrants is inter-generational closure. One of the reasons migrants face difficulties on the labour market is that they are not familiar with it. There are two ways in which social capital can compensate for this. Argued above, the first implies investing in bridging social capital. The second way is making use of the knowledge of other immigrants; particularly likely to be useful are that of the 'older' and host country-born generations (Waldinger 1994; Menjivar 1997; Livingston 2006; Nauck 2001). For instance, Massey and Espinosa (1997: 951) argue that: 'Since the head's relatives are relatives of the spouse and children as well, the social capital is clearly transferable because of the norms of reciprocity, bounded solidarity, and enforceable trust that generally suffuse kinship ties.' Thus, by possessing a strong family network with links to the older generation, one potentially accesses host country-specific knowledge of the labour market.

Most research on immigrants' bonding social capital deals with 'ethnic' networks.[2] Previous work finds that ethnic networks can be beneficial; often immigrants find a job through social networks (Mouw 2002; Elliott 1999; Garcia 2005; Waldinger 2005). Furthermore, the 'compensating discrimination' argument as outlined above for bridging social capital may also hold true for bonding social capital. It opens up a channel of access to the labour market that does not suffer from discrimination. The closure argument is rather the reverse: the main reason ethnic networks can be beneficial has to do with high levels of solidarity and trust as well as positive discrimination. In this book, bonding social capital is conceptualised as the family network and co-ethnic friendships. A strong family network may provide good opportunities for building ethnic networks since it, too, is an ethnic network. It is likely that people with a strong family network can more easily access wider ethnic networks and the potential benefits of the ethnic economy through insider referrals (Elliott 2001; Mouw 2002).

There is also some research on the effect of family-based networks for immigrants. Sanders, Nee and Sernau (2002), studying Asian immigrants in Los Angeles, find that job seekers ask their better-connected relatives, friends and acquaintances to serve as intermediaries. These networks provide resources to make headway on the labour market. Furthermore, Sanders and Nee (1996) find that family social capital – operationalised as being married and number of relatives – increases the likelihood of being self-employed for immigrants in the US. Nee and Sanders (2001a) conclude that social capital embodied in intra-family, kinship and ethnic ties serves as an important form of capital in the process of finding a job, although it increases the risk of getting low-paid jobs. Kahanec and Mendola (2007) find for ethnic minorities in Britain that core family structures increase the probability of self-employment. However, they also find that immigrants with mixed or non-ethnic networks increase the probability of finding paid employment among minority individuals. Sanders et al. (2002: 308) conclude that: '… our research helps explain how family- and ethnic-based social networks, through their properties of social capital and closure, influence the incorporation of immigrants into their host society'. In other words, due to closure in their social network, immigrants improve their position on the labour market. I follow the closure argument with a second hypothesis.

H2   There is a positive relationship between the level of immigrants' bonding social capital and labour market outcomes (i.e. the likelihood of employment, occupational status and income).

The few studies simultaneously assessing bonding and bridging social capital empirically find positive results for bridging and not for bonding. The studies that theoretically discuss the concepts hypothesise that bonding social capital forms a base for building bridges. Few authors explicitly discuss the interrelatedness of bonding and bridging (see also Patulny & Svendsen 2007; Schuller 2007). Williams warns against a too rigid use of a 'key binary hierarchy', such as the one between bridging and bonding, which implicitly also places bridging over bonding. Williams asks (2005: 261): 'What is so wrong with having deep relationships with other individuals rather than fleeting acquaintances?' However, for those authors explicitly discussing the interrelatedness of bonding and bridging, such a binary understanding seems not to be the case.

According to Woolcock and Narayan (2000), the most profitable network is one containing strong intra-community ties combined with weak inter-community ties. However, Leonard and Onyx (2003) conclude that in order to bridge socio-economic divides, mostly strong ties are used. They conclude that a distant colleague is contacted more easily if both ego and contact live in the same neighbourhood or have a mutual friend. According to Burt (2000, 2001, 2005), structural holes can add value to one's social network, but closure is critical to realising the value buried in structural holes. Schuller (2007: 15) states: 'One can have bonding without bridging but not vice versa.' Agnitsch, Flora and Ryan (2006) examine structural bonding and bridging social capital in neighbourhoods to explain community action and come to similar conclusions: both bonding and bridging significantly predict community action, though they are more effective when combined.

It is therefore suggested that bonding and bridging are related, and the main argument is that bonding social capital helps building bridges. Partly, this relatedness originates from the strong and weak ties distinction. Several authors conclude that both are needed, or are at least useful. For that reason, the strong versus weak ties distinction is not the key difference between bonding and bridging.

Furthermore, when analysing the economic returns of bonding and bridging social capital, whether the concepts are related or not is not of key importance. The main interest here is whether and, if so, to what extent bonding and bridging social capital result in better labour market outcomes. Whether or not bridging social capital is partly created by bonding, is not the question here. The objective is to analyse the returns of social capital, not its creation. However, some may argue that such an approach undervalues the potential effect of bonding social capital. Therefore, to analyse whether the effect of bonding social capital is being mediated by bridging social capital, the models are also estimated without bridging social capital. If there is a mediation effect, bonding social capital will show up as significant. When such effects are found, I report this.

Human capital

The main explanatory variable for labour market outcomes is human capital. One must therefore take it into account when analysing the effect of different forms of social capital. This is important for two reasons. First, the amount of human capital an individual possesses is the main variable that explains labour market outcomes. Human capital hence needs to be included to avoid finding spurious effects for social capital. The second reason to pay attention to human capital is the possible interaction effects it has with social capital. These points will be discussed consecutively.

The first argument is that of human capital as a necessary control variable. To give an example, Euwals, Dagevos, Gijsberts and Roodenburg (2007) identify an improvement in educational attainment and language proficiency as the main cause for labour force status disparity between the first and second generations. When analysing the role of human capital in the relation between social capital and labour force status, one can differentiate between a direct and an indirect effect.

The direct effect deals with the influence of possessing human capital on labour force status. Human capital has been used extensively to explain immigrants' economic integration. The general conclusion is that the possession of human capital contributes to economic equality[3] (see e.g. Borjas 1994), employment (Bevelander & Veenman 2004) and occupational status (Forrest & Johnston 2000). Furthermore, it is suggested that host country-specific human capital (i.e. capital acquired after arrival in the host society) has most impact on labour force status (Friedberg 2000).

The indirect effect of human capital on labour force status is through acquiring social capital. Human capital is often related to social capital. Coleman (1988) finds social capital to contribute to the creation of human capital. Boxman, De Graaf and Flap (1991) conclude that, in the process of income attainment, social capital adds to human capital rather than replaces it. They also conclude that human capital produces social capital. Janjuha-Jivraj (2003) concludes that through education and working experiences, younger-generation immigrants have developed more widely embedded networks. Sanders and Nee (1996) find that the combination of human capital and family relations can help explain the occurrence of immigrant self-employment in the US. Since human capital is also included in the regression models, the effect of social capital is therefore underestimated in the empirical analyses. However, by including interaction terms I test to what extent the effect of social capital is different for different levels of educational attainment.

When dealing with human capital and labour market outcomes, country-specific human capital is of particular importance. This may be because acquiring host country-specific human capital allows for bridging social capital to be built, since it enables immigrants to build contacts with natives (Kanas & Van Tubergen 2009). The positive effect of host country-specific social capital could thus be partly due to the fact that immigrants come into contact with natives and build bridging social capital. Kanas and Van Tubergen find for immigrants in the Netherlands that this is indeed partly the case.

Besides education in the host society, one of the most important country-specific skills is language proficiency. To give an example, Reitz and Sklar (1997) find that when seeking employment, immigrants are at a disadvantage if they speak their native language. Generally, host country-specific language proficiency is found to have a positive impact on labour force status, such as on employment (Van Tubergen, Maas & Flap 2004; Chiswick & Miller 2002), occupational status (Forrest & Johnston 2000) and income (Dustmann & Van Soest 2002). However, the 'penalty' seems to vary for each ethnic group (Kossoudji 1988). Also, there may be a negative effect of ethnic networks on language proficiency (Chiswick & Miller 1996). It may therefore be the case that bonding social capital negatively effects language proficiency and consequently has a negative effect on labour force status. On the other hand, one could expect that those with good proficiency in the host country language profit more from their bridging social capital than those who speak it poorly, since the former will be able to communicate better. Language proficiency is therefore also tested with interaction terms concerning whether the effect of social capital is different for various levels of language proficiency.

The second reason to give attention to human capital is that there may be differential effects of social capital for the several levels of human capital. For example, it is argued that when immigrants acquire more host country-specific human capital, the need for social capital may decline. This argument is most frequently made with reference to ethnic networks: social capital is particularly useful for immigrants who have minimal host country-specific skills, but extensive links to the immigrant community (Livingston 2006; Massey, Alarcon, Durand & Gonzalez 1987). However, as given in the isolation argument, there are indications that the economic advantages associated with social capital are not always shared among all members of the immigrant group (Portes & Zhou 1993; Lin 2001a). Boxman, De Graaf and Flap (1991) examine the interplay of human and social capital in the process of income attainment among Dutch managers to find an interaction between human and social capital. However, the interaction is unexpected: they find that social capital helps at all levels of human capital, but human capital does not make a difference at high levels of social capital. Van Alphen and Lancee (2008) find that for the likelihood of employment and income of early school leavers in Germany, some forms of social capital are indeed more effective than for those who completed their education. The more effective social capital for early school leavers is a social network that links to the employed population: a form of bridging social capital. The question, therefore, is whether the *same* type of social capital is differently effective for different levels of education.

By including interactions between the human capital variables (language proficiency and educational attainment), I analyse whether there is a difference in the effect of social capital. Since this is not the main research question of the book, and since there are no clear expectations on the differential effect of social capital, I do not formulate a general hypothesis on the interaction effect – with one exception: chapter 7 formulates a hypothesis to explore the effect of bridging social capital for different educational levels.

Social capital and labour market outcomes for men and women

It goes without saying that there are differences between men and women on the labour market. Because of these differences, labour market outcomes of men and women are often analysed separately. This is also what is done in this book.

There is also some research on the differences in the effect of social capital on labour market outcomes for female and male immigrants (Livingston 2006; Smith 2000; Hagan 1998). Fernandez and Harris (1992), examining the urban poor in the US, find that women have fewer ties and less multiplexity in their network. Livingston (2006), with respect to Mexican immigrants in the US, argues that migrant networks provide little relevant information for female job seekers. Because the men mostly arrived earlier than the women, more men work. Men also mainly work in male-dominated occupations. Female immigrants may have good access to female networks, but the little information they offer is mostly on socially isolated domestic work, which provides few opportunities for information-sharing, as compared to men's networks (Hagan 1998). Smith (2000) finds that the wage penalty of using social networks for Latina women in the US is twice as high as for men. Livingston (2006) finds for Mexican women in the US that, although overall *usage* of family and friends networks is similar for men and women, the returns differ. Contrary to men, women use their network more, the longer they are in the host country. Furthermore, Livingston finds that for women, using social networks significantly reduces chances of obtaining a job within the formal sector (while among men this was significantly positive). Hence, for women there is a negative return on use of their social network. This is partly supported by the qualitative studies of Hagan (1998) and Hondagneu-Sotelo (1994), who conclude that immigrant women are channelled into low-paying and informal sector jobs via their social ties.

Some studies, however, report other findings. Aguilera (2005) examines the economic returns of social capital for Puerto Rican immigrants in the US. He develops hypotheses to compare the effect of social capital, expecting that returns will be *lower* for women than for men. As it turns out, Aguilera finds that for women the returns of social capital are *higher*. More specifically, it appears that organisational involvement and having lived with non-family members from the respondent's town is positively associated with wages. In another study, Aguilera (2002) analyses the influence of social capital on labour market outcomes for immigrants and the US and concludes that, although there are differences between men and women, social capital is not less effective for women.

The aforementioned studies were all conducted in the US, mainly studying Mexican immigrants. As observed, the results are mixed. As Livingston (2006: 50) notes, research on gender and job-seeking among immigrants is extremely limited. I question thus to what extent these differences also apply to immigrant men and women in the Netherlands and Germany. It seems likely that the returns on social capital are lower for women than for men – perhaps with the exception for non-family-based social capital. According to the conceptualisation of bonding and bridging social capital, for bonding expected returns are lower for women than for men, but not necessarily for bridging social capital. To account for these possible differences, I therefore separate the analyses for men and women. As a general hypothesis, I formulate the following:

H3a The economic returns of bonding social capital are lower for women than they are for men.

H3b There is no difference between men and women in the economic returns of bridging social capital.

Notes

1   This is also one of the reasons bridging social capital is often thought to be more effective than bonding social capital: it is host country-specific capital. See also the isolation argument in this chapter's 'Hypothesis referring to bonding' section.

2   When it comes to the returns of ethnic networks, we also find a dilemma of closure versus isolation.

3   However, not surprisingly, education itself is not evenly distributed. Even after controlling for background characteristics, the educational attainment of immigrants is lower than that of natives in Germany (Riphahn 2003) and partly also for immigrants in the Netherlands (Crul & Schneider 2005; Van Ours & Veenman 2003).

5   The case of the Netherlands

Introduction

This chapter empirically analyses the influence of bonding and bridging social capital on the labour market outcomes of the four main non-Western ethnic minority groups in the Netherlands: Turks, Moroccans, Antilleans and Surinamese (see also Lancee 2010). The data used is the SPVA from 1998 and 2002 (Groeneveld & Weyers-Martens 2003; Martens 1999).[1] The SPVA survey is the main data source for monitoring the disadvantages experienced by ethnic minorities in the Netherlands (Guiraudon, Phalet & Ter Wal 2005). Spanning thirteen municipalities – which includes those in the country's four largest cities, along with more rural communities – the survey was taken with the objective of representing the Dutch immigrant population. The survey also contains a native Dutch sample, though they were not surveyed about social capital. The SPVA is a unique dataset, yet there are some limitations. First, the data are mainly cross-sectional, which implies that it is impossible to examine the causality of relationships. This is also addressed in the discussion. Second, the non-response rate was rather high (ranging from 48 per cent for the Turks and Moroccans to 56 per cent for the Surinamese). Although high, there are no indications for systematic non-response; furthermore, measures were taken to also include people who are less integrated culturally and economically (Groeneveld & Weyers-Martens 2003). Third, the SPVA sample is not representative of all socio-demographic characteristics. The ages 45-64 are slightly over-represented; those aged 15-29 are slightly under-represented (differences are maximally four percentage points when compared with register data) (Groeneveld & Weyers-Martens 2003). With respect to the first and second generations, there are some minor differences compared to the population. In the younger age category (15-29), those born in the Netherlands are slightly over-represented compared to first-generation immigrants (with the exception of Turks, whose numbers are the same as those of the native population). Last, unmarried adults are under-represented and parents with children are over-represented.

The sample includes heads of households only. Other household members were also surveyed, though they received a different questionnaire with some items omitted, for example, on language proficiency. Cases with a missing value on the dependent variable are deleted. The SPVA contains survey waves from 1988, 1991, 1994, 1998 and 2002. Unfortunately, although aimed at being longitudinal, these waves are mainly cross-sectional. Only a very small part of the sample appears in more than one wave and, if so, in almost all cases this is limited to two. I therefore rely on the 2002 wave of the SPVA for the cross-sectional analyses. This wave contains most suitable items for the measurement of the different forms of social capital. To better account for the causal argument made, a small panel design is used for each of the dependent variables. For those who participated in both the 1998 and 2002 waves (N = 764 for the likelihood of employment; N = 274 for income; N = 228 for ISEI), labour market outcomes in 2002 are predicted by bridging social capital and the relevant controls, while also controlling for the labour market outcomes in 1998. However, due to data availability limitations, this was only possible for structural bridging social capital.

Those in the 20-65 age range were analysed for likelihood of employment. For income and occupational status analysis, the sample comprises people who are active on the labour market,[2] hold a job and are between twenty and 65 years old. I selected this bottom age threshold because those older than twenty are assumed to have finished their studies and be active on the labour market; 65 is the official retirement age, hence the top age threshold. In Tables 5.1 and 5.2, a description of the sample is presented. Income is measured by the natural logarithm of the total net income. Occupational status is measured by the International Socio-Economic Index for Occupational Status (ISEI)[3] (Ganzeboom, De Graaf & Treiman 1992; a detailed discussion on the dependent variables used to measure the labour market performance can be found in chapter 4). I inputted missing values using imputation regressions; by including a dummy variable I checked if the imputed values significantly differed from the observed values. For the items belonging to the social capital measures, I used an imputation strategy developed specifically for missing values belonging to a scale (Van Ginkel & Van der Ark 2007). This is described in the appendix in more detail.

Method of estimation

Since the data are cross-sectional, the main method of estimation is logistic and ordinary least squares (OLS) regression. The main drawback of such an analysis is that one cannot rule out reversed causality or endogeneity and unobserved heterogeneity. In other words, it could be that one gains more social capital because one is working, or more useful contacts simply because one's position is higher (Mouw 2003). Since the data only provide a snapshot in time, this cannot be ruled out statistically. Finding an effect therefore supports the social capital argument (there is indeed a relation), but does not prove the causal ordering of events (the relation may or may not be causal). Finding no effect is less problematic in that respect: this would falsify the hypotheses formulated.

I tried to account for this lacuna in several ways. First, for the individuals in which this was possible, I constructed a panel with two time points (1998 and 2002). Taking all covariates in 1998, I predicted the labour market outcome in 2002 while controlling for the labour market outcome in 1998. This implies that if there is an effect of social capital in 1998 on income in 2002, while controlling for income in 1998, it is likely that the increase in income is due to having social capital. However, since cross-sectional analysis (as well as the mini-panel constructed here) relies on between-individual differences for the variation in the data, one cannot rule out possible effects of unobserved heterogeneity. There might be something else that influences both social capital and labour market outcomes. For example, people with a higher capacity for social capital may also be more often employed or earn more. In this case, it is not necessarily social capital that improves labour market outcomes, but people's own capabilities that are proxied by their social capital.

Naturally, by including control variables I tried to minimise such bias. That the effect of social capital is spurious with other variables shows, for example, when not including educational attainment in the models. In that case, the coefficients of social capital are much higher and the p-values are much lower. If this heterogeneity were not 'observed', then the effect of social capital would be greatly overestimated. I therefore chose to present only two models for each sub-group and dependent variable: Model 1 includes the measures for social capital; Model 2 is the full model, including all controls. Any conclusion or interpretation is based on the full model only. As mentioned, unobserved heterogeneity clearly is a limitation; the problem is, however, inherent to analysis with cross-sectional data.

Measures

To measure the different forms of social capital, two scaling techniques were applied. First was a non-parametric item response theory (IRT) model for developing cumulative scales, the so-called Mokken scaling method (Mokken 1996; Sijtsma & Molenaar 2002). The logic of IRT is based on an items pattern generated according to the number of people who gave a positive response, rather than the items simply being correlated. The advantage of IRT models – as opposed to reliability analysis – is that a Mokken scale deals with the ordinal structure between the items (Van Schuur & Kiers 2004). The following example illustrates this advantage. Few of the respondents in the sample have a partner who was born in the Netherlands, thus correlating relatively low with the other items that measure interethnic contacts. Yet it appears that those who have a native Dutch partner also score positively on the other items that measure interethnic contacts – though not necessarily the other way around. IRT models take into account such a stepwise ordering of the items. The most important measure that a set of items must meet to form an acceptable Mokken survey construct is Loevinger's homogeneity coefficient (H). The following cut-off values are conventional for judging a Mokken scale: H>.30 being a useful scale; H>.40 a medium-strong scale; and H>.50 a strong scale (Mokken 1996; Sijtsma & Molenaar 2002). As a second measure, the more conventional reliability of the scale is estimated with Cronbach's alpha. A Cronbach's alpha of .60 is an often cited threshold for a scale to serve as a reliable survey construct.

The two scales measuring bonding structural and cognitive social capital consist of twelve items that cover family ties and values (see Figure 5.1). The scale for structural bonding consists of six items that measure the strength of family ties by the frequency of giving or receiving help and/or advice from one's parents or children and by the frequency of contact with one's parents or children (H = .46, alpha = .73). Evidently, this measurement does not cover one's entire family network; moreover, it emphasises recent help, as opposed to support in the long run. Since it was unavailable in the survey, data concerning relations with siblings and long-term family support could not be included in the measurement. This is a drawback, especially because siblings are more likely to be closer in age to the respondent, making it more likely for them to have helpful contacts and applicable knowledge. Although selective, the scale does proxy the strength of family ties. It could hence be argued that a person who has strong relations with his or her parents and/or children also stays in good contact with

Figure 5.1 *Items that measure bonding social capital in the SPVA*

Structural bonding	Cognitive bonding
Received help from parent/child in past 3 months[1]	Trust family more than trust friends[3]
Helped parent/child in past 3 months[1]	Rather discuss problems with family than friends[3]
Got advice from parent/child in past 3 months[1]	Family members should be there for each other[3]
Gave advice to parent/child in past 3 months[1]	You can always count on family[3]
Saw parent/child in past 12 months[2]	In case of worries, the family should help[3]
Had contact with parent/child in past 12 months[2]	Family members keep each other informed[3]

[1] Range: no, sometimes, frequently
[2] Range: 1 never – 7 daily
[3] Range: 1 do not agree at all – 5 fully agree
Source: SPVA 2002; author's translation

Figure 5.2 *Items that measure bridging social capital in the SPVA*

Structural bridging	Cognitive bridging
More contact with native Dutch than own ethnic group[1]	Openness about sex is wrong[3]
Native Dutch friends or acquaintances (yes/no)	Contact between men and women is too liberal[3]
Receives visits at home from native Dutch friends or neighbours[2]	It is best if children live at home until they marry[3]
Contact with native Dutch in personal life[2]	It is fine for unmarried men and women to live together[3]
Partner born in the Netherlands (yes/no)	(Item reversed)
Member of an association containing mainly native Dutch (y/n)	

[1] Range: more own group, equal, more native Dutch
[2] Range: never, sometimes, often
[3] Range: 1 fully agree – 5 do not agree at all
Source: SPVA 2002, author's translation

his or her siblings. The same line of argumentation can be followed with respect to the emphasis on recent help: it is likely that those family members who provide support in the short term also do so in the long term. The scale for cognitive bonding consists of six items covering trust in and positive attitudes towards the family (see Figure 5.2). Since these items deal with the family in a general way, these items do not suffer the above-mentioned disadvantages. The values of Loevinger's H (.40) and the Cronbach's alpha (.77) clearly indicate that these items can be seen as a single construct.

Structural bridging is measured with a scale (H = .57, alpha = .71), based on six items that deal with interethnic contacts such as friendships or receiving visits from native Dutch and having a partner who was born in the Netherlands. Also included is being a member of an association that contains few or almost no members with the same ethnicity as the respondent does. The associations included in the survey are sports/hobby clubs, unions, NGOs, political parties and religious organisations. Last, cognitive bridging social capital is measured with a scale (H = .46, alpha = .73), based on the items that were used by Uunk (2003) to measure outward orientation: opinions about living together unmarried, contact between men and women and sexual openness.

Control variables

A number of control variables are included in the analyses. The crux of the difference in labour force status between immigrants themselves and between immigrants and the native population in the Netherlands is due to variation in educational attainment and language proficiency (Euwals et al.

2006, 2007; Bevelander & Veenman 2004; Lautenbach & Otten 2007). Furthermore, it is has been suggested that country-specific human capital (that is, human capital acquired after arrival in the host society) most impacts labour force status (Friedberg 2000). Besides education in the host society, one of the most important country-specific skills is language proficiency. Generally, language proficiency is found to have a positive impact on employment (Van Tubergen, Maas & Flap 2004; Chiswick & Miller 2002), occupational status (Forrest & Johnston 2000) and income (Dustmann & Van Soest 2002). As such, a (Mokken) scale of Dutch language proficiency is included as a control variable.[4]

Furthermore, the labour force status of an individual is affected by his or her socio-economic background (Erickson & Goldthorpe 2002; Solon 2002). To account for some notion of socio-economic background, the educational attainment of the parents (measured as the highest degree obtained by either the father or the mother) is included in the analysis. Besides that, I control for age, being married (Bevelander & Veenman 2004), rural versus urban domicile, ethnic group, first versus second generation, being self-employed, having a temporary job (as opposed to having tenure) and – with respect to income – the number of contracted working hours. First-generation immigrants are defined as those who were born in Turkey, Morocco, Suriname or the Netherlands Antilles. Second-generation ethnic minorities are those born in the Netherlands with at least one parent born in one of the aforementioned countries or those born abroad who migrated to the Netherlands before age six. These definitions are equivalent to those used by the SPVA survey.

Last, the duration of stay in the host society may have an impact on labour market outcomes (Li 2004). Logically, duration of stay also affects the creation of bridging social capital: it is likely that the time spent in a country increases the probability of building bridges and thin trust. Duration of stay will therefore partially incorporate the effect of social capital. Yet, the duration of stay also proxies other factors influencing economic outcomes, such as familiarity with the labour market and the institutional design of the host society (Büchel & Frick 2005). This is therefore included as a control variable.

Results

In Table 5.1 and Table 5.2, the mean and standard deviation of the included variables are presented, separated for men and women. A t-test is performed to see whether there is a difference between men and women, which is the case for most variables (not shown here). For this reason, the analyses are separated for men and women, except in the panel design, due to the otherwise too low N. As for the descriptive statistics, most

Table 5.1 *Descriptive statistics sample employment*

	Men		Women	
	Mean	SD	Mean	SD
Cognitive bonding (0-1)	0.71	0.16	0.69	0.17
Structural bonding (0-1)	0.39	0.25	0.43	0.28
Cognitive bridging (0-1)	0.41	0.22	0.45	0.22
Structural bridging (0-1)	0.32	0.23	0.31	0.22
Age	39.04	10.14	38.01	10.10
Duration of stay in years	20.38	9.74	18.34	9.38
Language proficiency (0-1)	0.64	0.30	0.69	0.31
	%	N	%	N
Employed	71.02	1,110	52.48	710
Educational attainment				
Primary	34.55	540	35.77	484
Lower secondary	22.58	353	26.46	358
Upper secondary	27.13	424	25.13	340
Tertiary	14.52	227	11.09	150
Education information missing	1.22	19	1.55	21
Parental education				
Parent primary	68.39	1,096	55.80	755
Parent lower secondary	11.00	172	14.86	201
Parent upper secondary	6.97	109	9.61	130
Parent tertiary	8.38	131	10.13	137
Parental education information missing	5.25	82	9.61	130
Married	65.77	1,028	30.45	412
Urban domicile	67.32	1,050	69.48	940
Ethnicity				
Moroccans	28.45	440	17.44	236
Turks	31.86	498	18.92	256
Dutch Antilleans	18.58	292	28.97	392
Surinamese	21.33	333	34.66	469
Second generation	12.73	199	16.04	217
Total	100	1,563	100	1,353

Source: SPVA 2002

respondents have a rather low educational attainment; as expected, this is even lower for their parents (around two thirds of respondents' parents highest degree obtained was that of primary education). Furthermore, I observed a large discrepancy in employment between men (71 per cent) and women (52 per cent). Last, a relatively small part of the sample can be classified as second-generation, and far fewer women than men are married (this is due to the fact that heads of household – almost always male – are analysed). Table 5.3 presents the means of the social capital scales for each ethnic group. Whereas on the bonding scales, the groups score rather similarly, the Antilleans and the Surinamese score substantially higher than the Turks and the Moroccans on bridging. Last, noting that .48 is the highest

Table 5.2   *Descriptive statistics sample income*

	Men		Women	
	Mean	SD	Mean	SD
ISEI	39.68	15.27	41.37	15.24
Income	1.594.07	786.35	1257.67	523.56
Cognitive bonding (0-1)	0.69	0.17	0.66	0.17
Structural bonding (0-1)	0.39	0.25	0.47	0.27
Cognitive bridging (0-1)	0.44	0.23	0.5	0.21
Structural bridging (0-1)	0.35	0.23	0.37	0.22
Age	38.05	9.20	37.34	9.23
Duration of stay (in years)	19.85	9.46	19.68	9.12
Language proficiency (0-1)	0.69	0.28	0.80	0.22
Contracted hours	37.08	7.98	31.50	9.60
	%	N	%	N
Educational attainment				
Primary	26.60	258	18.11	113
Lower secondary	23.71	230	27.88	174
Upper secondary	30.62	297	34.13	213
Tertiary education	17.94	174	17.95	112
Education information missing	1.13	11	1.92	12
Parental education				
Primary	63.81	619	44.55	278
Parent lower secondary	13.40	130	18.88	117
Parent upper secondary	7.94	77	13.30	83
Parent tertiary education	10.10	98	14.74	92
Parental education information missing	4.74	46	8.65	54
Married	64.54	626	24.20	151
Self-employed	7.42	72	2.24	14
Temporary job	11.55	112	15.78	99
Urban domicile	63.20	613	68.59	428
Ethnicity				
Moroccans	24.12	234	11.38	71
Turks	29.79	289	11.06	69
Dutch Antilleans	21.24	206	33.17	207
Surinamese	24.84	241	44.39	277
Second generation	15.57	151	18.91	118
Total	100	970	100	624

Source: SPVA 2002

Table 5.3   *Mean social capital in the Netherlands, by ethnic group*

	Cognitive bonding	Structural bonding	Cognitive bridging	Structural bridging
Turks	0.76	0.37	0.31	0.21
Moroccans	0.75	0.43	0.28	0.23
Surinamese	0.65	0.48	0.51	0.38
Dutch Antilleans	0.66	0.39	0.55	0.42
Total	0.71	0.42	0.42	0.31

Source: SPVA 2002

correlation coefficient (between structural and cognitive bridging), there is no need for concerns about multi-collinearity.[5] To account for a possible bias in the standard errors due to heteroskedasticity, Huber-White robust estimates of the standard errors are reported.

The likelihood of being employed

In Tables 5.4 and 5.5, men's and women's likelihood of being employed is predicted by the social capital variables and the relevant controls. When only including social capital, for both men and women, bridging social capital is positively associated with employment. For women, structural bonding also positively affects employment. However, when including the controls (Model 2), only structural bridging social capital significantly affects employment likelihood for both genders. None of the other social capital scales affect the employment status significantly. This implies that, even when controlling for language proficiency, educational attainment of the respondent and the respondent's parents, structural bridging social capital has an effect for both genders, but not for the other forms of social capital measured. Men, with a maximum score on structural bridging social capital, are 2.2 times more likely to be employed than those with a minimum score; women are 2.1 times more likely to be employed if they have a maximum score on structural bridging social capital. This effect remains when controlling for ethnic group, generation, age, duration of stay in the Netherlands, being married, educational attainment, Dutch language proficiency and educational attainment of the parents.

I also tested whether the effect of bridging social capital is different for certain levels of education or for ethnic groups (not shown here), but this did not appear to be the case. With respect to language proficiency, one effect was found: it appears that among women, the effect of structural bridging capital is less strong for those with good Dutch language proficiency. Or when reversed: the effect of structural bridging social capital is stronger for those who use Dutch less. For men, no significant interaction terms with language proficiency were found. There does appear to be an age effect for men, though: when the model is estimated for those between 25 and 45 years old, the results concerning significance of the coefficients remain the same and the coefficient of structural bridging goes up to 3.2 (not shown here). For women, this is not the case.

As expected, both controls of educational attainment and language proficiency strongly increase the odds of being employed. Men with a maximum score on the language proficiency scale are 3.2 times more likely to be employed than men with a minimum on the scale; for women, this is 2.98. For both genders, there is one difference between the ethnic groups in employment likelihood when taking into account the control variables. Moroccans have a lower likelihood than do the Surinamese. There is no

Table 5.4 *Logistic regression predicting employment likelihood among men, odds ratios*

	Model 1		Model 2	
	b	se	b	se
Cognitive bonding	.563	(.231)	.794	(.346)
Structural bonding	.787	(.186)	.717	(.186)
Cognitive bridging	2.592**	(.872)	1.631	(.685)
Structural bridging	5.195***	(1.748)	2.184*	(.866)
Age			.057***	(.039)
Ethnic group				
Surinamese			ref.	
Turkish			.632	(.151)
Moroccan			.522**	(.123)
Dutch Antillean			.681	(.158)
Second generation			1.106	(.306)
Duration of stay			.738	(.525)
Married			2.718***	(.458)
Urban domicile			.966	(.134)
Educational attainment				
Primary education			ref.	
Lower secondary			1.545*	(.265)
Upper secondary			1.879***	(.320)
Tertiary education			2.860***	(.707)
Education information missing			2.193	(1.469)
Language proficiency			3.252***	(.934)
Parental education				
Parent primary education			ref.	
Parent lower secondary			1.015	(.254)
Parent upper secondary			.854	(.251)
Parent tertiary education			.727	(.212)
Parental education information missing			.873	(.279)
Constant	1.739	(.643)	1.726	(.975)
Log-likelihood	-896.847		-816.346	
Pseudo-R-squared	.047		.132	
N	1,563		1,563	

* p < 0.05, ** p < 0.01, *** p < 0.001 (two-tailed tests); robust standard errors
Source: SPVA 2002

difference for Turks and Antilleans, when compared with the Surinamese. Furthermore, for men, there is no significant effect of being a second-generation ethnic minority, as opposed to being a first-generation immigrant. Women who belong to the second generation have a significantly lower likelihood of being employed, when compared to first-generation immigrants. The duration of stay does not affect the employment status, for neither men nor for women.

To better account for the causal ordering of events, I constructed a mini-panel covering two time periods and four years for structural bridging

Table 5.5 *Logistic regression predicting employment likelihood among women, odds ratios*

	Model 1		Model 2	
	b	se	b	se
Cognitive bonding	.491	(.188)	.695	(.286)
Structural bonding	1.774**	(.377)	1.295	(.329)
Cognitive bridging	5.530***	(1.744)	1.197	(.441)
Structural bridging	5.738***	(1.738)	2.141*	(.763)
Age			.420	(.253)
Ethnic group				
Surinamese			ref.	
Turkish			.703	(.162)
Moroccan			.510**	(.115)
Dutch Antillean			.845	(.152)
Second generation			.490**	(.115)
Duration of stay			2.603	(1.818)
Married			1.152	(.187)
Urban domicile			1.076	(.151)
Educational attainment				
Primary education			ref.	
Lower secondary			1.903***	(.316)
Upper secondary			3.932***	(.687)
Tertiary education			7.990***	(2.302)
Education information missing			2.696	(1.408)
Language proficiency			2.984***	(.865)
Parental education				
Parent primary education			ref.	
Parent lower secondary			1.313	(.261)
Parent upper secondary			1.417	(.350)
Parent tertiary education			1.579	(.424)
Parental education information missing			.920	(.206)
Constant	.389**	(.133)	.239**	(.119)
Log-likelihood	-858.827		-761.813	
Pseudo R-squared	.083		.186	
N	1,353		1,353	

* $p < 0.05$, ** $p < 0.01$, *** $p < 0.001$ (two-tailed tests); robust standard errors
Source: SPVA 2002

social capital. In Table 5.6, the descriptive statistics are presented. Since few people appear both in the 1998 and the 2002 waves, the sample size was reduced to 746, even when combining men and women. A potential drawback to this reduced N is non-random selection: people included in both waves could be distinct from those who participated only once. The descriptive statistics in Table 5.6 are slightly different from the complete 2002 sample, though not substantially.

In the panel design, all independent variables were measured for 1998; the dependent variable was measured for 2002. As for the controls, the

Table 5.6   *Descriptive statistics sample employment (SPVA panel 1998, 2002)*

	Employed and unemployed in 1998		Unemployed in 1998	
	Mean	SD	Mean	SD
Structural bridging social capital	0.39	0.27	0.31	0.24
Age	39.59	10.29	37.59	7.15
Duration of stay	19.52	11.63	16.16	7.48
Dutch language proficiency	0.62	0.33	0.54	0.32
	Percentage		Percentage	
Employed in 1998	57		0	
Ethnic group				
Surinamese	35		23	
Turkish	25		32	
Moroccan	18		19	
Dutch Antillean	22		25	
Second generation	14		5	
Female	43		58	
Married	43		38	
Urban domicile	65		67	
Educational attainment				
Primary	43		57	
Lower secondary	23		23	
Upper secondary	22		15	
Tertiary education	9		3	
Education information missing	3		2	
Total	746		206	

Source: SPVA 1998, 2002

models presented are similar to those of the cross-sectional analyses, except for the inclusion of being employed in 1998 as an extra control. Due to limited data availability, it was only possible to measure structural bridging social capital. This scale is the same as the structural bridging scale in the cross-sectional analyses.

When including all controls, the effect of structural bridging does not prove significant (Table 5.7). This implies that in a cross-sectional design, being employed is positively affected by structural bridging social capital. It does not, however, have an effect when assessing the likelihood of a *change* in employment. Put differently, when controlling for one's employment status in 1998, structural bridging social capital cannot *additionally* predict the employment status in 2002. Estimating the model using non-parametric bootstrapping with hundred replications yielded similar results. This does not necessarily mean that bridging social capital does not have an effect: there is little variation in employment status; the strongest predictor variable therefore is being employed in 1998. If only these people who did not work in 1998 are selected and the sample is restricted to those

Table 5.7 *Logistic regression predicting employment likelihood (SPVA panel 1998, 2002), odds ratios*

	Model 1		Model 2	
	b	se	b	se
Structural bridging social capital in 1998	8.042***	(2.378)	1.190	(.520)
Being employed in 1998			5.432***	(1.082)
Age			.959**	(.013)
Female			.798	(.192)
Ethnic group				
Surinamese			ref.	
Turkish			.577	(.199)
Moroccan			.650	(.222)
Dutch Antillean			1.946*	(.556)
Second generation			1.156	(.249)
Duration of stay			1.004	(.015)
Married			.843	(.213)
Urban domicile			.684	(.138)
Educational attainment in 1998				
Primary education			ref.	
Lower secondary			1.511	(.357)
Upper secondary			2.469**	(.688)
Tertiary education			3.716***	(1.471)
Education information missing			1.497	(.865)
Language proficiency in 1998			.826	(.363)
Parental education				
Parent primary education			ref.	
Parent lower secondary			.749	(.406)
Parent upper secondary			2.435	(2.273)
Parent tertiary education			.673	(.389)
Parental education information missing			.574	(.243)
Constant	.653**	(.086)	3.405	(2.544)
Log-likelihood	-482.030		-378.280	
N	752		746	

* $p < 0.05$, ** $p < 0.01$, *** $p < 0.001$ (two-tailed tests); robust standard errors
Source: SPVA 1998, 2002

under age 50, possessing structural bridging social capital does increase the likelihood of being employed in 2002; this model is presented in Table 5.8. Since this is an even smaller sample, chances of selection bias are bigger; still, a coefficient being significant is also less likely. Keeping the limitations in mind, there is some evidence that for those not working in 1998, possessing structural bridging social capital increases the likelihood of being employed in 2002. In fact, people with bridging social capital are 4.4 times more likely to be employed in 2002 than those who do not possess bridging social capital. This is not due to the employed having more bridging social capital: people not working in 1998 had a higher likelihood of working in 2002 once they had more structural bridging social capital.

Table 5.8   *Logistic regression predicting the employment likelihood in 2002 for*
            unemployed population aged < 50 in 1998, odds ratios

	Model 1		Model 2	
	b	se	b	se
Structural bridging social capital in 1998	4.911**	(2.956)	4.448*	(3.266)
Age			.950	(.029)
Female			1.060	(.453)
Ethnic group				
Surinamese			ref.	
Turkish			.827	(.490)
Moroccan			1.042	(.621)
Dutch Antillean			2.619	(1.341)
Second generation			.983	(.949)
Duration of stay			.973	(.028)
Married			.879	(.381)
Urban domicile			.546	(.194)
Educational attainment in 1998				
Primary education			ref.	
Lower secondary			1.414	(.562)
Upper secondary			2.961*	(1.514)
Tertiary education			3.648	(3.007)
Education information missing			4.261	(4.958)
Language proficiency in 1998			.641	(.455)
Parental education				
Parent primary education			ref.	
Parent lower secondary			.525	(.635)
Parent tertiary education			.536	(.484)
Parental education information missing			.200*	(.159)
Constant	.423***	(.101)	5.934	(9.059)
Log-likelihood	-136.670		-122.032	
N	207		206	

* p < 0.05, ** p < 0.01, *** p < 0.001 (two-tailed tests); robust standard errors
Source: SPVA 1998, 2002

Using this design, reversed causality is thus much less likely than in the
cross-sectional analysis.

Occupational status

In Table 5.9 and Table 5.10, occupational status (ISEI) is predicted by the
social capital measures and the relevant control variables. Taking into account all controls, only structural bridging social capital affects the occupational status among men; none of the measures affects occupational status
among women. For men, just as in the analysis of employment status, interethnic contacts can be associated with a higher occupational status. The
other measures of social capital do not significantly affect the ISEI score
although, for men, structural bonding is almost significant with a p-value

Table 5.9   *OLS regression predicting ISEI scores among men, standardised coefficients*

	Model 1		Model 2	
	b	se	b	se
Cognitive bonding	-5.481	(3.065)	-.756	(2.524)
Structural bonding	4.261*	(1.842)	3.070	(1.612)
Cognitive bridging	13.832***	(2.646)	.114	(2.394)
Structural bridging	14.512***	(2.135)	3.926*	(1.967)
Age			-5.972	(4.572)
Ethnic group				
Surinamese			ref.	
Turkish			-3.265*	(1.357)
Moroccan			-2.929*	(1.280)
Dutch Antillean			.749	(1.340)
Second generation			-.637	(1.526)
Duration of stay			9.710*	(4.488)
Married			-.289	(.943)
Urban domicile			.959	(.803)
Temporary job			-1.079	(1.208)
Contracted hours			.537	(4.810)
Self-employed			8.161***	(1.813)
Educational attainment				
Primary education			ref.	
Lower secondary			1.507	(1.033)
Upper secondary			5.463***	(1.045)
Tertiary education			23.256***	(1.495)
Education information missing			-.214	(4.339)
Language proficiency			3.193	(1.758)
Parental education				
Parent primary education			ref.	
Parent lower secondary			1.720	(1.413)
Parent upper secondary			-1.215	(1.679)
Parent tertiary education			2.221	(1.588)
Parental education information missing			-.488	(2.087)
Constant	27.494***	(2.828)	27.443***	(3.874)
Adjusted R-squared	.187		.464	
N	934		934	

* $p < 0.05$, ** $p < 0.01$, *** $p < 0.001$ (two-tailed tests); robust standard errors
Source: SPVA 2002

of .057. If the people between 60 and 65 years old are excluded from the analysis, structural bonding social capital also significantly affects men's occupational status. Thus, where structural bridging social capital can be associated with a higher occupational status for all men, structural bonding only has a positive effect for men younger than 60 years old. When using the whole sample and including an interaction between age and structural bonding, this is not significant. It is therefore not the case that the effect of structural bonding is stronger for younger people; the effect is not

Table 5.10   *OLS regression predicting ISEI scores among women, standardised coefficients*

	Model 1		Model 2	
	b	se	b	se
Cognitive bonding	1.548	(3.560)	-.809	(2.956)
Structural bonding	-14.569**	(5.232)	2.683	(1.991)
Cognitive bridging	18.686***	(3.179)	5.532	(2.832)
Structural bridging	23.165***	(5.437)	-1.479	(2.639)
Age			-15.875**	(5.518)
Ethnic group				
Surinamese			ref.	
Turkish			1.007	(1.828)
Moroccan			-.417	(1.777)
Dutch Antillean			2.375	(1.343)
Second generation			1.744	(1.839)
Duration of stay			9.476	(5.982)
Married			1.237	(1.176)
Urban domicile			1.562	(1.083)
Temporary job			1.976	(1.443)
Contracted hours			24.018***	(4.370)
Self-employed			-6.587*	(3.320)
Educational attainment				
Primary education			ref.	
Lower secondary			4.955***	(1.417)
Upper secondary			8.303***	(1.453)
Tertiary education			20.804***	(1.993)
Education information missing			5.759	(3.142)
Language proficiency			9.703***	(2.343)
Parental education				
Parent primary education			ref.	
Parent lower secondary			.772	(1.421)
Parent upper secondary			2.867	(1.627)
Parent high school/university			2.432	(1.767)
Parental education information missing			-1.965	(2.094)
Constant	27.446***	(3.073)	11.702**	(3.799)
Adjusted R-squared	.145		.414	
N	605		605	

* p < 0.05, ** p < 0.01, *** p < 0.001 (two-tailed tests); robust standard errors
Source: SPVA 2002

significant for people between 60 and 65 years old. This could be due to the fact that the family network is not useful for these respondents, or because occupational status does not change so much at the end of people's careers.

None of the measures significantly affects occupational status for women. However, there is one borderline case. The p-value of cognitive bridging is .51. When including an interaction term between age and cognitive bridging, this is significant: for younger women the effect of cognitive bridging is stronger than for older women. When only the younger part of the sample is selected, cognitive bridging social capital is now indeed significant.

The coefficients of the control variables do not show surprising results. As expected, education and language proficiency strongly affect occupational status. Furthermore, for men, there are significant differences between being Turkish and Surinamese and between being Moroccan and Surinamese: both groups have a significantly lower occupational status than the Surinamese. Antilleans do not significantly differ from the Surinamese. For women, once all controls are taken into account, there are no significant differences between the ethnic groups. For men, duration of stay positively affects occupational status, as does being self-employed. For women, those who are self-employed have a lower occupational status than those who are not. It could be the case that seemingly self-employed women actually work in an enterprise with their husband, who – as the male family breadwinner – claims the 'highest' occupational status. Whereas self-employment has a positive effect on occupational status for men, women are pushed into a lower position when self-employed. Last, for men, there is no effect of age, although for women there is a strong negative effect.

By including the relevant interaction terms, I also analysed whether the effect of social capital differs for ethnic groups, levels of education and language proficiency. It appears that for men, there is a significant interaction between having upper secondary education and structural bridging social capital: for those with an upper secondary education, structural bridging is more effective than for those with a primary education (not shown here). There were no significant differences found for the ethnic groups or for Dutch language proficiency.

In Table 5.11, the descriptive statistics for the panel are presented (N = 228 for occupational status, N = 274 for income). The values differ slightly, though not substantially from the 2002 sample. All variables are measured in 1998, except for the dependent variable, which is measured in 2002.

Table 5.12 presents the regression model for occupational status. For this analysis, the sample contains only those between 25 and 45 years old. The analysis was also carried out to include those between 45 and 65 years old. The latter showed no significant effect for structural bridging social capital. This implies that, with respect to occupational status, the effects of bridging social capital are more prevalent for the younger part of the labour force. When analysing only the younger part – although their sample size is much smaller – the coefficient for bridging is significant at the p = 0.05 level. Taking into account the regular controls and occupational status (measured in 1998), bridging social capital proves to positively affect occupational status in 2002. This implies that people who have more structural

Table 5.11 *Descriptive statistics sample income and occupational status panel SPVA 1998-2002*

	Income		Occupational status (ISEI)	
	Mean	SD	Mean	SD
Structural bridging social capital	0.46	0.27	0.5	0.27
Age	37.77	9.17	35.04	5.57
Duration of stay	19.49	10.49	18.33	11.12
Dutch language proficiency	0.7	0.3	0.72	0.28
Number of hours worked	35.37	9.51	35.35	9.04
Income in 1998/ISEI in 1998	1,150.15	429.36	40.49	14.13
	%		%	
Ethnic group				
Surinamese	41		43	
Turkish	22		21	
Moroccan	11		11	
Dutch Antillean	26		26	
Second generation	16		16	
Female	37		43	
Married	40		37	
Urban domicile	60		62	
Self-employed	4		4	
Education				
Primary	28		20	
Lower secondary	24		25	
Upper secondary	31		37	
Tertiary	13		15	
Education information missing	3		3	
Total	274		228	

Source: SPVA 1998, 2002

bridging social capital can be associated with a higher occupational status four years later. This is not due to variation in educational attainment, language proficiency, parental education or between ethnic groups.

With respect to the control variables, the strongest predictor of occupational status in 2002 is, first and foremost, occupational status in 1998. Furthermore, having tertiary education has a positive effect, compared to having only primary education. Furthermore, respondents whose parents have a lower secondary education have a lower occupational status than parents with just primary education. By including an interaction term in the model, I also checked whether the effect of bridging on occupational status is significantly different for men and women, but this did not appear to be the case.

Table 5.12 *OLS regression predicting ISEI scores (SPVA panel 1998, 2002), for those aged 25-45, standardised coefficients*

	Model 1		Model 2	
	b	se	b	se
Structural bridging social capital in 1998	18.772***	(3.177)	7.080*	(3.454)
ISEI in1998, standardised			25.826***	(5.575)
Age			-.354	(.185)
Female			-1.215	(1.672)
Ethnic group				
Surinamese			ref.	
Turkish			-4.580	(3.290)
Moroccan			-5.998	(3.252)
Dutch Antillean			-.346	(2.018)
Second generation			-.714	(1.797)
Duration of stay			.233	(.139)
Married			.955	(2.394)
Educational attainment in 1998				
Primary education			ref.	
Lower secondary			-2.635	(2.391)
Upper secondary			1.081	(2.340)
Tertiary education			10.668**	(3.409)
Education information missing			.788	(4.445)
Language proficiency in 1998			-6.286	(4.928)
Parental education				
Parent primary education			ref.	
Parent lower secondary			-6.377*	(3.178)
Parent upper secondary			7.174	(8.511)
Parent tertiary			-.305	(2.806)
Parental education information missing			-3.718	(3.046)
Constant	32.957***	(1.762)	43.093***	(8.707)
Adjusted R-squared	.110		.427	
N	231		228	

* $p < 0.05$, ** $p < 0.01$, *** $p < 0.001$ (two-tailed tests); robust standard errors
Source: SPVA 1998, 2002

Income

The findings with respect to income are rather similar (Table 5.13 and Table 5.14).[6] For men, the only social capital measure that positively affects income is structural bridging. For women, only cognitive bridging social capital has a positive effect. None of the bonding measures significantly affects income of men or women. Whereas among men interethnic contacts are associated with a higher income, for women, it is an attitude that is congruent with that of Dutch society. For all, closure in the family network does not translate into better opportunities on the labour market, i.e. a higher income.

Table 5.13 *OLS regression predicting income (ln) among men, standardised coefficients*

	Model 1		Model 2	
	b	se	b	se
Cognitive bonding	-.159	(.085)	-.027	(.073)
Structural bonding	.045	(.051)	.008	(.044)
Cognitive bridging	-.063	(.077)	-.122	(.070)
Structural bridging	.413***	(.063)	.208**	(.064)
Age			.142	(.114)
Ethnic group				
Surinamese			ref.	
Turkish			-.053	(.037)
Moroccan			-.109**	(.036)
Dutch Antillean			-.068	(.035)
Second generation			-.036	(.044)
Duration of stay			.479***	(.115)
Married			.076**	(.028)
Urban domicile			.039	(.022)
Temporary job			-.164***	(.039)
Contracted hours			.891***	(.172)
Self-employed			.182*	(.073)
Educational attainment				
Primary education			ref.	
Lower secondary			.045	(.031)
Upper secondary			.104***	(.030)
Tertiary education			.315***	(.040)
Education information missing			.029	(.064)
Language proficiency			.053	(.051)
Parental education				
Parent primary education			ref.	
Parent lower secondary			.014	(.037)
Parent upper secondary			-.016	(.041)
Parent tertiary education			.035	(.042)
Parental education information missing			-.009	(.055)
Constant	7.268***	(.078)	6.547***	(.120)
Adjusted R-squared	.068		.325	
N	970		970	

* $p < 0.05$, ** $p < 0.01$, *** $p < 0.001$ (two-tailed tests); robust standard errors
Source: SPVA 2002

With respect to the control variables included in the model, Moroccan men have a significantly lower income than the Surinamese and there is no discrepancy in income between the ethnic groups for women. Being second-generation shows no significant impact, but the longer men have been in the Netherlands, the higher their income. The number of hours worked has a positive impact. Men who have a temporary job have a lower income than those with a tenured job; type of work contract makes no difference for women. Just as in the analysis of occupational status, men who are

Table 5.14   *OLS regression predicting income (ln) among women, standardised coefficients*

	Model 1		Model 2	
	b	se	b	se
Cognitive bonding	.126	(.102)	.084	(.084)
Structural bonding	.083	(.064)	.036	(.053)
Cognitive bridging	.448***	(.096)	.224**	(.080)
Structural bridging	.117	(.086)	.067	(.073)
Age			.141	(.143)
Ethnic group				
Surinamese			ref.	
Turkish			-.078	(.047)
Moroccan			.037	(.053)
Dutch Antillean			-.039	(.036)
Second generation			-.040	(.047)
Duration of stay			.245	(.137)
Married			-.038	(.034)
Urban domicile			-.002	(.031)
Temporary job			-.076	(.040)
Contracted hours			2.041***	(.190)
Self-employed			-.307	(.165)
Educational attainment				
Primary education			ref.	
Lower secondary			.022	(.040)
Upper secondary			.083*	(.039)
Tertiary education			.350***	(.049)
Education information missing			-.021	(.090)
Language proficiency			.096	(.069)
Parental education				
Parent primary education			ref.	
Parent lower secondary			-.005	(.038)
Parent upper secondary			.001	(.042)
Parent tertiary education			-.058	(.049)
Parental education information missing			.007	(.049)
Constant	6.658***	(.087)	5.824***	(.124)
Adjusted R-squared	.056		.476	
N	624		624	

* $p < 0.05$, ** $p < 0.01$, *** $p < 0.001$ (two-tailed tests); robust standard errors
Source: SPVA 2002

self-employed have a higher income; for women, the effect is negative. This is in line with Constant and Schachmurove (2003), who find that self-employed immigrant men in Germany earn 22 per cent more than salaried immigrants. Parental education has no significant effect. Neither does language proficiency or age.

By including interaction terms, I analysed whether the effects of social capital differ for ethnic groups, different levels of education and language proficiency. This did not appear to be the case.

Table 5.15 predicts income in a mini-panel design. As in the cross-sectional model including men and in the models predicting occupational status and employment likelihood, structural bridging capital positively affects income four years later. In other words, those who possess more structural bridging social capital in 1998 have a higher income in 2002. An interaction term between being female and structural bridging social capital was included, though this was not significant. Note, however, that due to limited data availability for 1998, only structural bridging social capital was included. It is likely that the effect of cognitive bridging social capital found in the cross-sectional analysis for women is now manifested in structural bridging social capital.

Table 5.15 *OLS regression predicting income (ln) (SPVA panel 1998, 2002), standardised coefficients*

	Model 1		Model 2	
	b	se	b	se
Structural bridging social capital in 1998	.388***	(.088)	.274**	(.104)
Income in 1998			.477***	(.093)
Age			-.002	(.003)
Female			-.190***	(.055)
Ethnic group				
Surinamese			ref.	
Turkish			-.003	(.107)
Moroccan			-.032	(.116)
Dutch Antillean			-.004	(.056)
Second generation			-.044	(.043)
Duration of stay			.005	(.003)
Married			-.106*	(.051)
Self-employed			-.069	(.141)
Urban domicile			.051	(.046)
Contracted hours			-.008*	(.003)
Educational attainment in 1998				
Primary education			ref.	
Lower secondary			.070	(.058)
Upper secondary			.156*	(.066)
Tertiary education			.306***	(.084)
Education information missing			.121	(.172)
Language proficiency in 1998			-.235	(.134)
Parental education				
Parent primary education			ref.	
Parent lower secondary			.058	(.150)
Parent upper secondary			.026	(.112)
Parent tertiary education			.040	(.089)
Parental education information missing			.169	(.125)
Constant	6.999***	(.044)	4.102***	(.619)
Adjusted R-squared	.058		.313	
N	277		274	

* p < 0.05, ** p < 0.01, *** p < 0.001 (two-tailed tests); robust standard errors
Source: SPVA 1998, 2002

Conclusion

Figure 5.3 summarises the results of this chapter.

Certain limitations should be kept in mind with the findings of this study. The first is the cross-sectional nature of the data used. As several scholars point out (Mouw 2002; Offe & Fuchs 2004), many studies on social capital are challenged by an endogeneity problem. On the one hand, social capital may contribute to economic success. On the other hand, economic participation may also enhance social capital. Constructing a mini-panel partly solves this by making it possible to estimate the effect of bridging social capital in 1998 on the outcome variable in 2002, while controlling for the labour market position in 1998. This reduces the possibility of bias due to reversed causality and unobserved heterogeneity. A limitation of the panel approach, though, is that the sample is very small; it could thus be the case that there was non-random selection in this regard.

The second limitation concerns the measurement of structural bonding social capital. Due to limited data availability, the measurement of structural bonding was limited to the strength of family ties with one's parents and/or children. Being unable to include other information – for example, on siblings or co-ethnics overall – means not capturing potentially valuable information about respondents' family members who are close in age. Whereas one can argue that this measurement serves as a proxy for the strength of all family ties, it is likely that the effect is underestimated. Further research would be necessary to answer this question. Also in this case, analysis of the labour market position of immigrants in Germany may improve the understanding of the effect of bonding social capital, since in the German data there is more extended information available on the family network.

Furthermore, the relation between structural bridging social capital and labour market outcomes cannot be ascribed to the *network* effect of social capital only. It could very well be that measurement of interethnic contacts to some extent also captures unobserved characteristics related to other dimensions of integration (be it social or psychological). So it is not only social capital, per se, that is positively associated with performance on the

Figure 5.3 *The returns of bonding and bridging social capital in the Netherlands*

	Likelihood of being employed		Occupational status		Income	
	Men	Women	Men	Women	Men	Women
Cognitive bonding						
Structural bonding			X			
Cognitive bridging				(X)		X
Structural bridging	X	X	X		X	

Source: Author

labour market; certain dimensions of integration into the host society are also captured by the factor of 'having interethnic contacts'. On this point, the German data allow for better measurement because it was possible to include two variables that proxy the propensity to integrate.

In light of these limitations, my findings have several implications for immigrants in the Netherlands. H2, stating that bonding social capital is positively associated with labour market outcomes, must be rejected, albeit with the exception for the occupational status of men. Bonding social capital, measured as closure in the densest network – that of the family – does not influence the labour market outcomes of immigrants in the Netherlands. This supports the 'isolation' rather than the 'closure' argument: high closure in the family network may indicate a high level of solidarity and enforceable trust, but it does not provide a gateway to valuable new information useful in finding a job or better-paid employment. This type of network is therefore not effective for making headway on the labour market.

An explanation for this finding may be the different function of family-based social capital. It may be that a strong family network mainly implies 'giving'. That is, a high closure network may also have negative externalities, other than those posed in the isolation argument. Having a high-quality family network implies investing in relations: spending time, care and resources that do not necessarily have returns. As the title of Portes' (2000) article indicates, there are 'two meanings of social capital'. In this case, bonding social capital does not have negative externalities; there is simply no difference in terms of labour market outcomes between people indicating high closure in their family network and people that do not. Although some scholars report positive effects of family-based social capital for immigrants on self-employment or job-seeking, in general (Sanders & Nee 1996; Sanders, Nee & Sernau 2002; Alesina & Giuliano 2007), these positive effects cannot be corroborated for immigrants in the Netherlands.

In one case, bonding social capital affected labour market outcomes. Men with more structural bonding social capital had a higher occupational status. It seems that men with a strong family network found different types of jobs than men not possessing such a network. The former group's jobs, however, were not better paid (as structural bonding does not affect income).

On the other hand, H1 stated that bridging social capital positively affects labour market outcomes. I did indeed find that networks comprising interethnic contacts are positively associated with labour market outcomes. People with a high level of bridging social capital are more likely to be employed than those who don't possess bridging social capital. Among those who have work, bridging social capital is associated with higher income and higher occupational status. Yet, there is no effect of social capital on women's occupational status. For men, structural bridging has a positive effect on income whereas, for women, cognitive bridging has a positive effect. Nevertheless, possessing bridging social capital generally seems to pay off; both in terms of access to the labour market and income and occupational status.

The results also indicate a difference in the effect of cognitive and structural social capital. It seems that cognitive social capital mostly does not have an effect, while structural social capital does. One could argue that this is simply because the process of finding a job is an action, hence it is actions (i.e. structural social capital) and not mere attitudes that yield positive returns. Yet such an argument would discard almost any claim about the impact of attitudes. Particularly in the field of social capital research, attitudinal measures are frequently used (e.g. trust or solidarity). One could also argue that attitudes (cognitive) result in behaviour (structural) rather than the other way around. Since they also capture attitudes, it seems logical that the 'structural' scales behave better in the analyses. However, estimating the models without the scales of structural social capital does not result in the cognitive scales being significant. If there was an indirect effect, this should be the case.

My last conclusion is that the results are rather similar for each dependent variable analysed. That is, one may perhaps speak of a more general pattern for economic returns to immigrants' social capital. Bridging social capital positively affects labour market outcomes. Bonding has no effect on them. The reasoning behind bonding and bridging as applied in this book seems similar for both access to and performance on the labour market.

Notes

1   The SPVA consists of a stratified sample of the population in a number of cities, including the four biggest cities in the Netherlands. For a detailed description of survey and sampling techniques, see Groeneveld and Weyers-Martens (2003).

2   Being active on the labour market foresees working more than eleven hours per week (Groeneveld & Weyers-Martens 2003).

3   In the SPVA, occupation is coded with the standard 1992 classification of the Dutch Central Bureau of Statistics (CBS). Bakker, Sieben, Nieuwbeerta and Ganzeboom (1997) describe how this can be converted into an ISEI score.

4   For a description of the scale construction, see the appendix.

5   Furthermore, the highest VIF value is 3, which is much below the often cited threshold of 10.

6   Models were also estimated using the equivalised household income as a dependent variable. Results are very similar to the models presented here. One difference appeared: for men, cognitive bonding negatively affects family income. This can be explained by the fact that men who value family more highly are more likely to have more children and therefore a lower equivalised household income (since in this case, the household income is divided by the square root of the number of household members). As discussed in chapter 4, this is the main reason to use personal income as a dependent variable in the regressions.

6 The case of Germany

Introduction

Using data from the German Social Economic Panel (GSOEP), this chapter analyses the effect of bonding and bridging social capital on the labour market outcomes of immigrants in Germany (see also Lancee forthcoming). The ethnic groups included are Turks, Greeks, Italians, Spaniards and Portuguese (the latter two combined in one category), migrants from former Yugoslavia and migrants from Eastern Europe (Romania, Poland, Hungary, Bulgaria, Czech Republic), plus 'Other', a category for the 'rest' mainly comprising immigrants from Western European countries.

Data and measurement

Sample

The GSOEP is a household-based panel study that has conducted a yearly questionnaire since 1984 (Wagner, Burkhauser & Behringer 1993). In 1996, 2001 and 2006, the survey included a module on social networks. The panel used in my analyses is therefore restricted to the years 1996 to 2007. Although the GSOEP is not specifically geared towards immigrant studies, it does include an immigrant sample, containing questionnaire items specifically designed for immigrants, such as contacts with the native population. The GSOEP is therefore very suitable for studying immigrants, and is frequently used to analyse their labour market outcomes in terms of types of employment (Kogan 2004, 2007a), income (Constant & Massey 2005; Dustmann & Van Soest 2002) and occupational mobility (Bauer & Zimmermann 1999).

The sample consists of all people who are not 'native German'. A native German is defined as somebody who was born in Germany and holds German nationality. A person is classified as an ethnic minority if his or her country of birth is not Germany or his or her nationality is not German. This classification is different from the one used in the case of the Netherlands (for GSOEP respondents the country of birth of the parents in the GSOEP is often missing, as well as the country of birth, in case this is not Germany). However, using only the country of birth as a criterion

overlooks the second generation; using only nationality misses the naturalised first generation and part of the second generation. Hence, those with
a country of birth other than Germany and those who arrived in Germany
at age six or older are classified as first-generation immigrants. 'Second'-
generation minorities comprise those who were born in Germany or arrived
in Germany before age six and hold a foreign nationality and those who
hold German nationality but were not born in Germany (i.e. naturalised
immigrants).

The sample for the analysis of employment likelihood consists of all
people between twenty and 65 years old who answered at least one of the
items used to measure social capital. For the years between the measurements of social capital items, respondents were assigned the last known
value of this item. Thus, the value of an indicator measured in, for example, 2001 remains the same until its next measurement in 2006. To respect
the causal ordering of events, the social capital items were always replaced
with information from earlier waves. The age thresholds were chosen as
such because, on average, at age twenty, most people are on the labour
market; 65 years old is official retirement age in Germany. Furthermore,
people in school, performing military or civil service and those who have
retired before age 65 are excluded from the sample. For the analyses of
income and occupational status, the sample is restricted to those with either
full-time or regular part-time work. Missing values are replaced with information available from earlier waves. Remaining missing values are
imputed using imputation regressions; I checked with a dummy if imputed
cases differ significantly from the observed cases.

Method of estimation

A problem in research on social capital and its effects is that of reversed
causality. It may be that more social capital results in better labour market
outcomes, but it is also likely that a better position on the labour market
results in more social capital (for a recent review on the measurement of
causality in social capital, see Mouw 2006). Another problem in cross-
sectional research is the problem of unobserved heterogeneity: if a correlation is found between some form of social capital and labour market outcomes, this can also be due to enduring differences between people, rather
than having acquired social capital. There is some research that deals with
the endogeneity problem by using longitudinal data, for example, for estimating the effect of using personal contacts on the likelihood of finding a
job (Mouw 2002, 2003, 2006). However, not much research has been done
that estimates the effect of immigrants' social capital on labour market outcomes using longitudinal data.

I estimate both random-effects and fixed-effects models. The fixed-
effects model (also referred to as the fixed intercept model) estimates an

intercept for each individual and can hence estimate only coefficients that have within-individual variation (Rabe-Hesketh & Skrondal 2008). Since it only uses within-individual information, the fixed-effects model has the advantage of being able to control for all stable individual characteristics: each subject truly serves as his or her own control. By eliminating unobserved heterogeneity, fixed-effects models can therefore better deal with the endogeneity problem. In other words, since only time-varying variables are included, there is no omitted variable bias with regard to time-constant variables. Reviewing the studies on social capital that aim to estimate a causal relationship, Mouw (2006) favours those that apply fixed-effects models. The disadvantage of fixed-effects models, however, is that it is not possible to estimate the effect of time-invariant covariates, such as ethnic origin.

The random-effects model (also referred to as the random intercept model) assumes a randomly varying intercept, which is a draw from some distribution for each unit that is independent of the error for a particular observation. An advantage of this model is that it uses within-individual and between-individual information, hence also being able to estimate coefficients for time-constant variables. The major drawback is that the random intercept is assumed to be uncorrelated with the covariates; it therefore cannot control for unobserved individual characteristics. Although random-effects models use the panel structure of the data, they thus fail to solve the problem of unobserved heterogeneity. I apply random-effects models to show the effects of time-constant covariates and the between-individual variation. Furthermore, since the items used to measure social capital are only measured every five years, they have little within-individual variation. The effects of social capital, as reported in the fixed-effects models, may therefore be underestimated.

A problem with fixed-effects and random-effects models is that they are sensitive to period effects. Time dummies for each survey year are therefore included in each model. This controls for a general time trend in the labour market and a changing macro-context.

Measures

The dependent variables that I analysed are the likelihood of full-time or regular part-time employment, as opposed to being unemployed, looking for a job or not working. The occupational status is measured by the ISEI score (Ganzeboom, De Graaf & Treiman 1992) and monthly net income in logs. Also see chapter 4 for a discussion of the dependent variables.

With respect to bonding social capital, five measures are constructed, taken from various survey years. First, in 1996, 2001 and 2006, the GSOEP includes the module 'Social networks and persons to confide in'. In this module, respondents are asked to mention up to three people outside their household who are important to them. In Figure 6.1, the exact wording of the items is presented. The 1996 and 2006 surveys' wording differs slightly though reflects the same substantial content. The three cited people are subsequently classified by whether they are or are not related to the respondent and what their country of origin is.

The validity of this item has its limits. The social ties being explored through these items are classified as either 'coming from East/West Germany', or as 'coming from another country'. If the latter is selected, respondents are asked whether they come from the same country as the cited people. A pitfall is the ambiguity of the phrase 'coming from'. While, for first-generation immigrants, this should pose no problem – it is clear that they were born abroad – if the person cited is a second-generation ethnic minority (or a first-generation immigrant holding German nationality), the individual could well be classified as 'coming from another country' or as 'coming from East/West Germany'. Which box is ticked depends on the perception of ego.

This has two potential consequences. First, in the most extreme case, it is theoretically possible that *all* ties classified as 'coming from East/West Germany' are in fact to second-generation immigrants or immigrants holding German nationality – thus not native Germans. Second, it is possible that the most 'integrated' ethnic minorities are included in the measure of bridging and the least integrated, in the measure of bonding. Put differently, if bonding proves ineffective and bridging, effective, we might chalk this up to how respondents classify their ties on the basis of 'coming from East/West Germany' or 'coming from another country'.

However, this may be less problematic than it seems. First of all, in 98 per cent of the cases where respondents indicated the tie was from another country, they stated in the follow-up question that they are from the same

Figure 6.1   *Items in the GSOEP differentiating interethnic and intra-ethnic ties*

Now some questions about your friends and acquaintances:
Please think of *three friends or relatives* or other people whom you go out with or meet with often.
Please do not include relatives or other people who live in the same household as you.
Please provide us with the following information about these friends or relatives:

Are you related? (Yes/No)

Where does this person come from?
From the former West Germany / From the former East Germany
From another country

If 'From another country' selected:
Are you from the same country? (Yes/No)

Source: GSOEP 2001; translation from German by GSOEP

country as the tie mentioned. This implies that the bonding ties can be seen as truly co-ethnic ties. With respect to bridging, it appears that migrants interpret the country meant in the phrase 'coming from' as 'coming from the original country of origin', rather than coming from Germany. When selecting only those born in Germany though not holding German nationality, the respondents indicate in the follow-up question that they are from the same country as 93 per cent of the ties classified as 'coming from another country'. When only selecting those that hold German nationality but were born abroad, this figures at 90 per cent. Thus, when second-generation ethnic minorities classify their ties as *not* coming from Germany, they are classifying them as coming from the same country as themselves. That is, the country referred to when indicating 'coming from' is the 'original' country of origin. It seems that people classified as not from Germany are perceived as being from the same country as the second generation. In sum, first- *and* second-generation ethnic minorities refer to their *original* country of origin when they are asked to classify ties as coming from Germany or not.

Another argument for why this is not as problematic as it may seem relates to the resource argument, as discussed in chapter 4. It is not so much the ethnic divide that is bridged, but accessing a resource-rich (i.e. host country-specific) network that matters. If ties are being perceived as coming from Germany, the ties are also likely to provide host country-specific resources.

For the measurement of bonding social capital, only ties linking to the same ethnic group are included. This results in two measures: friends who come from the same country and family members outside of the household who are important to ego and come from the same country.

In 1996 and 2001, an additional module is available containing items on the relatives of ego outside the home. From these items, a construct called 'Family strength' is built. Respondents were asked to cite types of family members, indicating whether they have such a family member and how strong their relationship is to each of them. The module introduction[1] reads: 'Now a question concerning family members who don't live at home: which ones and how many of the following relatives do you have?' Family member categories comprised: mother, father, former spouse, current spouse if not living in the household, son/s, daughter/s, brother/s, sister/s, grandchild/-ren, grandparent/s, other relatives with whom you have close contacts (aunts, uncles, cousins, nephews, nieces). Subsequently, respondents were asked: 'With those relatives that you do have, how close is your relationship (no relationship, fleeting, average, close, very close)?' Reliability analysis (for 1996 Cronbach's alpha = .82; for 2001: Cronbach's alpha = .81) clearly shows that these items can be seen as underlying measures of a single construct. The scale consists of the average relation strength of all relatives mentioned. Furthermore, the module contains items measuring the number of family members each respondent has. As a proxy for family network size, this is also included as a measure of bonding social capital. The construction of these scales is discussed in more detail in the appendix.

Survey waves 1996 and 2001 also include two items on the social support people receive through their network. The first item asks: 'If you came down with the flu and had to stay in bed for a couple of days, whom would you ask for help with, for example, shopping?' The second items asks: 'Hypothetically: whom would you turn to for help if you need long-term help, e.g. after a bad accident?' Respondents are asked to mention up to two people and to classify them by relation type (family or non-relatives such as friends, co-workers and social workers). The items were separated into family members versus non-family members. With respect to social support and care, the friends who are listed also indicate some level of closure in one's network (albeit not in the family network), as contrasted with people indicating they have nobody. Hence, the analyses for social support were also done when including all ties mentioned. This did not make any difference in the results. Reliability analysis was also done for these items (for 1996 Cronbach's alpha = .73, Loevinger's H = .68; for 2001 Cron-bach's alpha = .74, Loevinger's H = .69). Consequently, the items were summed up.

The following measures are constructed for bridging social capital. First, the items described as 'Coming from East/West Germany' are used to measure interethnic friendships and family ties. Following the survey item 'Please think of three friends or relatives or other people whom you go out with or meet often' are two subsequent questions: 'Where does this person come from?' and 'Do you come from the same country?' Those ties that are classified as co-ethnic are included in the bonding measure described above. The ties that are interethnic are used as a measure of bridging social capital: one through relatives, one through friends.

The second measure for bridging social capital is a construct labelled 'Interethnic contacts'. In 1997, 1999, 2001, 2003, 2005 and 2007, respondents were asked whether they had paid a social visit to Germans the previous year (yes or no) and whether they had received social visits by Germans in the previous year (yes or no). Reliability analysis (Cronbach's alpha ranging from .80-.87 over the survey years) and cumulative scaling (Loevinger's H = .85) shows that these items can be seen as dimensions of a single construct. Consequently, the items were summed up. In the appendix, a table with the exact values of Cronbach's alpha and Loevinger's H for each survey year can be found.

Limitations

Measures of social capital should be seen in the light of some limitations. First, the GSOEP does not provide information on cognitive social capital.

The attitudinal dimension of immigrants' bonding and bridging social capital can therefore not be analysed for the German case. The second limitation concerns their time-variation. Since social capital is not measured every survey year, but every five years (apart from visiting or receiving social visits, which is measured every second year), there is little within-individual variation. One could furthermore argue that one's stock of social capital is relatively constant over time. This complicates the estimation of its causal effect and would imply that a between-individual comparison is sufficient: since social capital is relatively time-constant, one can only compare individuals with high and low social capital and analyse to what extent their labour market outcomes are different. This problem is partly solved by estimating random-effects models, which include between individual information. However, when fixed-effects models do indicate a significant impact of social capital on labour market outcomes, this is strong evidence for the existence of a causal relationship.

A third limitation concerns the relative diversity of social capital measures available in the GSOEP. As a result, the measures used to measure bonding and bridging are not symmetrical. For example, with respect to bridging, the interethnic contacts measured are the three closest people outside one's household who are of native German origin, plus an indicator for whether one receives social visits from native Germans. It is therefore not possible to have an indicator for network size of one's bridging social capital. Also, since the three cited people are most important to the respondent, the construct does not measure one's weakest ties. The visiting Germans variable most likely does not compensate for this: when one visits people at home, the people visited are most likely not the weakest ties in one's network. It could therefore be the case that bridging social capital is underestimated.

For bonding, there is much more information available. One could argue that bonding social capital is better measured than bridging social capital.

Figure 6.2   *Items that measure bonding and bridging social capital in the GSOEP*

Social capital	Bonding	Bridging
Structural	Network closure • Strength of family relations • Number of family members outside the household • Social support • Intra-ethnic family ties outside the household • Intra-ethnic friendships	Structural holes • Interethnic friends • Interethnic family members (outside the household) • Visiting/receiving social visits from native Germans
Cognitive	(Thick trust)	(Thin trust)

Source: Author

This can only be solved by excluding some items aimed at measuring bonding social capital. I chose not to do that since it would imply omitting potentially valuable information to test the hypothesis on bonding social capital (especially since it is found not to affect labour market outcomes in the Dutch case). However, in chapter 7, on the duration of unemployment of Turkish immigrants, the measures are symmetrical. Another disadvantage of the measures used for bonding is that they all exclude members in the household itself, expect for the measure of support.

Although being limited in the measurement of both bonding and bridging social capital, I argue that the measures are a proxy of the social capital available to the respondents. First, the measures used are assumed to proxy the theoretical constructs. Second, although perhaps not covering all family relations, someone scoring high on the measured indicators is also likely to do so on those that are not measured. It is thus likely that if a respondent mentions interethnic contacts as one of the three people with whom he or she goes out and meets often, this is a good proxy for potential other (unmeasured) interethnic contacts in one's social network.

Control variables

I controlled for human capital by including the educational attainment of the respondent, as measured with the ISCED classification (UNESCO 1997) and a scale for language proficiency. Measured in 1997, 1999, 2001, 2003 and 2005, language proficiency is determined by a three-item scale, specifying: 'Own opinion of spoken German', 'Own opinion of written German', 'Language usually spoken (German, mostly that of country of origin, both equally)'. Reliability analysis (Cronbach's alpha varies between waves from .83 until .86) as well as cumulative scaling with Mokken analysis (Loevinger's H varies between waves from .74 to .79) show that these items can be seen as a single construct. Consequently, the items were summed up.

I also controlled for the number of years of working experience (and squared the years). I controlled for the years of working experience rather than age (which is highly collinear with it) since experience is more likely to capture any potential social capital that is gained through earlier experiences on the labour market. In other words, it could be that those with more working experience have an advantage on the labour market just because they had more time to build experience and have more job-related ties.

Furthermore, I controlled for the highest educational degree obtained by either the father or the mother as well as whether the respondents held German nationality, their age at immigration separated according to three dummy variables: born in Germany, age of immigration when younger than six and age of immigration when older than six), marital status (being single or divorced/widowed versus being married) and ethnic origin. For the analyses of income and occupational status, a dummy variable for working part-time was included as was the number of hours worked per week. Last, to control for differences across regions, I included a dummy variable for each federal state in the random-effects models.[2] These dummies are meant to capture any regional factors affecting labour market outcomes, such as regional unemployment levels or job opportunities (Constant & Massey 2005).

Last, one can argue that the potential effect of social capital (especially that of the bridging type) is not only due to the network effect. It could be that possessing bridging social capital captures unobserved variation related to some dimensions of immigrant adaptation, social or psychological. Thus, it is not social capital, per se, that has a positive effect on labour market performance, but the fact that having bridging social capital proxies some level of integration and/or adaptation. Hence, it may be the case that bridging social capital proxies something like the 'propensity to integrate'. For example, Haug (2008) finds for Italian migrants in Germany that host country-specific social capital negatively impacts the intentions of return migration, since these immigrants are better 'socially' integrated. This implies that an effect of bridging on labour market outcomes is not necessarily due to social capital, but rooted in a more positive attitude or higher ability towards integration. Estimating a fixed-effects model partly solves this problem. Since these models only take into account within-individual changes, it controls for any between-individual differences in propensity to integrate. Only a changing propensity to integrate within an individual over time could therefore possibly be spurious with any found effects of social capital. Two control variables are therefore included that control for propensity to integrate. First, every year people were asked whether they have the desire to stay in Germany indefinitely (yes, no). Second, in 1997, 1999, 2001 and 2003 people were asked: 'To what extent do you feel German (completely, for the most part, in some respects, hardly at all, not at all)?' It is likely that those who feel more German or have a desire to stay in Germany have a higher propensity to integrate. By including these controls, I thus tried to control for possible other dimensions of integration that could be inadvertently captured in the measurement of social capital.

Results

In Table 6.1 and Table 6.2, descriptive statistics for the employment sample and the income analysis sample are presented. Since the sample of occupational status is very similar to that of income it is not presented in a separate table. Table 6.3 shows the means of the social capital measures

Table 6.1 *Descriptive statistics sample employment*

	Men		Women	
	Mean	*SD*	*Mean*	*SD*
Interethnic friendships	0.28	0.36	0.26	0.34
Interethnic family outside the household	0.07	0.2	0.07	0.21
Receives visits from Germans/visits Germans	0.85	0.33	0.82	0.36
Intra-ethnic friendships	0.37	0.38	0.34	0.37
Intra-ethnic family outside the household	0.22	0.33	0.27	0.35
Strength of family ties	0.72	0.18	0.75	0.17
Number of family members	0.11	0.11	0.11	0.1
Support from friends and family	0.57	0.17	0.59	0.18
German language proficiency	9.47	2.52	8.99	2.91
Working experience full-time in years	17.83	12.02	8.34	9.45
Feels German	2.76	1.14	2.69	1.2
Intention to stay in Germany indefinitely	0.63	0.48	0.64	0.47
	%		%	
Employed	80		46	
Ethnic groups				
Turkish	35		34	
Former Yugoslavian	17		18	
Greek	10		9	
Italian	18		15	
Spanish/Portuguese	6		4	
Eastern European (EU-10)	5		8	
Other	9		12	
Age at immigration				
German-born	16		15	
Age at immigration <6	8		6	
Age at immigration >=6	71		74	
Age at immigration missing	5		5	
German nationality	7		8	
Educational level				
Inadequately schooled/general elementary	37		49	
Middle vocational	43		31	
Vocational Abitur/higher vocational	10		12	
Higher education	9		7	
Education information missing	1		2	
Marital status				
Single	17		10	
Divorced/separated/widowed	7		12	
Married	76		78	
Highest education parents				
Parent secondary degree	28		29	
Parent intermediate school/technical	4		6	
Parent upper secondary	3		4	
Parent other degree	22		17	
Parent no school/no degree	35		34	
Parental education information missing	9		10	

Table 6.1 *(continued)*

	Men	Women
	%	%
Number of observations	6,896	7,259
Number of individuals	1,313	1,344

Source: GSOEP 1996-2007

Table 6.2 *Descriptive statistics sample income*

	Men		Women	
	Mean	SD	Mean	SD
Income	1662.68	730.07	974.01	506.23
ISEI score	36.05	12.55	35.9	14.16
Interethnic friendships	0.28	0.36	0.3	0.35
Interethnic family outside the household	0.07	0.2	0.08	0.22
Receives social visits from Germans/visits Germans	0.86	0.33	0.89	0.3
Intra-ethnic friendships	0.35	0.38	0.32	0.35
Intra-ethnic family outside the household	0.21	0.32	0.22	0.32
Strength of family ties	0.72	0.18	0.73	0.18
Number of family members	0.36	0.14	0.37	0.15
Support from friends and family	0.57	0.17	0.59	0.17
German language proficiency	9.58	2.48	9.79	2.52
Working experience full-time in years	18.23	11.54	11.93	10.22
Feels German	2.78	1.13	2.92	1.16
Intention to stay in Germany indefinitely	0.63	0.48	0.65	0.47
Actual work time per week	42.32	8.43	33.74	11.08
	%		%	
Ethnic group				
Turkish	33		21	
Former Yugoslavian	17		23	
Greek	10		11	
Italian	19		17	
Spanish/Portuguese	7		6	
Eastern European (EU-10)	6		10	
Other	9		12	
Age at immigration				
German-born	15		17	
Age at immigration <6	9		7	
Age at immigration >=6	71		71	
Age at immigration missing	5		6	
German nationality	7		10	
Educational level				
Inadequately schooled/general elementary	34		42	
Middle vocational	44		35	
Vocational Abitur/higher vocational	11		14	
Higher education	10		8	
No information on education	1		1	

Table 6.2   *(continued)*

	Men	Women
	%	%
Marital status		
Single	15	15
Divorced/separated/widowed	7	17
Married	78	68
Part-time	2	35
Self-employed	7	3
Highest degree parents		
Parent secondary degree	28	29
Parent intermediate school/technical	4	6
Parent upper secondary	3	3
Parent other degree	23	19
Parent no school/no degree	35	34
Parent information missing	9	9
Number of observations	5,516	3,344
Number of individuals	1,144	809

Source: GSOEP 1996-2007

Table 6.3   *Mean bonding and bridging social capital in Germany, by ethnic group*

	Turkish	Former Yugoslavia	Greek	Italian	Spanish/ Portuguese	Eastern European (EU-10)	Other
Bridging social capital							
Interethnic friendships	0.17	0.29	0.29	0.27	0.47	0.26	0.45
Interethnic family outside the household	0.06	0.04	0.04	0.07	0.07	0.19	0.10
Receives social visits from Germans/visits Germans	0.75	0.87	0.87	0.85	0.92	0.92	0.92
Bonding social capital							
Intra-ethnic friendships	0.41	0.39	0.39	0.34	0.18	0.30	0.26
Intra-ethnic family outside the household	0.32	0.23	0.23	0.26	0.23	0.18	0.12
Strength of family ties	0.73	0.74	0.74	0.77	0.73	0.69	0.71
Number of family members	0.12	0.11	0.11	0.11	0.11	0.08	0.11
Support from friends and family	0.56	0.60	0.60	0.54	0.59	0.60	0.66

Source: GSOEP 1996-2007

per ethnic group. Table 6.4 depicts the percentage of observations in each respective survey year and in the federal states.

As can be seen in the tables, the main ethnic groups are Turks, followed by migrants from the former Yugoslavia. Around 20 per cent were born in

Table 6.4   *Descriptive statistics, by survey year and federal state*

Survey year	%
1996	11
1997	11
1998	8
1999	8
2000	7
2001	10
2002	8
2003	8
2004	7
2005	7
2006	8
2007	8
Federal state	
Baden-Wuerttemberg	27
Bavaria	15
Berlin	3
Bremen	1
Hamburg	1
Hesse	11
Lower Saxony	7
North Rhine-Westphalia	27
Rhineland-Palatinate	5
Saarland	1
Schleswig-Holstein	2
Brandenburg/Mecklenburg-Western Pomerania/Thuringia Saxony/Saxony-Anhalt	1

Source: GSOEP 1996-2007

Germany or migrated before age six. The rest migrated at an older age. For a small percentage, the age of immigration is missing. Only 7 per cent of the men and 8 per cent of the women have German citizenship. The educational attainment according to the ISCED scheme is predominantly 'inadequately/general elementary' (37 per cent men, 49 per cent women), and 'middle vocational' (42 per cent men, 32 per cent women). More or less the same holds for parental education. Furthermore, the majority of the people in the sample are married (around 80 per cent). Whereas almost none of the men work part-time, this percentage is considerably higher among women (35 per cent).

The likelihood of being employed

Table 6.5 presents a random-effects model predicting the likelihood of men being employed. Besides the presented coefficients, the model includes dummies for each survey year to correct for the general trend and dummies for the federal states to correct for regional differences. The standard errors are corrected for clustering on the individual. As can be seen in the model, both interethnic friendships and relatives outside the household increase employment likelihood. Also, men indicating stronger family ties have a higher likelihood here. The number of family members has a negative impact on employment, although the coefficient is very close to one. The other measures of social capital do not significantly affect likelihood. From the random-effects model, we would thus conclude that men's interethnic contacts outside the household increase the likelihood of being employed.

With respect to the controls, there is no significant difference between those that were born in Germany and those who migrated themselves. Furthermore, migrants from Southern and Eastern European countries have a higher employment likelihood than Turks. Migrants from the former Yugoslavia do not significantly differ from the Turks. There are strong effects of educational attainment, while years of work experience and German language proficiency also positively affect employment chances. As for a propensity to integrate, 'feeling German' increases employment likelihood slightly; the intention to stay does not have an effect. Being single (as opposed to married) negatively affects the likelihood of being employed. Only respondents with parents who have an unknown educational level are more likely to be employed than people with parents who just have secondary education. Perhaps parents who indicate they have another degree are more likely to be self-employed and are therefore more able to provide employment for their children. It could also be that the effect of parental education with respect to the other degrees is already captured by the other covariates in the model.

Although the random-effects model takes into account the longitudinal design, it includes between-individual information in the estimates and therefore cannot deal conclusively with the problem of unobserved heterogeneity. It could be that due to respondents' unobserved characteristics (such as personal ability or effects of human capital not captured by the included variables), the effect actually captures enduring differences between individuals rather than estimating a 'pure' effect of social capital. In other words, it might be that immigrants with higher ability (or whatever unobserved characteristics) have more social contacts, but they might also be more often employed. The fixed-effects model solves this problem by only including within-individual variation. Model 2 of Table 6.5 presents such a fixed-effects model. Since they do not provide any within-individual information, the time-invariant covariates are dropped. Naturally, due to these more stringent model restrictions, the number of observations is much lower in the case of a logistic fixed-effects model.[3] However, the coefficients of having interethnic contacts remain significant. This implies that the effect in the random-effects model is not due to unobserved

heterogeneity, but can be interpreted as a 'true' effect of bridging social capital: people that reported an increase in their interethnic contacts are more
likely to be employed at a later point in time than people who do not report
such an increase. Since this is a fixed-effects model, this effect is not due
to differences between individuals or unobserved time-stable characteristics. Furthermore, with respect to possible time-variant characteristics, the
model controls for changes in educational attainment, changes in marital
status and in labour market experience. Besides, potential over-time
changes in the propensity to integrate are controlled for in a dynamic way.
Although possible effects of differences between individuals with respect
to propensity to integrate are ruled out by the design of the fixed-effects
model, possible time-variant effects are being controlled for. Since the
model includes dummies for the survey year, the effect cannot be spurious
with a common trend. The effect of the number of family members outside
the household, found in the random-effects model, could be a between-individual difference. Men with more family members are less likely to be
employed than those who report fewer members, but a change in the number of relatives does not affect one's employment status. This indicates unobserved heterogeneity, though it could also be that the reduced sample
size results in the effect no longer being significantly different from zero.

I do not formulate explicit hypotheses on the differences in the strength
of the effect of social capital between any ethnic groups or educational
levels. However, to make sure that the effects are not driven by one group
only, as well as to detect possible extreme differences in effect size, it is in-
sightful to know to what extent the results differ. To analyse whether there
is a difference among the ethnic groups with respect to the effect of the
social capital measures, interaction terms with the ethnic groups were thus
included in the models. Since fixed-effects models cannot deal with time-
invariant covariates, this is done with the random-effects models. The interaction models were estimated separately for each measure of social capital.
Since this implies estimating many models and since no explicit hypotheses are formulated with regard to ethnic differences, the results are summarised rather than presented in full length.

The results indicate some differences among ethnic groups. For immigrants from Eastern Europe (as compared to Turks), receiving social visits
from native Germans has a positive effect on the likelihood of being employed. Furthermore, with respect to bonding social capital, the strength of
family ties has a stronger effect for migrants from the former Yugoslavia.
The number of family members outside the household positively affects
employment likelihood for migrants from Southern Europe, as compared
with the Turks. However, it must be kept in mind that this variation may
be due to initial unobserved differences between ethnic groups, not necessarily inherently different effects.

Table 6.5 *Panel regression predicting the likelihood of employment among men, random-effects and fixed-effects models, odds ratios*

	Random-effects model		Fixed-effects model	
	b	se	b	se
Social capital				
Interethnic friendships	1.344*	(.187)	1.543*	(.265)
Interethnic family outside the household	1.732***	(.287)	2.040***	(.392)
Receives social visits from Germans/visits Germans	1.090	(.106)	1.032	(.116)
Intra-ethnic friendship	1.178	(.160)	1.332	(.216)
Intra-ethnic family outside the household	1.173	(.161)	1.301	(.210)
Strength of family ties	1.235	(.133)	.900	(.130)
Number of family members	.984*	(.007)	.993	(.009)
Support from friends and family	.880	(.102)	.822	(.130)
Ethnic group				
Turkish	.257***	(.096)		
Former Yugoslavian	.449	(.183)		
Greek	.828	(.414)		
Italian	ref.			
Spanish/Portuguese	.899	(.549)		
Eastern European (EU-10)	.942	(.592)		
Other	.327*	(.168)		
Age at immigration				
German-born	ref.			
Age at immigration <6	1.514	(.833)		
Age at immigration >=6	.670	(.279)		
Age at immigration missing	.547	(.346)		
German nationality	.657	(.264)	392	(.204)
German language proficiency	1.201***	(.050)	1.089	(.059)
Educational attainment				
Inadequately/general elementary	.902	(.169)	1.620	(.418)
Middle vocational	ref.		ref.	
Vocational Abitur/higher vocational	3.111***	(.909)	4.698***	(1.770)
Higher education	9.591***	(3.538)	28.707***	(17.909)
Education information missing	2.557	(1.651)	6.275*	(4.897)
Working experience full-time in years	1.507***	(.053)	1.707***	(.129)
Working experience full-time squared	.991***	(.001)	.985***	(.001)
Feels German	1.145	(.082)	1.173	(.101)
Intention to stay in Germany indefinitely	1.065	(.147)	1.063	(.164)

Table 6.5   *(continued)*

	Random-effects model		Fixed-effects model	
	b	*se*	*b*	*se*
Marital status				
Married	ref.		ref.	
Single	.348***	(.105)	.810	(.346)
Divorced/separated/widowed	.602	(.170)	.976	(.336)
Parental education				
Parents secondary education	ref.			
Parent intermediate school/ technical	.855	(.517)		
Parent upper secondary	.480	(.331)		
Parent other degree	2.517*	(.952)		
Parent no school/no degree	.982	(.297)		
Parental education information missing	1.453	(.657)		
Constant	10.579***	(1.125)		
Log-likelihood	-2,338.8		-801.4	
Number observations	6,896		2,492	
Number subjects	1,313		354	

Note: Models include dummies for each survey year; the random-effects model also includes dummies for the federal states.
* p < 0.05, ** p < 0.01, *** p < 0.001 (two-tailed tests); standard errors corrected for clustering on the individual
Source: GSOEP 1996-2007

I also include interaction terms to detect possible variation across educational levels. With respect to educational attainment, it appears that the strength of family ties and the family members who belong to the same ethnic group mentioned (intra-ethnic family outside the household) are more effective for those with higher educational attainment (not shown here). This could be explained by the fact that the higher educated also have family networks containing more valuable resources. They hence profit more from their bonding social capital than do the lower educated. However, as mentioned above, no hypotheses have been formulated with respect to these interaction effects. Further research explicitly hypothesising and theorising these differences would be needed to provide more conclusive answers.

Table 6.6 gives the likelihood of being employed predicted for women. The same covariates are included as for men, though there is one difference. In the model for women, the ethnic groups category 'other' is omitted. This category contains mainly Western European migrants. Initially, models were also estimated including this category, but this resulted in none of the social capital measures being significant. Instead of presenting such a model, I chose to omit this category. The results therefore have to be interpreted as only valid for the ethnic groups included.[4]

Just as in the model predicting men's employment, a random-effects model is estimated first. Two indicators of bridging social capital increase employment likelihood: interethnic family members and receiving social visits and visiting native Germans. Of the indicators measuring bonding social capital, the only significant one is receiving support from friends and family, though its coefficient is negative. As with the results for men, interethnic contacts seem to matter, not a strong family network.

When estimating a fixed-effects model, none of the social capital indicators is significant (middle model in Table 6.6). However, this appears to be solely due to the presence of migrants from Eastern Europe. In the last model, the same fixed-effects model is estimated, now excluding migrants from Eastern Europe. Coefficients for bridging social capital are now significant. In contrast to the models in Table 6.5, interethnic relatives and visiting or receiving visits from native Germans at home increases women's likelihood of being employed. This could be due to the fact that women, as opposed to men, are more often at home and therefore more isolated. Those receiving visits at home hence profit more. For men, these contacts do not necessarily take place at home: for them, having interethnic friendships has a positive effect. Last, the results were not found to be valid for women from Eastern Europe: for them, none of the social capital indicators had an effect.

Looking at the controls, we see that the coefficients do not differ from the male sample. There are differences across the ethnic groups: all groups except Greeks have a higher employment likelihood than Turkish women. Given the more traditional role that Turkish women have, this is not a surprising finding. Furthermore, being single, divorced, widowed or separated (as opposed to being married) has a positive effect. This is also unsurprising: these are likely to be women who stayed at home while married and entered the labour market when their marriage ended.

To check the robustness of the results, I analysed whether the effects of social capital varied between ethnic groups and across educational levels. The analytical strategy was the same as explained above for the models including men. As discussed, the effect of bridging social capital was not found for women from Eastern European countries. Furthermore, it appears that for women from Southern European countries (Greece, Italy, Spain and Portugal), visiting or receiving social visits from native Germans has a less positive effect on employment when compared to the experience of Turkish women. Conversely, for Southern European women, the strength of family ties has a more positive effect on the likelihood of being employed, when compared with Turkish women. With respect to levels of education, one difference was found. Interethnic friendships do have a positive effect for the lower educated, and less so for the higher educated.

Table 6.6 *Panel regression predicting employment likelihood among women, random-effects and fixed-effects models, odds ratios*

	Random-effects model All		Fixed-effects model All		Fixed-effects model Excluding Eastern EU and Other	
	b	se	b	se	b	se
Social capital						
Interethnic friendship	1.191	(.143)	1.062	(.145)	1.251	(.197)
Interethnic family outside household	1.348*	(.185)	1.235	(.191)	1.453*	(.250)
Receives visits from Germans/visits Germans	1.334***	(.112)	1.183	(.113)	1.278*	(.132)
Intra-ethnic friendship	1.203	(.142)	1.097	(.148)	1.291	(.196)
Intra-ethnic family outside household	1.019	(.122)	.946	(.131)	1.082	(.168)
Strength of family ties	1.189	(.114)	1.070	(.127)	1.192	(.162)
Number of family members	1.005	(.007)	.999	(.010)	1.005	(.011)
Support from friends and family	.747**	(.071)	.868	(.104)	.711*	(.098)
Ethnic group						
Turkish	.340**	(.120)				
Italian	ref.					
Former Yugoslavian	1.140	(.432)				
Greek	.866	(.391)				
Spanish/Portuguese	1.446	(.827)				
Eastern European (EU-10)	1.367	(.659)				
Other	.361*	(.156)				
Age at immigration						
German-born	ref.					
Age at immigration <6	2.225	(1.100)				
Age at immigration >=6	1.299	(.449)				
Age at immigration missing	2.585	(1.408)				
German nationality	.609	(.193)	.683	(.286)	.471	(.274)
German language proficiency	1.234***	(.044)	1.100*	(.050)	1.123*	(.057)
Educational attainment						
Inadequately schooled/ general elementary	.881	(.167)	.917	(.234)	1.203	(.354)
Middle vocational	ref.		ref.		ref.	
Vocational *Abitur*/ higher vocational	1.720*	(.405)	2.336**	(.729)	1.619	(.622)
Higher education	2.482**	(.858)	3.931*	(2.110)	5.695*	(4.833)
Education information missing	.476	(.254)	.392	(.227)	.700	(.467)

Table 6.6   *(continued)*

	Random-effects model All		Fixed-effects model All		Fixed-effects model Excluding Eastern EU and Other	
	b	se	b	se	b	se
Working experience full-time in years	1.330***	(.038)	1.019	(.072)	1.198*	(.099)
Working experience full-time squared	.994***	(.001)	.986***	(.003)	.976***	(.003)
Feels German	1.062	(.065)	.986	(.072)	.967	(.077)
Intention to stay in Germany indefinitely	1.014	(.117)	1.092	(.137)	1.126	(.153)
Marital status						
Married	ref.		ref.		ref.	
Single	6.501***	(1.627)	4.904***	(1.532)	4.685***	(1.736)
Divorced/separated/widowed	2.345***	(.486)	2.110**	(.523)	1.930*	(.566)
Parental education						
Parent secondary education	ref.					
Parent intermediate school/technical	.536	(.242)				
Parent upper secondary	.373	(.201)				
Parent other degree	.862	(.286)				
Parent no school/degree	1.325	(.359)				
Parental education information missing	1.276	(.477)				
Constant	.003***	(.002)				
Constant	9.320***	(.867)				
Log-likelihood	-3,057.2		-1,163.9		-929.2	
Number observations	7,259		3,016		2,440	
Number subjects	1,344		423		317	

Note: Models include dummies for each survey year; the random-effects model also includes dummies for the federal states.
* p < 0.05, ** p < 0.01, *** p < 0.001 (two-tailed tests); standard errors corrected for clustering by individual
Source: GSOEP 1996-2007

Occupational status

Table 6.7 shows how the effect of social capital on the occupational status for men is predicted. All coefficients are standardised between zero and one to make them comparable within the models. This means that, since all coefficients have the same range, one can compare effect sizes. However, the disadvantage is that the coefficients do not represent increases in the indicators. For example, it cannot be seen from the current models how much increase in occupational status is associated with an

Table 6.7 *Panel regression predicting ISEI scores among men, random-effects and fixed-effects models, standardised coefficients*

	Random-effects model		Fixed-effects model	
	b	*se*	*b*	*se*
Social capital				
Interethnic friendships	3.050**	(1.157)	2.866*	(1.321)
Interethnic family outside the household	1.325	(1.421)	1.493	(1.504)
Intra-ethnic friendships	1.321	(1.007)	1.425	(1.176)
Intra-ethnic family outside the household	1.603	(1.197)	1.568	(1.377)
Receives social visits from Germans/visits ans	.369	(.421)	.540	(.462)
Number of family members	-1.496	(3.574)	-1.434	(5.703)
Strength of family ties	-.655	(1.333)	-.978	(1.611)
Support from friends and family	-1.184	(.993)	-1.215	(1.218)
Control variables				
Ethnic group				
Italian	ref.			
Turkish	-1.941*	(.850)		
Former Yugoslavian	-1.859*	(.931)		
Greek	1.626	(1.230)		
Spanish/Portuguese	.453	(1.207)		
Eastern European (EU-10)	.875	(1.506)		
Other	4.451**	(1.609)		
Age at immigration				
German-born	ref.			
Age at immigration <6	-4.134**	(1.322)		
Age at immigration >=6	-4.468***	(1.076)		
Age at immigration missing	2.411	(2.291)		
German nationality	.267	(.893)	-1.283	(.980)
German language proficiency	5.473***	(1.155)	.577	(1.371)
Educational attainment				
Inadequately schooled/general elementary	-.294	(.478)	.267	(.589)
Middle vocational	ref.		ref.	
Vocational *Abitur*/higher vocational	-.190	(1.166)	-2.180	(1.547)
Higher education	10.815***	(2.004)	-1.115	(2.915)
Education information missing	-.184	(1.350)	-.361	(1.227)
Working experience full-time in years	10.554*	(4.929)	-5.744	(24.193)
Working experience full-time squared	-13.581**	(5.143)	-21.546**	(6.618)
Self-employed	4.807***	(.945)	4.633***	(1.106)
Feels German	-1.031	(.719)	-1.468	(.806)
Intention to stay in Germany indefinitely	-.108	(.353)	.156	(.361)

Table 6.7   *(continued)*

	Random-effects model		Fixed-effects model	
	b	*se*	*b*	*se*
Marital status				
Married	ref.		ref.	
Single	-.205	(.655)	-.313	(.938)
Divorced/separated/widowed	-.683	(.813)	-.140	(1.033)
Working part-time	.775	(1.164)	1.258	(1.215)
Actual work time per week	5.132**	(1.713)	4.568*	(1.909)
Parental education				
Parents secondary education	ref.			
Parent intermediate school/ technical	2.167	(1.722)		
Parent upper secondary	5.132	(2.656)		
Parent other degree	1.884*	(.912)		
Parent no school/no degree	-.112	(.691)		
Parental education information missing	-1.171	(1.002)		
Constant	30.199***	(2.649)	37.123***	(7.446)
Overall R-squared	.34		.04	
Within R-squared	.03		.04	
N observations	5,073		5,075	
N subjects	1,082		1,082	

Note: Models include dummies for each survey year; the random-effects model also includes dummies for the federal states.
* $p < 0.05$, ** $p < 0.01$, *** $p < 0.001$ (two-tailed tests); standard errors corrected for clustering on the individual
Source: GSOEP 1996-2007

additional year of labour market experience. The advantage is that it is possible to compare the effect size of labour market experience with that of social capital. Since this is of greater interest for the topic at hand, I chose to standardise all variables in a range from zero to one. The variables included in the models for occupational status and income are the same as for employment, expect for two extra variables: working part-time (as opposed to full-time) and the actual number of hours worked in a week.

In the random-effects model (left panel of Table 6.7), only interethnic friendships affect men's occupational status in a positively significant way. None of the other social capital indicators affect the occupational status. High closure in one's family network thus does not correspond with better labour market outcomes, when operationalised as occupational status. Diversifying one's network by building interethnic friendships does result in a higher occupational status. When estimating the fixed-effects model, these effects remain (second model of Table 6.7).

When excluding the ethnic category 'Other' (Table 6.8), interethnic family members outside the household significantly affect one's occupational

Table 6.8   *Panel regression predicting ISEI scores among men, excluding immigrants from category 'Other', random-effects and fixed-effects models, standardised coefficients*

	Random-effects model		Fixed-effects model	
	b	se	b	se
Social capital				
Interethnic friendships	2.833*	(1.136)	3.035*	(1.253)
Interethnic family outside the household	2.328*	(1.142)	3.146*	(1.236)
Receives social visits from Germans/visits Germans	1.346	(1.008)	1.636	(1.133)
Intra-ethnic friendships	1.930	(1.128)	2.240	(1.267)
Intra-ethnic family outside the household	.323	(.426)	.505	(.468)
Strength of family ties	-1.603	(3.671)	-2.017	(5.879)
Number of family members	-.673	(1.357)	-.222	(1.611)
Support from friends and family	-.554	(.981)	-.447	(1.180)
Ethnic group				
Italian	ref.			
Turkish	-2.153*	(.845)		
Former Yugoslavian	-1.823*	(.916)		
Greek	1.898	(1.202)		
Spanish/Portuguese	.444	(1.210)		
Eastern European (EU-10)	.800	(1.551)		
Age at immigration				
German-born	ref.			
Age at immigration <6	-3.705**	(1.337)		
Age at immigration >=6	-4.089***	(1.135)		
Age at immigration missing	3.002	(2.318)		
German nationality	.794	(.902)	-.937	(.960)
German language proficiency	5.262***	(1.076)	1.219	(1.245)
Educational attainment				
Inadequately schooled/general elementary	-.288	(.482)	.339	(.590)
Middle vocational	ref.		ref.	
Vocational *Abitur*/higher vocational	-.514	(1.241)	-2.241	(1.621)
Higher education	11.158***	(2.478)	-1.519	(3.851)
Education information missing	-.276	(1.334)	-.293	(1.251)
Working experience full-time in years	6.864	(4.833)	4.809	(23.620)
Working experience full-time squared	-10.858*	(4.722)	-21.729***	(6.227)
Self-employed	4.839***	(1.039)	4.878***	(1.208)
Feels German	-.934	(.734)	-1.267	(.800)
Intention to stay in Germany indefinitely	-.104	(.323)	-.002	(.331)

Table 6.8   *(continued)*

	Random-effects model		Fixed-effects model	
	b	*se*	*b*	*se*
Married	ref.		ref.	
Single	-.364	(.696)	-.363	(1.037)
Divorced/separated/widowed	.244	(.734)	.775	(.865)
Part-time	-.058	(1.354)	-.534	(1.468)
Actual work time per week	5.606**	(1.815)	5.046*	(1.989)
Parental education				
Parents secondary education	ref.			
Parent intermediate school/ technical	1.289	(1.955)		
Parent upper secondary	5.183	(3.610)		
Parent other degree	1.390	(.921)		
Parent no school/no degree	.085	(.681)		
Parental education information missing	-.862	(1.002)		
Constant	30.015***	(2.678)	31.284***	(7.147)
Overall R-squared	.29		.05	
Within R-squared	.03		.05	
N observations	4,737		4,739	
N subjects	979		979	

Note: Models include dummies for each survey year; the random-effects model also includes dummies for the federal states.
* $p < 0.05$, ** $p < 0.01$, *** $p < 0.001$ (two-tailed tests); standard errors corrected for clustering on the individual
Source: GSOEP 1996-2007

status. In other words, as in the case of employment, interethnic contacts (either friends or relatives outside the household) result for Turkish, Southern European and former Yugoslav male migrants in a higher occupational status. Since these effects remain significant in the fixed-effects model, these effects are not biased by unobserved heterogeneity. That is, the found effects are not due to selection: it is not the case that men with interethnic contacts already have a higher position, or that the effect is due to other unobserved factors.

With respect to the control variables, contrary to employment likelihood, the age at immigration does affect occupational status: those not born in Germany have a significantly lower occupational status than those born in Germany. The difference could be due to the fact that having work is a necessity for everybody; the second generation is therefore not more likely to be employed than first-generation immigrants. With respect to job quality, men born in Germany do profit from growing up in the host society. Furthermore, better German language proficiency results in a higher occupational status, but this effect disappears in the fixed-effects model. Hence, this effect might be biased by unobservables such as unmeasured ability.

Table 6.9 *Panel regression predicting ISEI scores among women, random-effects and fixed-effects models, standardised coefficients*

	Random-effects		Fixed-effects	
	b	se	b	se
Social capital				
Interethnic friendships	.451	(1.136)	.077	(1.285)
Interethnic family outside the household	-.829	(1.508)	-.561	(1.715)
Receives social visits from Germans/visits Germans	-.840	(.563)	-.626	(.574)
Intra-ethnic friendships	-.567	(1.203)	-.956	(1.378)
Intra-ethnic family outside the household	.271	(1.153)	.168	(1.326)
Strength of family ties	.288	(1.452)	-.633	(1.680)
Number of family members	4.040	(3.096)	4.566	(4.353)
Support from friends and family	-2.192	(1.312)	-2.189	(1.429)
Ethnic group				
Italian	ref.			
Turkish	-.796	(1.308)		
Former Yugoslavian	-.753	(1.349)		
Greek	1.717	(1.586)		
Spanish/Portuguese	2.018	(1.931)		
Eastern Europe (EU-10)	1.329	(1.832)		
Other	1.756	(1.799)		
Age at immigration				
German-born	ref.			
Age at immigration <6	1.399	(1.798)		
Age at immigration >=6	-5.243***	(1.291)		
Age at immigration missing	-4.565*	(1.859)		
German nationality	1.100	(1.095)	-1.838	(1.151)
German language proficiency	4.718***	(1.392)	-.259	(1.618)
Educational attainment				
Inadequately schooled/general elementary	-2.478*	(1.034)	-.138	(1.438)
Middle vocational	ref.		ref.	
Vocational *Abitur*/higher vocational	.547	(1.189)	-1.261	(1.492)
Higher education	10.261***	(2.265)	2.653	(2.490)
Education information missing	3.049	(1.792)	2.024	(1.168)
Working experience full-time in years	15.965**	(5.663)	-2.946	(10.591)
Working experience full-time squared	-19.298*	(7.812)	-12.025	(10.949)
Self-employed	5.419**	(2.035)	4.553	(2.329)
Feels German	.262	(.885)	-.322	(.981)
Intention to stay in Germany indefinitely	.271	(.410)	.240	(.408)

Table 6.9   *(continued)*

	Random-effects		Fixed-effects	
	b	*se*	*b*	*se*
Marital status				
Married	ref.		ref.	
Single	1.556	(.918)	-.283	(1.166)
Divorced/separated/widowed	-.022	(.707)	.234	(.831)
Part-time	.771	(.534)	.579	(.565)
Actual work time per week	11.373***	(1.821)	10.236***	(1.945)
Parental education				
Parents secondary education	ref.			
Parent intermediate school/ technical	5.732**	(1.835)		
Parent upper secondary	11.937***	(2.601)		
Parent other degree	1.282	(1.319)		
Parent no school/no degree	-2.245*	(1.048)		
Parental education information missing	-.968	(1.465)		
Constant	28.141***	(2.973)	33.354***	(3.317)
Overall R-squared	.40		.05	
Within R-squared	.03		.05	
N observations	3,141		3,141	
N subjects	777		777	

Note: Models include dummies for each survey year; the random-effects model also
includes dummies for the federal states.
* $p < 0.05$, ** $p < 0.01$, *** $p < 0.001$ (two-tailed tests); standard errors corrected for
clustering on the individual
Source: GSOEP 1996-2007

Taking into account the controls, migrants from Southern Europe have
higher occupational status than Turks, while migrants from the former
Yugoslavia do not differ significantly from Turks. The category 'Other',
comprising mainly Western European immigrants, has a significantly higher occupational status, as compared to Italians. Holding German nationality
does not have a significant effect on occupational status, neither does the
desire to stay in Germany nor feeling German. Men with a higher education have a significantly higher occupational status, but there is no significant effect in the fixed-effects model. Since educational attainment does
not change much over time, the variable not being significant could be due
to the little variation. The number of hours that one works significantly
and strongly affects one's occupational status. Last, there is no significant
effect of marital status and parental education.

Just as in the analysis of employment status, I also analysed whether the
effect differs across ethnic groups and across educational levels. As said,
the effects were not found for the category 'Other'. For the other ethnic
groups, no significant differences were found for the effects of social

capital. When including interaction terms between the various educational levels and the measures of social capital, no substantial differences were found.

Table 6.9 presents the models predicting women's occupational status. The categories 'Eastern European' and 'Other' are also included. The picture rather varies from that of the male sample. None of the measures for social capital significantly affects women's occupational status. These results do not change when excluding ethnic groups, as occurred in the case of the men. Social capital, as operationalised here, does not affect women's occupational status. The controls show similar coefficients as with the male sample. A difference is the strong effects for parental education on women's occupational status and, as with women's employment, the positive effect of divorce, separation or becoming a widow.

When including interaction terms with ethnic groups and the measures of social capital, one effect is different. For women from Eastern European countries, the effect of visiting native Germans and receiving social visits from native Germans as well as interethnic friendships negatively affects occupational status.

Income

In Table 6.10, the logged income is predicted for men. The included covariates are identical to the model of occupational status. In the models for income, all ethnic groups are included. In the random-effects model (left panel), we can see how having interethnic and intra-ethnic friendships and relatives outside the household significantly increases income. Thus, men having more friends and relatives (either interethnic or intra-ethnic) report a higher income. In the fixed-effects model, it appears that the effect in the random-effects model is overestimated: the coefficients drop and its p-values increase. Intra-ethnic friendships do not affect income once all between-individual information is taken into account. However, men reporting more interethnic friendships and relatives also have a higher income. This is not due to changes in labour market experience, education, a general time trend, the place where they live, their educational attainment (or that of their parents), their German language proficiency or because they have a higher propensity to integrate. Since the effect remains in the fixed-effects model, this is also not due to unobserved heterogeneity.

Unlike in the analysis of employment and occupational status, one indicator of bonding social capital is significant in the fixed-effects model: people reporting more family members (of their own ethnic group) outside of their household as being important to them have a significantly higher income.

The control variables show no differences between ethnic groups or age at immigration. German language proficiency positively affects income, but this effect disappears when looking at within-individual information

Table 6.10   *Panel regression predicting income (ln) among men, random-effects and fixed-effects models, standardised coefficients*

	Random-effects model		Fixed-effects model	
	b	se	b	se
Social capital				
Interethnic friendships	.079***	(.022)	.053*	(.027)
Interethnic family outside the household	.084**	(.028)	.071*	(.031)
Receives social visits from Germans/visits Germans	.005	(.013)	.004	(.014)
Intra-ethnic friendships	.048*	(.021)	.036	(.025)
Intra-ethnic family outside the household	.068**	(.024)	.062*	(.028)
Strength of family ties	-.023	(.033)	-.068	(.037)
Number of family members	-.021	(.074)	-.066	(.105)
Support from friends and family	-.016	(.032)	-.019	(.039)
Ethnic group				
Turkish	ref.			
Former Yugoslavian	-.051	(.029)		
Greek	-.021	(.033)		
Italian	-.032	(.024)		
Spanish/Portuguese	.014	(.037)		
Eastern European (EU-10)	.036	(.043)		
Other	.000	(.045)		
Age at immigration				
German-born	ref.			
Age at immigration <6	.021	(.043)		
Age at immigration >=6	-.066	(.035)		
Age at immigration missing	-.000	(.056)		
German nationality	-.039	(.035)		
German language proficiency	.086*	(.036)	.021	(.043)
Educational attainment				
Inadequately schooled/general elementary	-.012	(.013)	.016	(.017)
Middle vocational	ref.		ref.	
Vocational Abitur/higher vocational	.004	(.021)	.001	(.026)
Higher education	.227***	(.047)	.012	(.067)
Education information missing	-.008	(.050)	.009	(.064)
Working experience full-time in years	1.354***	(.129)	2.809**	(.853)
Working experience full-time squared	-1.085***	(.131)	-1.035***	(.169)
Self-employed	.144***	(.044)	.150**	(.056)
Feels German	.037	(.025)	.025	(.029)
Intention to stay in Germany indefinitely	-.014	(.011)	-.015	(.011)

Table 6.10   *(continued)*

	Random-effects model		Fixed-effects model	
	b	*se*	*b*	*se*
Marital status				
Married	ref.		ref.	
Single	-.172***	(.028)	-.175***	(.042)
Divorced/separated/widowed	-.104***	(.024)	-.074*	(.030)
Part-time	-.486***	(.057)	-.347***	(.060)
Actual work time per week	.372***	(.072)	.314***	(.079)
Parental education				
Parents secondary education	ref.			
Parent intermediate school/ technical	.032	(.054)		
Parent upper secondary	.211**	(.077)		
Parent other degree	.055*	(.028)		
Parent no school degree	-.004	(.023)		
Parental education information missing	-.052	(.032)		
Constant	6.748***	(.069)	6.394***	(.250)
Overall R-squared	.34		.07	
Within R-squared	.22		.23	
N observations	5,516		5,518	
N subjects	1,144		1,144	

Note: Models include dummies for each survey year; the random-effects model also includes dummies for the federal states.
* p < 0.05, ** p < 0.01, *** p < 0.001 (two-tailed tests); standard errors corrected for clustering on the individual
Source: GSOEP 1996-2007

only. Unsurprisingly, those working part-time have a lower income; those who work more hours have a higher income. Married men and self-employed men have a higher income. The strongest effect is that of years of working experience. Most likely this also explains why the effect of educational attainment is rather weak.

By including interaction terms, I analysed to what extent the strength of the effect differs for ethnic groups and educational levels. It appears that visiting or receiving visits from native Germans positively affects income for former Yugoslavs and Southern Europeans. With respect to education, no significant differences were found.

Table 6.11 shows predictions for women's income. The results are similar to that of occupational status: none of the measures of social capital significantly affects income. Apparently, for working women, social capital is not effective in making headway on the labour market. These results do not change when excluding ethnic groups or when including interaction terms with the ethnic groups. With respect to education, no substantial differences were found either.

Table 6.11　*Panel regression predicting income (ln) among women, random-effects and fixed-effects models, standardised coefficients*

	Random-effects model		Fixed-effects model	
	b	se	b	se
Social capital				
Interethnic friendships	.015	(.043)	-.014	(.047)
Interethnic family outside the household	.012	(.048)	-.005	(.052)
Receives social visits from Germans/visits Germans	.002	(.020)	.000	(.021)
Intra-ethnic friendships	.025	(.042)	-.001	(.046)
Intra-ethnic family outside the household	.014	(.041)	-.011	(.046)
Strength of family ties	-.001	(.054)	.004	(.061)
Number of family members	.148	(.097)	.141	(.154)
Support from friends and family	-.058	(.053)	-.067	(.063)
Ethnic group				
Turkish	ref.			
Former Yugoslavian	.024	(.038)		
Greek	.067	(.048)		
Italian	.009	(.037)		
Spanish/Portuguese	.089	(.054)		
Eastern European (EU-10)	.036	(.059)		
Other	.077	(.050)		
Age at immigration				
German-born	ref.			
Age at immigration <6	-.012	(.066)		
Age at immigration >=6	-.053	(.043)		
Age at immigration missing	-.060	(.053)		
German nationality	.042	(.048)	.039	(.068)
German language proficiency	-.019	(.056)	-.097	(.069)
Educational attainment				
Inadequately schooled/general elementary	-.021	(.027)	.022	(.038)
Middle vocational	ref.		ref.	
Vocational Abitur/higher vocational	.034	(.031)	-.011	(.044)
Higher education	.256***	(.054)	.082	(.083)
Education information missing	-.042	(.063)	-.001	(.065)
Working experience full-time in years	1.358***	(.150)	.597	(.338)
Working experience full-time squared	-1.179***	(.179)	-.949***	(.255)
Self-employed	-.098	(.090)	-.121	(.106)
Feels German	.042	(.030)	.028	(.035)
Intention to stay in Germany indefinitely	.014	(.015)	.018	(.015)

Table 6.11 *(continued)*

	Random-effects model		Fixed-effects model	
	b	*se*	*b*	*se*
Marital status				
Married	ref.		ref.	
Single	.088**	(.031)	.082	(.042)
Divorced/separated/widowed	.088**	(.027)	.072*	(.036)
Part-time	-.241***	(.027)	-.227***	(.029)
Actual work time per week	1.197***	(.109)	1.081***	(.113)
Parental education				
Parents secondary education	ref.			
Parent intermediate school/ technical	.065	(.055)		
Parent upper secondary	.190*	(.078)		
Parent other degree	.039	(.041)		
Parent no school/no degree	-.006	(.031)		
Parental education information missing	-.082	(.051)		
Constant	5.946***	(.100)	6.216***	(.115)
Overall R-squared	.58		.48	
Within R-squared	.35		.35	
N observations	3,245		3,245	
N subjects	794		794	

Note: Models include dummies for each survey year; the random-effects model also includes dummies for the federal states.
* $p < 0.05$, ** $p < 0.01$, *** $p < 0.001$ (two-tailed tests); standard errors corrected for clustering on the individual
Source: GSOEP 1996-2006

Conclusion

The effect of bonding and bridging social capital was analysed on employment status, occupational status and income for men and women. A pattern can clearly be noted.

With respect to men, bridging social capital improves both access to and performance on the labour market: it increases the likelihood of being employed, occupational status and income. Bonding social capital was not found to be effective. Only in the case of income, one indicator of bonding social capital was found to affect income significantly.

For women, bridging social capital was only found to be effective in getting access to the labour market, and only when excluding women from Eastern Europe and the category 'Other' from the analysis. For women, having interethnic contacts significantly increases employment likelihood. For women who are working, none of the indicators of social capital had a significant effect. This supports the argument of chapter 4 that women profit less from their social networks. As Livingston (2006) argues with respect to Mexican immigrants in the US: since men arrived mostly earlier and work in male dominated occupations, migrant networks provide little relevant information for female job seekers. Thus, migrant women may have good networks, but these provide little information and mostly on domestic work. According to Hondagneu-Sotelo (1994) and Hagan (1998), migrant women are channelled into low-paying and informal sector jobs via their social ties. This conclusion can also be drawn in the case of female migrants in Germany. It may be that in the possible event that the GSOEP survey items do not record the informal sector employment,[5] the model underestimates the effect for women, since migrant women often perform domestic service jobs.

How does this relate to the formulated hypotheses? Apparently, high closure in one's network does not improve labour market outcomes. The family is not found to be, as Nee and Sanders (2001b) argue, a central pillar in the process of incorporation in the labour market. They see the family as the primary basis of trust and collective action. Nee and Sanders (2001b: 389) emphasise that 'social ties associated with common ethnicity are unlikely to replicate the household communism and solidarity of the family household or to be as strong as the social ties within extended family networks'. However, this does not mean that family relations are not beneficial in terms of labour market outcomes. Having interethnic family members in one's close social circle has a significantly positive effect on labour market outcomes. This holds for men and, with respect to the likelihood of being employed, also for women. Perhaps having interethnic family members in one's close circle combines the advantages of both network closure (hence high solidarity and reciprocity) and spanning structural holes (hence a more diversified network and more host country-specific information).

On the other hand, interethnic contacts seem to pay off: for men, they increase the likelihood of being employed, occupational status and income. This effect remains when controlling for ethnic group, age at immigration, holding German nationality, years of labour market experience, educational attainment, parental education, marital status, German language proficiency, the propensity to integrate, a common time trend and regional differences. Furthermore, this effect remains when eliminating unobserved time-constant heterogeneity and using within-individual information only.

These results have to be seen in the light of some limitations. As already discussed above, there are some limitations to the available measures of social capital. None of the measures is available every survey year, some were measured only twice in the period of observation. Since there may be much less variation in the data than when measured every year, the effect of social capital might be underestimated. However, this does not affect the differences between bonding and bridging social capital, notably not in the case of the interethnic and intra-ethnic friendships and relatives outside of the household. Since this latter measure is symmetric with respect to bonding and bridging, differences in its effect cannot be attributed to differences in measurement frequency.

Another limitation may be the relatively rough measure of the propensity to integrate. One may argue that any social capital effects found can, due to the rough measure, be also an effect of having a higher propensity to integrate rather than a pure network effect. However, the fixed-effects models eliminate any between-individual differences. Therefore, this limitation only holds with respect to possible time-varying effects of the propensity to integrate. These time-varying effects are likely to be small; in any case they are captured (at least partly) by the 'rough' measure of propensity to integrate that is also included in the fixed-effects models.

Notes

1   The 2001 wording is the same.
2   Some categories were collapsed due to the low N found in some of the states; Mecklenburg-Western Pomerania, Brandenburg, Saxony, Saxony-Anhalt and Thuringia were collapsed into one category.
3   As Halaby (2004) notes, estimating fixed-effects models is not throwing away information, but making use of the panel structure of the data.
4   For men, models were also estimated excluding the category 'Other', though this did not substantially change the results.
5   However, this is not necessarily the case. The questionnaire refers to paid employment, which can also be informal.

7 Interethnic and intra-ethnic friendships and unemployment duration for Turkish immigrants and native Germans[1]

Introduction

This chapter investigates to what extent bonding and bridging social capital can help reduce the duration of unemployment for Turkish immigrants and native residents in Germany. More specifically, I analyse whether having interethnic and intra-ethnic friendships can be associated with shorter unemployment duration.

The research design in this chapter differs from the two previous chapters in two ways. First, the only immigrant group included is that of Turks. Moreover, I compare Turks with native Germans. Second, the dependent variable is different. By estimating event history models, I analyse the duration of unemployment and the transition from unemployment to work. The sample in this chapter starts in the first survey year with all unemployed people and models the timing and duration of a transition into employment.

A possible disadvantage to this approach is that the concepts of bonding and bridging are measured differently from in previous chapters. Here, bonding social capital is operationalised as intra-ethnic friendships and bridging, as interethnic friendships. This implies that because bonding and bridging are measured symmetrically, not all measures are included that were previously defined as bonding social capital. For example, visiting or receiving social visits from native Germans is not included, nor is family-based social capital and the support construct.

Still, the advantages of this approach seem to triumph. The effect of social capital on the duration of unemployment is being compared between Turks and native Germans. This procedure makes it possible to analyse whether social capital is more beneficial for Turkish immigrants than it is for native Germans. Another advantage is that the focus with respect to bonding is not on the family, but on ties with co-ethnics. Hence, I focus on a type of social capital that is less dependent on one's background.

Despite the large body of literature on social capital on the labour market, only a few studies compare the effect of bridging social capital across ethnic groups (Battu, Seaman & Zenou 2004; Kalter 2006). In view of the disadvantages of Turkish immigrants on the labour market (see Kogan 2004, 2007a; Uhlendorff & Zimmerman 2006; Hartung & Neels 2009), this chapter contributes to the existing body of literature on social capital and labour market outcomes by simultaneously analysing the effect of having interethnic and intra-ethnic friendships for persons with and without a migration background.

As a consequence of the different design, hypotheses are formulated separately in this chapter. The arguments underlying them are nonetheless similar to the ones developed in chapter 4.

Hypotheses

As shown in the book's earlier chapters, social capital of the bridging type is especially useful for making headway on the labour market. The argument is that bridging ties (such as interethnic friendships) diversify one's network and consequently create opportunities for upward mobility on the labour market.

However, the idea of social capital being *capital* implies that by building connections between people, valuable resources come into reach. Put differently, a relevant question regarding bridging social capital is: to what extent do ties tap into resource-rich networks? To gain more insight in the effect of a tie bridging across ethnic groups and the effect of a tie providing access to valuable resources, one would need to compare bridging ties for a resource-rich and a resource-poor group.

Family and friends cover several of these dimensions and can therefore be considered as multiplex, while relatives, colleagues and acquaintances are rather uniplex in the sense of functional differentiation – their support is relatively limited to one or some of these dimensions (compare Petermann 2002; Hollstein 2001; Plickert, Côté & Wellman 2007). In other words, friends compared to acquaintances are sources of support for labour market outcomes in more than one regard. From a utilitarian perspective, people will 'invest' in relations with others because of the prospective value of the resources made available by these relations (Flap & Völker 2004). From this perspective, a social network is considered capital that can produce returns on these investments.

Studies on the impact of friendships on labour market outcomes often refer to a hypothesis of the strength of weak ties (Granovetter 1973), predicting that weak ties, such as remote friends and acquaintances, are more profitable than strong ties, such as family members and close friends. Yet according to Burt (2001), it is not necessarily weak ties that are profitable. He argues that in order to access valuable information, it is essential to 'span structural holes', either through strong or weak ties. Friendships in general are found to coincide with labour market success (both for migrants and natives), such as higher wages and occupational status (De Graaf & Flap 1988; Lin 1999) and job search (Patacchini & Zenou 2008; Granovetter 1995; Flap & Boxman 2001; Aguilera 2002; Drever & Hoffmeister 2008; Battu, Seaman & Zenou 2004). As a general hypothesis, one would therefore expect all friendships to be helpful for finding a job, irrespective of their being interethnic or intra-ethnic. As for the effect size, however, one can expect differences.

Bridging and bonding social capital and the resource argument

Looking at native Germans and Turkish immigrants, Kalter (2006) analyses the effect friendships with native Germans have on employment likelihood. Also drawing on the GSOEP data, he finds a positive effect of having friendships with Germans. I also anticipate a positive effect of friendships with native Germans, both for the Turkish minority and native Germans, though this effect is not expected to be the same. The argument stems from more recent discussions on social capital, which distinguish between bonding and bridging ties (Gitell & Vidal 1998; Putnam 2000; Woolcock & Narayan 2000; Leonard & Onyx 2003; Schuller 2007).

In this chapter, bridging ties are defined as interethnic relations and bonding ties as ties with co-ethnics. The 'Measures' section operationalises this as interethnic and intra-ethnic friendships. Whereas the operationalisation of bridging is the same as in former chapters, bonding social capital is operationalised differently. In this chapter, bonding ties are not operationalised as closure in the family network, but as friendships with co-ethnics. Instead, the concept of bonding refers to that of connecting to the ethnic community. As such, the argument of closure in the network is now made on the level of the ethnic community.

This approach has both merits and drawbacks. It is disadvantageous in the way that closure is less likely to have an effect, since the ethnic community is so much bigger than the family network. As Sanders and Nee (1996) argue, a limitation of solidarity based on ethnic ties, per se, is that they are difficult to enforce on the community level. The reason is that when opportunities are available outside the ethnic community, one is less dependent on ethnic resources. This weakens the mechanism that maintains bounded solidarity and enforceable trust within the ethnic group. Furthermore, increasing ethnic heterogeneity in a country results in more porous ethnic boundaries and hence a greater variety of identities, making ethnic solidarity less likely (Light, Sabagh, Bozorgmehr, & Der-Martirosian 1993). Within the family, solidarity is likely to be less vulnerable.

Yet there is also a clear advantage. A main critique of family-based social capital is that the family network is too small, not sufficiently linked to the labour market and therefore cannot provide valuable information to make headway on it. There is, however, ample research that argues that the ethnic community as such provides an environment of higher trust and solidarity (Fennema 2004). Furthermore, there is research suggesting that ethnic networks function as a means to make headway on the labour market, since these networks rely on ethnic solidarity and enforceable trust (see e.g. Portes & Sensenbrenner 1993; Portes 1995b; Patacchini & Zenou 2008). By building ties with co-ethnics, immigrants may therefore benefit from the ethnic economy (Light et al. 1995; Greve & Salaff 2005). Taking friendships with co-ethnics as bonding social capital has two advantages: friendship ties are more likely to tap into a wider network than do family ties; ties with co-ethnics can provide access to the 'ethnic economy'. As hypothesised above, all friendships are expected to reduce unemployment duration, including for Turkish immigrants.

Social capital of the bridging type is often thought to be useful to make headway on the labour market as it spans – by definition – gaps across socio-economic variables such as class, ethnicity and age (Portes 1998; Narayan 1999). These gaps in networks, called structural holes, can disrupt the flow of information between people (Burt 2001). Ties bridging such structural holes are thought to be more effective than non-bridging ties, since unique information and opportunities come into reach (Putnam 2000: 22). Bonding ties, on the other hand, connect to a network where the same information is being circulated, therefore not necessarily providing job market information of additional value (see e.g. Nannestad et al. 2008).

Yet this does not simply imply that bridging is effective and bonding is not. The resource argument refines this perspective. Social capital being *capital* – in the sense that it yields positive returns – is based on the assumption that social relations connect people with valuable resources. The statement that bonding social capital is to 'get by' while bridging social capital is to 'get ahead' (Narayan 1999; Putnam 2000) is predominantly argued from the perspective of a *resource-poor* group. When taking the perspective of the *resource-rich* group, one would expect bonding ties to be beneficial, but bridging ties not. The question is to what extent ties are accessing a network that contains useful resources on the labour market.

It is too simplistic to classify Turkish migrants as resource-poor and the native population as resource-rich. There is, for example, evidence that social capital of the bonding type yields positive returns for migrants, since intra-ethnic ties provide access to an 'ethnic' economy (see e.g. Waldinger 1994; Elliott 2001; Sanders, Nee & Sernau 2002). Yet, the distinction between resource-rich and resource-poor is based on access to the host country and labour market-specific resources that migrants have less of than natives. Hence, immigrants building connections to the native population gain access to host country-specific resources. It is well established in the literature that migrants need host country-specific skills to integrate onto the local labour market (Friedberg 2000; Duleep & Regets 1999;

Zeng & Xie 2004; Borjas 1994). The argument is predominantly made with respect to skills such as education and language proficiency (Chiswick & Miller 2002; Kanas & Van Tubergen 2009), though forms the core of bridging social capital. By building interethnic contacts, immigrants realise access to resources they themselves typically have little of (depending on their length of stay in the host country) and that are in high demand on the labour market.

Haug (2003: 719) points out how *host country-specific social capital* is particularly beneficial for labour market outcomes: 'Since […] in Germany most employers are Germans, it is useful for immigrants to have contacts to Germans.' Kazemipur (2006: 6) also states:

> The ethnic diversity of social networks is particularly important in the case of immigrants. A less diverse social network would mean a lower frequency of contacts with the larger society and, potentially, a slower process of language acquisition and cultural adaptation, not to mention the presence of fewer job choices. In some extreme cases, immigrants with ethnically homogeneous networks have to rely on their ethnic enclaves as the only source of employment.

Being resource-rich does not refer to social class or occupational prestige. Rather, it implies possessing host country-specific resources, such as providing help with applications and job-seeking, pointing to vacancies, dealing with employment agencies, translating cover letters, knowing employers or being employers themselves. In this study thus, German natives are seen as the resource-rich group, as compared to the Turkish first generation.[2] Bridging social capital is expected to be more effective for Turkish immigrants than for native Germans, as it represents (potential) access to information and structures important for the host country's labour market (Haug 2007). For native Germans, on the other hand, interethnic friendships have a diversifying effect, though represent a link to a resource-poor or resource-poorer group. As such, the bridging argument holds, but the resource argument does not. Interethnic friendships are therefore expected to be less beneficial for native Germans. This is formulated in the following hypothesis:

H1a The positive effect of interethnic friendships on finding employment is larger for first generation Turkish migrants than it is for native Germans.

By the same token, the opposite is expected with respect to *intra*-ethnic friendships, which are more favourable for native Germans than for immigrants. The argument is that they tap into a resource-rich environment for

Germans but not for immigrants. This is formulated in the following hypothesis:

H1b: The positive effect of having intra-ethnic friendships on finding employment is larger for native Germans than it is for first-generation Turkish migrants.

Social and human capital

Contrary to Kalter's aforementioned study (2006), I expect the returns of social capital to differ across educational levels. The effect of having access to a resource-rich network is likely to be largest for people who possess the least resources themselves. People with fewer educational credentials are, on average, less proficient at finding a job through formal methods (Marsden & Hurlbert 1988; Elliott 2001). Drever and Hofmeister (2008) indeed find that lower-educated migrants in Germany make more use of their personal network to find a job (this also proves true in the US, see Elliott 2001; Stainback 2008). If the lower educated are less proficient at finding a job through formal channels, the effect of social capital is likely to be larger for them than for the higher educated, who have more alternatives available. Along that line of reasoning, social capital connecting to a resource-rich environment is more valuable for people who possess relatively few resources themselves. In other words, for the low educated, having friendships with native Germans is more beneficial than it is for those with more educational credentials. This is formulated in the following hypothesis:

H2a: The positive effect of having friendships with German natives on finding employment is larger for those with a low education level, as compared to those with a high education level.

However, this reasoning particularly applies to first-generation migrants, rather than to native residents. Connecting to a resource-rich network is especially crucial for the first generation, who generally possess little host country-specific knowledge, language proficiency or education (Aguilera & Massey 2003; Drever & Hoffmeister 2008). This is formulated in the following hypothesis:

H2b: The mechanism of H2a is stronger for Turkish migrants than for German natives.

Data and measurement

Data and construction of the sample

The analyses in this chapter again draw on the GSOEP. The GSOEP provides a detailed monthly activity calendar, showing if a person is in school, works or is unemployed. Due to limited availability of information on friendships, the observation period is limited to 1996 to 2007.

With regard to the sample construction, I first selected all unemployment periods from the monthly activity calendar, meaning only the working-age population also active on the labour market was included. Direct transitions to work were defined as realising part-time or full-time work at the end of the unemployment spell (up to three months after) and the employment lasting at least three months. Taking only the native Germans and the Turkish migrants, male and female, and excluding left-censored spells, this resulted in a person period file (N = 7,803) with multiple unemployment spells per person (N = 5,047), of which only 37.6 per cent end in a transition to work, while 16.5 per cent are right-censored. Persons exiting the labour market were treated as censored in the analysis yielding thus event-specific hazard models (compare Singer & Willett 2003).

It is important to note that the monthly calendar information was matched with other variables measured on a yearly basis. As most of the information besides the labour market status record is collected in yearly intervals, a limitation posed by this study is not being able to assign individual information to the exact monthly timing of the beginning of the spell.

Ethnic groups

There is no consensus in the literature on how ethnic groups are to be defined. Depending on the source, the definition can include notions of a shared culture in addition to common ancestry. Despite the theoretical complexity of the phenomenon (for a more detailed discussion, see Sollors 1996), ethnic group membership is a concept that is difficult to measure adequately. Quantitative data have severe limitations in this regard. Since the options to operationalise ethnic group membership in the GSOEP are limited or entail a heavy selection when using more recently added indicators, the ethnic groups are identified via nationality and place of birth. Persons born in Germany and holding German nationality are defined as native Germans. Turkish migrants were born in Turkey and hold either Turkish or German nationality – hence inclusion of the naturalised first generation in the sample (for the descriptive statistics of the sample, see Table 7.1). Persons born in Germany who hold Turkish nationality are considered second generation and are thus excluded from the sample.

Table 7.1 *Descriptive statistics sample event history analysis, by ethnic group*

	Native German		First-generation Turkish	
	Mean	SD	Mean	SD
Interethnic friendships	0.04	0.24	0.43	0.82
Intra-ethnic friendships	1.35	1.27	0.98	1.16
Age	36.96	12.59	34.39	11.16
Years full-time work experience	11.92	11.67	9.34	9.66
German language proficiency	13	0	9.36	2.94
Years of stay in Germany	38	0	20.13	9.47
	%		%	
Female	47		35	
Educational attainment				
Inadequately/General elementary	18		58	
Middle vocational	60		29	
Vocational *Abitur*/higher vocational	10		5	
Higher education	12		6	

Source: GSOEP 1996-2007

Interethnic and intra-ethnic friendships

Interethnic and intra-ethnic friendships are measured identically to the measures used in Chapter six. However, since this chapter focuses on friendships, I use only non-related ties and subsequently recode them on the basis of the nationality specified. For a Turkish person, interethnic friendships are those with German nationals. Interethnic friendships for a German refer to the number of friends that hold a nationality other than German. Intra-ethnic ties are coded inversely: for native Germans, these are friendships with German nationals; for Turkish migrants these are friendships with people not holding German nationality. The friendships are matched to the unemployment spells in such a way that the time of measurement falls closest to the beginning of the spell, but not before unemployment has started.[3]

The GSOEP survey does not allow for a much more refined review of the ethnic differences in social capital. What is analysed therefore is not the network of ethnic minorities compared to natives, but rather the differences in background characteristics between persons with and without interethnic and intra-ethnic friendships. Furthermore, since the measurement is limited to ethnic differences in social capital, it is not possible to measure the actual resources available in ego's network. This implies that spanning structural holes can only be observed with respect to the ethnic divide, and not when it concerns socio-economic differences. I therefore assume that social connections with native Germans as such imply having access to valuable resources. This is clearly a limitation; data on the socio-economic status of the friends would be desirable to describe the social composition of the networks. In that way, one could examine which socio-economic characteristics are bridged in addition to ethnicity.

Important to note is that this study considers friendships ties in one's larger network. It remains a question wether these are weak ties in Granovetter's (1973) sense. Moreover, in earlier literature there is consensus that the ties mentioned in name generator items (like the ones used in this study) are biased towards strong ties (see e.g. Van der Gaag & Snijders 2004). The ties mentioned in the survey are therefore likely to be close rather than remote friendships. Since the GSOEP survey only allows for distinguishing between family relations and friendships, I concentrate on friendships as the least strong ties measured.

Control variables

As a first control variable, educational attainment was introduced. Operationalised according to the ISCED scheme, the following categories were used: 1) inadequately schooled, 2) general elementary, 3) middle vocational, 4) vocational plus Abitur (A levels), 5) higher vocational education and 6) higher education (UNESCO 1997). For the analysis, (1) and (2) as well as (4) and (5) were collapsed into single categories. In addition, I controlled for years of full-time working experience (also squared), age (also squared) and gender. For the Turkish migrants, I further controlled for German language proficiency and the duration of stay in Germany in years. The latter two control variables were included to test their spuriousness with interethnic friendships: it could be that those having interethnic friendships also speak German well, or that those who are in Germany for longer are also the ones that have interethnic friendships. Finally, a dichotomous variable was included to control for regional differences (the former East Germany vs. West Germany) and dummies for each survey year to control for a time trend.

Method of estimation

Many studies that analyse the returns of social capital suffer from an endogeneity problem, since the direction of the association between labour market outcomes and social capital is not clear (compare Mouw 2002; Offe & Fuchs 2004). Both theoretical arguments are plausible: on the one hand, social capital may contribute to economic success, but economic participation may, on the other hand, also enhance social capital. Panel studies can isolate the effects. Applied in this study thus was an event history design, a longitudinal record of changes in variables and their timing (Blossfeld, Golsch & Rohwer 2007). The data were set up as such that the predictors always preceded the timing of the event. In this way, the temporal order of cause and effect is unambiguous (Singer & Willett 2003). Event history analysis can, moreover, exploit censored data in a more efficient way than other panel techniques (Allison 1984: 11).

The hazard and survival functions are key means to investigate the transitions from one state to another. The continuous-time hazard $\lambda(t)$ is a time-specific failure rate measuring the 'conditional probability of event occurrence per unit of time' (Singer & Willett 2003: 474):

$$\lambda(t) = \lim_{\Delta t \to 0+} \frac{pr(t \leq T < t + \leq T)}{\Delta t} \tag{1}$$

with T denoting the failure time measured here in months (Cox 1972: 187). The equation indicates that the event – the transition from unemployment to work – occurs at T in the interval t to t+Δt, given that it has not occurred before. The rate is measured in Δt units. The continuous-time survivor function F(t) refers to the probability of surviving at least until time t (Singer & Willett 2003: 472; Cox 1972: 187):

$$F(t) = pr(T \geq t) \tag{2}$$

The event time T of the event exceeds thus time t.

Not making assumptions regarding the shape of the hazard function, Cox proportional hazards models are used to estimate the impact of the covariates. Cox regressions can generally be formulated as:

$$h(t_{ij}) = h_0(t_j)e^{\beta_1 X_{1ij} + \beta_2 X_{2ij} + \ldots + \beta_k X_{kij}} \tag{3}$$

with $\log h_0(t_j)$ as the unspecified general baseline log cumulative hazard function and with $e^{\beta_1 X_{1ij} + \beta_2 X_{2ij} + \ldots + \beta_k X_{kij}}$ as the covariate effects.

As the sample contains multiple records per person, which are not expected to be independent, the standard errors are allowed to be intra-group-correlated (clustering). In that way, independence across (but not necessarily within) groups is assumed. All variables included in the analysis are treated as time-constant. The estimates are obtained by the Breslow method handling tied events as though the order of the events is unknown. Finally, the proportionality assumption has been relaxed by including interactions with time when significant.

Results

Table 7.2 displays the average number of interethnic and intra-ethnic friendships for native Germans and first-generation Turkish migrants, split by educational level.[4] With respect to the dependent variable, only 37 per cent of the unemployment spells end with a transition to employment in

Table 7.2   *Average number of interethnic and intra-ethnic friendships, by level of education and ethnic group*

| | Interethnic friends | | | | Intra-ethnic friends | | | |
| | Native German | | First-generation Turkish | | Native German | | First-generation Turkish | |
	Mean	SD	Mean	SD	Mean	SD	Mean	SD
Inadequately schooled/ general elementary	0.05	0.01	0.39	0.04	1.25	0.03	1.03	0.06
Middle vocational	0.03	0.00	0.48	0.06	1.35	0.02	0.89	0.09
Vocational *Abitur*/ higher vocational	0.05	0.01	0.68	0.19	1.52	0.04	0.81	0.22
Higher education	0.04	0.01	0.37	0.14	1.44	0.04	1.14	0.21

Source: GSOEP 1996-2007

Figure 7.1   *Kaplan-Meier survival estimates for the transition from unemployment to employment for native Germans and first-generation Turks*

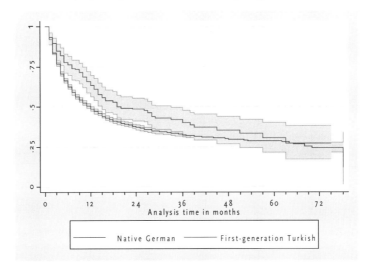

Note: Estimates include 95 per cent confidence interval.
Source: GSOEP 1996-2007

the observed time span. Figure 7.1 visualises the survival curve for this transition for native Germans and first-generation Turkish immigrants. Turkish immigrants make a significantly slower transition to employment than do Germans.[5] Naturally, these survival curves are a univariate picture of the transition from unemployment to employment. To account for other individual characteristics as well, multivariate models are estimated in the following section.

Table 7.3 presents Cox regressions predicting the duration of the transition from unemployment to employment for Turkish migrants and native Germans separately. Models 1 and 2 include interethnic and intra-ethnic friendships, plus all controls. When looking at native Germans only (Model 1), the results with regard to social capital indicate that having friends of a different ethnic background does not impact the transition from unemployment to work. On the other hand, each friend within the same ethnic group accelerates the process of finding a job by almost 4 per cent. Model 2, including only the Turkish first generation, suggests that Turkish migrants profit from interethnic friendships. For them, each native German friend accelerates the process of finding a job by 46 per cent.

Contrary to native Germans, having intra-ethnic friendships does not affect the process of finding a job for Turkish migrants. There is hence no advantage of co-ethnic friendships, for example, with respect to the ethnic economy. This could be explained by Smith's (2003) findings. Smith concludes that due to lacking trust and thus collective efficacy, the resources and support mobilised through the ethnic network differ across ethnic communities. Poor blacks in the US were found to lag behind other ethnic communities in these terms (Smith 2003). It might be that such processes also apply to the Turkish community.

These findings only partly confirm the first hypothesis that despite a varying effect size, all friendships reduce unemployment duration. Although intra-ethnic friendships are beneficial for native Germans, they are not for Turkish migrants. Similarly, interethnic friendships are beneficial for Turkish migrants but not for native Germans. From Models 1 and 2 it can be concluded that having friendships with native Germans accelerates the process of finding a job, rather than interethnic or intra-ethnic friendships as such.

In Model 3 analysing both ethnic groups jointly, I therefore combine the interethnic friendships for the Turkish migrants and the intra-ethnic friendships for the native Germans in one variable: the number of native German friends. As can be seen from Model 3, having German friends shortens the transition to employment for both native Germans and Turkish migrants, though this effect is much stronger for the latter. This result supports the resource-argument and thus also Haug's (2007) thesis on host country-related social capital. It seems that friendships with Germans are effective in smoothening the transition to employment. This holds both for native Germans and Turkish migrants. However, friendships that bridge across the ethnic divide and tap into a resource-rich environment prove even more effective.

With respect to the controls (gender, age, level of education, language skills, labour market experience), the findings are in line with the literature (see e.g. Kogan 2004; Hartung & Neels 2009). Previous research indicates that immigrant men and women use their social networks differently (see

Table 7.3   *Cox regression predicting the effect of interethnic and intra-ethnic friendships on the transition to employment, hazard ratios*

	Model 1 Native German	Model 2 First-generation Turkish	Model 3 All
Female	.577***	.596~	.577***
	(.025)	(.166)	(.025)
Age	1.063**	1.022	1.062**
	(.020)	(.110)	(.020)
Age squared	.998***	.999	.998***
	(.000)	(.001)	(.000)
Years full-time work experience	1.084***	1.198***	1.085***
	(.010)	(.058)	(.010)
Years full-time work experience squared	.999***	.995***	.999***
	(.000)	(.002)	(.000)
Educational attainment			
Inadequately schooled/ general elementary	.673***	.851	.685***
	(.045)	(.201)	(.043)
Middle vocational	ref.	ref.	ref.
Vocational plus *Abitur*/ higher vocational	1.183**	1.234	1.191**
	(.077)	(.629)	(.077)
Higher education	1.566***	.650	1.490***
	(.090)	(.638)	(.105)
German language proficiency		1.098~	1.057
		(.054)	(.044)
Years of stay in Germany		.962*	.966**
		(.015)	(.011)
Interethnic friendships	1.047	1.460**	
	(.082)	(.168)	
Intra-ethnic friendships	1.036*	1.016	
	(.017)	(.088)	
Native German			ref.
First-generation Turkish			.483*
			(.143)
German friends			1.034*
			(.017)
German friends * First-generation Turkish			1.259*
			(.135)
Number of observations	7,503	313	7,803
Number of failures	2,830	113	2,938
Log-likelihood	-21,826.345	-480.730	-22,749.222
AIC	43,714.690	1,027.460	45,568.444
BIC	43,929.305	1,151.085	45,812.123

Note: Models include dummies for each survey year, a dummy for former East Germany and interactions with time where model improving (survey year, higher education, female). p < 0.10 * p < 0.05, ** p < 0.01, *** p < 0.001, two-tailed tests, robust standard errors clustered by individual
Source: GSOEP 1996-2007

Table 7.4 *Cox regression predicting the effect of friendships with Germans for high and low educated on the transition to employment, hazard ratios*

	Model 4 Native German	Model 5 First-generation Turkish	Model 6 Low education only
Female	.571***	.558*	.569***
	(.025)	(.157)	(.030)
Age	1.095***	1.048	1.072**
	(.020)	(.113)	(.023)
Age squared	.998***	.999	.998***
	(.000)	(.001)	(.000)
Years full-time working experience	1.078***	1.199***	1.091***
	(.010)	(.057)	(.013)
Years full-time working experience squared	.999***	.994***	.999***
	(.000)	(.002)	(.000)
German language proficiency		1.118*	1.092~
		(.059)	(.049)
Years of stay in Germany		.959*	.971*
		(.016)	(.012)
High education	ref.	ref.	
Low education	.644***	.341**	
	(.051)	(.131)	
German friends	1.008	.758	1.046*
	(.031)	(.248)	(.020)
Low education * German friends	1.039	2.185*	
	(.037)	(.744)	
Native German			ref.
First-generation Turkish			.502*
			(.151)
German friends * First-generation Turkish			1.406***
			(.141)
Number of observations	7,493	312	6,080
Number of failures	2,827	112	2,225
Log-likelihood	-21,829.751	-476.122	-16,671.655
AIC	43,717.502	1,012.244	33,405.311
BIC	43,918.232	1,124.534	33,613.406

Note: Models include dummies for each survey year, a dummy for former East Germany and interactions with time where model improving (survey year, higher education, female). p < 0.10 * p < 0.05, ** p < 0.01, *** p < 0.001, two-tailed tests, robust standard errors clustered by individual
Source: GSOEP 1996-2007

e.g. Moore 1990; Livingston 2006). Therefore, as a robustness check, an interaction term between interethnic and intra-ethnic friendships and sex for both native German and Turkish migrants was included; the results did not appear significant (output omitted).

To test the hypothesised interaction between having German friends and educational attainment the models are again differentiated by ethnic group (Table 7.4). The variable education is dichotomised into 'high' education (higher vocational and higher education) and 'low' or no education (middle vocational, general elementary and inadequate education). To test whether the effect of having friendships with Germans is more effective for those with a low education, I include an interaction term in Model 4. The effect of having friendships with Germans does not differ for high- or low-educated native Germans, herewith rejecting H2a. However, in line with H2b, lower-educated migrants profit much more from friendships with Germans, as compared to the higher educated (Model 5). Finally, to test whether the effect of having friendships with Germans for Turkish migrants with a low education is also greater than it is for the native Germans, I turn to Model 6. Here the higher educated are removed from the sample and the two ethnic groups are analysed jointly. The results confirm what was found earlier (Model 3): friendships with native Germans have an accelerating impact on finding a job both for low-educated native Germans and Turkish migrants. However, the return of this form of social capital is much higher for the Turkish first generation, when compared to native Germans. Low-educated Turkish migrants hence profit most from having friendships with native Germans, more so than do native Germans and higher-educated migrants.

Conclusion

The results of this chapter partly confirmed my expectations. For the Turkish first generation, interethnic friendships had a positive impact on the transition to employment, while for the native Germans, intra-ethnic friendships did. Rather than friendships, per se, it is having friendships with native Germans that reduced unemployment duration. Hence, intra-ethnic friendships are more effective for Germans; interethnic friendships are more effective for Turkish migrants. Finally, friendships with native Germans are most effective for low-educated Turkish migrants, more so than for higher-educated Turks and low-educated native Germans. The role of social capital for the structural integration of migrants into the receiving society has not gained much attention. Yet, the findings suggest that the receiving country-specific resources made available through one's network do contribute to reducing the ethnic gap on the labour market.

Again, these results must be seen in light of a few limitations. The higher impact of having German friends for the Turkish minority may also be explained alternatively. It could well be that Turkish migrants 'knowing Germans' also captures – besides the impact of social capital – unobserved characteristics related to other dimensions of integration, be it social or psychological (compare Mouw 2003). In other words, it is not only social capital that has a positive effect on the transition to work, but possibly also other dimensions of integration into the host society, measured by an indication of 'having German friends'. Unfortunately, due to data limitations, these dimensions cannot be disentangled here.

In addition, the effects could be overestimated for migrants if they make more frequent use of their social ties to find employment (Drever & Hoffmeister 2008). Mouw (2002), for instance, argues that job-seeking costs increase for minorities vis-à-vis discrimination. To reduce search costs, migrants may therefore rely more heavily on their social networks than natives do. Unfortunately, it was not possible to include information on whether the interethnic ties were actually used for the job search. Furthermore, one could interpret the differences between migrants and natives as a composition effect since migrants are, on average, less educated than natives and since the lower educated more frequently use their social networks to find employment. Yet, when only including the low educated (Model 6), the effect of social capital also proves larger for Turkish migrants than for native Germans, thus indicating that the difference in the effect of social capital cannot only be due to disparity in educational attainment.

A third limitation relates to the limited number of friendships recorded in the data and the bias of this name generator measurement instrument towards strong ties. In this way, close friendships rather than acquaintances were included and it was not possible to estimate the global effect of weak ties in Granovetter's (1973) sense. Future research could remedy this situation by investigating the entire network of a person. Better measurement of weaker ties is necessary to analyse to what extent results differ when taking into account the weakest ties in people's networks.

Nevertheless, it was possible to confirm that accessing resources available through contacts to the native population is an effective strategy to accelerate the transition from unemployment to employment, both for migrants and native residents. Friends can provide valuable information on job vacancies and/or support in the application process. As a result, persons with native German friends find a job more quickly than do people without such friends. This holds for native Germans, but even more so for migrants. It is, however, important to note that data on the socio-economic status of the friends would be desirable in order to examine if – in addition to ethnicity – other socio-economic characteristics are bridged as well. On the basis of the analysis, which sustains the temporal order required for making causal statements, it can be concluded that, in order to make the transition from unemployment to work, friendships are most 'profitable' when accessing a resource-rich environment, in combination with diversifying one's social network by building interethnic contacts. Thus, Turkish migrants with a low education profit most from having native German friends, more so than native Germans and higher-educated Turkish migrants.

Notes

1   This chapter is based on Lancee and Hartung (2012).
2   In this regard, it would be interesting to include the second generation. However, case numbers for the second generation were very low.
3   Due to a scarcity of cases, friendships are treated as time-invariant. The friendship measure used falls closest to the start of the unemployment spell, but not before. Analyses were also run with the measurement of friendships closest to the end of the unemployment spell, but this did not yield substantially different results.
4   Note that the sample includes pooled multiple unemployment spells from several years and can therefore not be claimed as representative for the whole population at a particular point of time.
5   Naturally, these results do not say anything about either the initial probability of *entering* unemployment or the transitions into different types of employment (for the latter, see Hartung & Neels 2009).

8 Conclusions on immigrants' bonding and bridging social capital

The question posed in this book is to what extent different forms of social capital help immigrants in making headway on the labour market. More specifically, I analysed the effect of bonding and bridging social capital on employment, income and occupational status. The economic incorporation of immigrants in their host society is of great interest to scholars studying the consequences of migration. Researchers have suggested that social capital contributes to economic outcomes such as access to the labour market (Aguilera, 2002; Drever & Hoffmeister 2008), wages (Aguilera 2005; Boxman, De Graaf & Flap 1991) and occupational status (Lin 1999). For immigrants, social capital is especially important, since relying on social networks is a way to reduce job-seeking costs, for example, in the presence of discrimination (Mouw 2002).

Conceptual differentiation in various forms of social networks and social capital is not new. In 1973, Granovetter had introduced the 'strength of weak ties hypothesis'. According to this hypothesis, weak ties provide more useful information, since the emphasis is on relations between groups. This is beneficial to making headway on the labour market (Granovetter 1973, 1995). The identification of 'bridges' in networks (Burt 1992) is not new either. Equally, the strength of strong ties (Lin, Ensel & Vaughn 1981) and the concept of network closure (Coleman 1988) have been discussed extensively. The term 'bridging and bonding social capital' was coined at the end of the 1990s (Gitell & Vidal 1998; Woolcock 1998; Narayan 1999). Putnam's book *Bowling alone* (2000) made the concepts central to the discussion of social capital. Simultaneously, the concepts of bonding and bridging are being used to analyse the social capital of immigrants, although not always named as such (Portes 1995b, 2000). In the past decade, a growing body of empirical studies on specific forms of immigrants' social capital has been published.

And yet, studies that compare different forms of social capital of immigrants simultaneously are rare, especially those that make use of survey data. This book has aimed to contribute to the research field by carrying out such an analysis in Germany and the Netherlands. The results indicate how useful it is to differentiate forms of social capital. Social connections are not beneficial as such; it depends on the type of relation whether social relations can be associated with better labour market outcomes. A main

contribution of this book is simultaneously analysing the impact of two basic forms of social capital for immigrants. By taking into account different
labour market outcomes, two countries, multiple ethnic groups and both
men and women, this book provides a detailed analysis of the economic
returns of immigrants' bonding and bridging social capital.

A second contribution of this book lies in the conceptualisation of bonding and bridging social capital for immigrants. Many studies on immigrants' social capital apply the bonding and bridging terminology, but the
specification of the concepts is often limited to within-group and between-
group connections. Building on the principles of network closure and
structural holes, I conceptualised bonding and bridging social capital specifically for immigrants. What is more, I discussed the arguments that
explain the mechanisms between bonding and bridging and labour market
outcomes.

Overview

With the main research questions laid out in chapter 1, chapter 2 discussed
social capital and the concepts of bonding and bridging. Social capital was
defined as the collection of resources owned by the members of an individual's personal social network that may become available to the individual
as a result of the history of these relationships, plus the collection of
resources that may become available to all members of the group/s one
belongs to. I differentiated between structural and cognitive social capital.
As opposed to cognitive social capital, structural social capital involves a
behavioural component. The structural component refers to the 'wires' in
the network: the intensity and quantity of connections between people. It
consists of a collection of ties characterised by the relation between the
people connected and the possible institutional embeddedness of these ties.
The cognitive component refers to the 'nodes' in a network: attitudes and
values, such as perceptions of support, reciprocity and trust that contribute
to the exchange of resources.

Bonding social capital implies having dense ties and thick trust. The underlying principle is that of network closure: in a network with closure, the
members of the network have ties with all members (Coleman 1988). In
terms of structural social capital, the concept of bonding is based on the
idea of the 'strength of strong ties' (Lin, Ensel & Vaughn 1981; Coleman
1990). I defined bonding structural capital as ties that closely connect people and increase the degree of network closure. Cognitive bonding social
capital was defined as the attitudes and values (such as trust) that contribute to the exchange of resources among the members of an individual's
close and dense network. The clearest case of a network with a high degree
of closure is probably the family. Besides family ties, those with co-ethnics

also contribute to a dense network with closure. Bonding social capital was hence operationalised as the strength of family ties and ties with co-ethnics.

A person's bridging social capital is characterised by a network of cross-cutting ties and thin trust. Structural bridging social capital refers to the collection of ties that form an individual's 'wide' social network, i.e. one that contains structural holes (Burt 2001). Structural holes are gaps in networks, for example, across socio-economic characteristics, such as ethnicity. A bridge is a tie that spans a structural hole (Burt 2001). Structural bridging social capital was defined as the ties in an individual's network that cut across the ethnic divide. Cognitive bridging social capital is characterised by thin or particular trust, that is, the attitudes and values such as outward orientation that contribute to the exchange of resources in one's wide social network.

Chapter 3 dealt with the macro-context of Germany and the Netherlands. I discussed the migration history, the immigration and integration policy, the labour market and the macro-differences in social capital. The histories and policies of Germany and the Netherlands are rather different. The migration regime in Germany is often described as exclusionary, while that of the Netherlands, as multicultural. Although both countries have a large share of immigration consisting of guest workers and family reunification, they differ in terms of the arrival of ethnic Germans and refugees in Germany and migration from former colonies in the Netherlands. With respect to the structure of the labour market, there is also variation. The Dutch labour market is more open and accessible to immigrants than the German one. The employment ratio (the employment rate of the immigrants relative to that of the natives) is much lower in Germany than in the Netherlands. There are also discrepancies in levels of individual social capital: levels seem to be higher in the Netherlands than in Germany (Pichler & Wallace 2007).

Chapter 4 discussed the dependent variable and individual-level hypotheses. The dependent variable of this study is 'labour market outcomes'. This is operationalised as the likelihood of being employed and, for those employed, income and occupational status. I formulated three hypotheses in this chapter.

The first hypothesis (H1) of the book states that there is a positive relationship between bridging social capital and labour market outcomes. Forming the basis of the hypothesis, I differentiated between the diversification argument, the resource argument and the argument of compensating and circumventing discrimination. The diversification argument stated that one's social network becomes more diverse by spanning structural holes as such and hence enables access to new and useful information, resulting in better labour market performance. The resource argument explains why it is effective for immigrants to span structural holes across the ethnic divide.

By doing so, one realises access to resources specific to the host country, such as labour market information. This is particularly useful for immigrants, since they are less familiar with the labour market than are native residents. The third argument is that bridging social capital is useful for immigrants as it opens up another channel of access to the labour market. This is particularly useful as an alternative to the discrimination that immigrants are faced with in more formal channels. Furthermore, by establishing connections with native residents, immigrants may be able to overcome initial barriers of distrust and prejudice that exists with employers, current or prospective. Along this line of reasoning, bridging social capital can function as a way to compensate the negative effects of prejudice and insecurity forming the basis of discrimination.

The second hypothesis (H2) stated that bonding social capital is positively associated with labour market outcomes. Yet there are two competing arguments. The closure argument states that strong within-group connections – in this case, family relations and co-ethnic friendships – result in a network with high solidarity and high-quality communication. Especially for immigrants, this may be important, for example, in order to realise employment in the ethnic economy (Waldinger 2005). The second argument was labelled the isolation argument, according to which within-group connections do not result in valuable new information and hence do not result in opportunities to make headway on the labour market. When being embedded into ethnic networks, successful upward mobility may be impeded due to social obligations, pressure to conformity or 'downward levelling norms' (Portes 1998). Such mobility traps can consequently lead to ethnic segmentation or 'downward assimilation' (Portes 1995).

Hypothesis three (H3) dealt with differences in the returns of social capital for men and women. Previous studies show that, although overall usage of networks is similar for men and women, returns may differ (see e.g. Livingston 2006). Compared to men, women are more likely to be channelled into informal or lower-quality jobs through their networks. It is unclear wether this also is the case when differentiating between bonding and bridging social capital. Returns to bonding social capital are expected to be lower for women than for men, since within-group connections are more likely to be non-work-related for women than for men. With respect to bridging, I hypothesised that there is no difference between men and women, as these connections are expected to link people to valuable host country-specific resources.

Chapters 5, 6 and 7 contain the study's empirical results. In chapter 5 (see also Lancee 2010), the effect of bonding and bridging social capital on labour market outcomes was analysed for Turkish, Moroccan, Antillean and Surinamese immigrants in the Netherlands. I made use of the Dutch Social Position and Use of Utilities Immigrants survey (SPVA) for the years 1998 and 2002. Models were estimated with OLS regression, using cross-sectional data as well as a small panel. Scales for social capital were constructed using Mokken analysis. The results indicate that bonding social capital is not associated with labour market outcomes. On the other hand, bridging social capital is positively associated with most labour market outcomes. This, however, holds for the structural rather than for the cognitive element of bridging social capital, and the effect is more pronounced for men than for women. Chapter 6 analysed the effect of bonding and bridging social capital in Germany. I made use of the German Socio-Economic Panel Survey (GSOEP) for the years 1996 to 2007. I estimated models using both random-effects and fixed-effects regression. Results are similar to those of the Netherlands: bonding indicators were mostly not associated with labour market outcomes; bridging indicators have a positive effect on being employed, income and occupational status. In Germany, results for bridging were also more pronounced for men than for women. In chapter 7, I applied an event history design. The chapter analysed the effect of interethnic and intra-ethnic friendships on the transition from unemployment to employment for Turks and native Germans in Germany. Models were estimated with Cox regression, making use of the monthly employment and unemployment spells given in the GSOEP. In line with my findings in chapters 5 and 6, bridging social capital for first-generation Turks reduced unemployment duration. Also for native Germans, connections with other natives reduced unemployment duration. However, having connections with native Germans was significantly more beneficial for Turks than it was for native Germans. In short, there seems to be a premium for bridging the ethnic divide.

Findings

In a nutshell, the results of this book are as follows: bridging social capital helps immigrants make headway on the labour market, but bonding social capital does not. Bridging social capital helps immigrants in both Germany and the Netherlands to find employment. Among those employed, it is associated with higher income and higher occupational status. On the other hand, this study found only marginal effects with respect to bonding social capital. Family relations (both within and outside the household), and co-ethnic friendships were not generally associated with labour market outcomes. In the following sections, I discuss how the empirical results relate to the hypotheses formulated.

Germany and the Netherlands

Expectations with respect to macro-level influences are not clear-cut. Several reasons were discussed why one could expect differing results in

Germany and the Netherlands. First, as discussed in chapter 3, the two countries' migration histories as well as their policies towards ethnic minorities have been rather distinct. There are also some differences with respect to the structure of the labour market. The second reason one could expect variation is the data used. The analyses for the Netherlands are almost solely based on cross-sectional data, while those for Germany, on a long-running panel. Turks aside, the included ethnic groups differ. Moreover, the items used to measure social capital are not identical in both datasets.

Despite these differences on the macro-level and in measurement, findings are very similar in Germany and the Netherlands. This is evidence favouring a generalisation of the individual-level relationship studied: identified differences between Germany and the Netherlands do not influence the relation between immigrants' social capital and their labour market outcomes. Nevertheless, the macro-contexts of Germany and the Netherlands are similar in many aspects, particularly when compared with Mediterranean countries or liberal welfare states. It is therefore unclear to what extent the results can be generalised for countries that are distinct. Conclusions might be different if one were to make a cross-national comparison with a more diverse range of countries. To generalise such findings and better examine the influence of macro-level characteristics, a comparison including more and more varied countries would be necessary (see also 'Open questions' section).

Bonding and bridging social capital

H1, stating that bridging social capital is positively associated with labour market outcomes, was largely confirmed. Most indicators of bridging social capital indeed appeared to be positively associated with the labour market outcomes identified, both in Germany and the Netherlands. Thus, connections with native residents proved beneficial to immigrants. There were, however, differences between men and women in this regard.

In chapter 3, I developed three arguments that form the basis of the hypothesis on the effect of bridging social capital. It remains open for discussion which of the arguments is dominant in explaining the found effect. The data do not allow for a test of the validity of each argument separately. For example, in the case of the diversification argument, only *ethnic* bridges are measured. It was not possible to examine wether socio-economic differences are bridged as well. The diversification argument is therefore an explanation of bridging social capital as such, rather than a specific explanation of *immigrants'* bridging social capital. The results indicate that spanning structural holes across the ethnic divide is beneficial in terms of labour market outcomes. This, however, does not exclude the possibility that spanning structural holes across other socio-economic characteristics is useful as well. Yet, the analyses in chapter 7 show that bridging the ethnic divide is more beneficial for Turks than it is for native Germans. This supports the idea that, for immigrants, bridging the ethnic divide is indeed more than 'just' spanning structural holes and other arguments are needed to explain its effect.

The resource argument and the compensating discrimination argument provide such immigrant-specific explanations. Also for these arguments, it is difficult to empirically disentangle their explanatory power. For example, there is no data on the actual resources a tie provides access to. The resource argument is therefore necessarily based on the assumption that the native population has more knowledge of or connections to the labour market than immigrants do. The discrimination argument is difficult to test separately: the effect of bridging social capital can be due to circumventing and compensating discrimination. At the same time, bridging social capital may provide access to host country-specific resources. However, favouring the compensating discrimination argument is the fact that the effect of bridging social capital does not differ much between the first and second generations: the resource argument is more difficult to make for the latter group because they were born in the host society.

Bonding social capital was expected to be associated positively with labour market outcomes (H2). Based on the present study, this hypothesis has to be rejected. Few bonding indicators could be statistically associated with labour market outcomes and, if they were, they were sometimes even negatively associated. Since no effect was found with respect to bonding social capital, it seems that the isolation argument offers a better explanation than the closure argument. Closure in the family and co-ethnic networks may indicate a high level of solidarity and enforceable trust, but it does not provide ego with new or valuable information useful for job-seeking. The results in chapter 7 suggest that the isolation argument is immigrant-specific: intra-ethnic friendships – a bonding indicator – are not beneficial in finding employment for Turks, but they are for native Germans. In other words, it seems that within-group connections are ineffective only when it concerns a group that has few resources, e.g. Turkish immigrants.

However, this does not mean that family ties as such are not useful on the labour market: both in Germany and the Netherlands, I found that inter-ethnic family ties have a positive impact on labour market outcomes.

With regard to cognitive and structural social capital, the findings show some clear differences. In the Netherlands, for both the bonding as well as the bridging type, no substantial relation between cognitive social capital and labour market outcomes was found. One could explain this by arguing that the process of finding a job is an action, hence it is relations (i.e. structural social capital) that yield positive returns, not attitudes. Such an argument would, however, discard almost any claim about the impact of attitudes. Another explanation might be that there is a problem with the internal validity of the construct. It could be that the items used to measure cognitive social capital measure something else, like the importance of family in a 'lonesome' world in the case of bonding, or attitudes to gender relations that are currently outdated in the case of bridging.

One could further argue that there is a causal ordering of cognitive and structural social capital. For example, attitudes (cognitive) result in behaviour (structural) rather than the other way around. Since they will also capture attitudes, it is likely that the 'structural' scales behave better in the analyses. However, estimating the models without the scales of structural social capital did not result in the cognitive scales being significant. If there is an indirect effect of cognitive social capital, this should be the case. I therefore conclude that my hypotheses referring to bonding and bridging cannot be confirmed when it concerns cognitive social capital.

Men and women

H3 stated that the economic returns of bonding are lower for women than for men. With regard to bridging social capital, I hypothesised that there was no difference between men and women. Both hypotheses have to be rejected. The effect of bonding social capital does not differ for men and women: for *both,* bonding social capital cannot be associated with labour market outcomes. With respect to bridging, however, there are differences. Whereas for men bridging is generally beneficial, for women, it is only partly beneficial with respect to employment and not beneficial once on the labour market (in terms of income and occupational status).

A possible explanation for these discrepancies is that, as discussed in chapter 4, networks of female migrants are less diverse and women have fewer ties than men. For example, Livingston's (2006) study on Mexican women in the US finds that although overall use of family and friends networks is similar for men and women, the returns differ. Making use of their social network significantly reduces women's chances of finding work in the formal sector (while for men this effect was positive). This might be the case for women's bridging social capital as well. As for the smaller effect with regard to employment, it could be that women indeed use their bridging capital in order to find work. Since this partly takes place in the informal sector, it is less likely to be recorded in surveys. This explains why the effect of bridging social capital on employment likelihood is less pronounced for women than for men. It may also explain why there is no effect with respect to income and occupational status. As Livingston (2006) finds, women use their social networks to find employment, but the jobs are not of better quality. Hagan (1998) and Hondagneu-Sotelo (1994) also conclude that migrant women are channelled into low-paying jobs and informal sector jobs via their social ties. For women, connections with native residents do seem to provide access to the labour market, but the quality of these connections is not sufficient to climb the occupational ladder. As discussed in the following 'Open questions' section, data that specify the socio-economic status of ties would allow for a better analysis in this respect.

Open questions

Further research might be undertaken with different objectives, such as improving theory, improving measurement and generalisation or replication. I raise some suggestions for each of these objectives.

From a theoretical point of view, one of the remaining questions regarding bridging social capital concerns which structural holes are spanned exactly. That is, to what extent is bridging the ethnic divide also bridging socio-economic differences? Moreover, what matters more? Unfortunately, the current measurement does not enable me to differentiate interethnic and socio-economic bridges. Improvements in theory could also be made in exploring the underlying mechanism of bridging social capital in more detail. Why exactly is bridging social capital effective for immigrants? Is it because of network diversification, circumventing discrimination or the signalling value to employers as a form of social homophily? To what extent is it a combination of all three, or does it depend on the specific situation? Disambiguating those arguments would allow for a better understanding of the mechanisms at work.

Questions also remain about the impact of macro-level characteristics on the relation between immigrants' social capital and labour market outcomes. This is both a matter of generalisation as well as of theory-building. To find out if the results can be extended to other ethnic groups and countries, it is necessary to replicate the study in differing contexts. A substantial reason for doing so refers to the possible impact of macro-level characteristics. As concluded by this book, there are some differences between Germany and the Netherlands, but results did not differ with respect to returns of social capital. It could be that macro-level characteristics do matter, for example, when considering other welfare state regimes or labour markets that have a different structure from that of Germany and the Netherlands. A cross-national study incorporating various types of countries could well tackle these questions.

To improve measurement results, there is a need for better data. Improvement is necessary with respect to the labour market position of immigrants in general. The identification of immigrants and their descendants is desirable, as is investing in longitudinal data. Furthermore, cross-national data that include social capital items specifically for immigrants would be desirable for a better international comparison of the effect of social capital. Improvements can also be made in the measurement of social capital. In the first place, measuring should be more symmetrical for immigrants and native residents. This allows for a better analysis of the differential effect of social capital. Secondly, measures can be better with respect to the resources available through ties and to longitudinal measures of social capital. For example, social capital-related measures in the GSOEP have been improved considerably since 2006, but a social network module is included only every five years.

Notwithstanding these open questions and limitations, the findings on bonding and bridging social capital are comparable for employment, occupational status and income – variables that stand for rather distinct labour market outcomes. The mechanism behind bonding and bridging, as applied in this book, seems to be similar for both access to and performance on the labour market, although it is less pronounced for women than for men. Furthermore, results are similar in Germany and the Netherlands. Keeping in mind the approach taken in this study, the statement that 'whereas bonding is to get by, bridging is to get ahead' (Putnam 2000: 20) also seems to apply to the case of immigrants in Germany and the Netherlands.

Appendix

The measurement of social capital using cumulative scaling

The Netherlands

For the scales that measure social capital in the Netherlands, Item Response Theory (IRT) was used. The logic of IRT is based on the order of the proportion of people that give a positive response to an item. For example, few of the respondents have a native Dutch partner. Having a native Dutch partner therefore correlates relatively low with the other items that measure interethnic contacts. However, marrying a native Dutch person may very well be the upper part of a scale that measures interethnic contacts: those who have a native Dutch partner also score positively on the other items. In the example, having a partner who was born in the Netherlands is the item with the lowest proportion of positive responses and thus the most 'difficult' item on the scale: those who marry a native Dutch partner also score positively on the other items, but not necessarily the other way around (this is supported by the high item- H, see Table A.3). Thus, IRT does account for such an ordinal structure and may therefore be more appropriate for scale construction than, for example, factor analysis (Van Schuur & Kiers 2004). Moreover, since social capital is often understood in terms of 'more' and 'less', IRT is especially suitable for the measurement of social capital (Van der Gaag & Snijders 2004).

A non-parametric IRT model for finding cumulative scales was thus used, the so-called Mokken scaling method.[1] This resulted in four scales. The relevant coefficients are presented in Tables A.1 through A.4. There are several criteria that a set of items has to meet to form an acceptable Mokken scale. The most important measure is Loevinger's H. The following cut-off values are conventional to judge a Mokken scale: >.30 being a useful scale; >.40 a medium-strong scale; and >.50 a strong scale (Mokken 1996; Van Schuur 2003). For each of the scales used in this book, H is at least .40. Furthermore, the test for monotone homogeneity (i.e. the positive response to each item is a function of the positive response to easier items in the same scale) and double monotonicity (to assess whether the degree of difficulty across items is the same for all individuals) is positive. Last, the Cronbach's alpha for the scales is satisfactory.

The actual scale consists of the sum of the items. Before this computation, missing values for the individual items were imputed using two-way imputation (described in Sijtsma & Van der Ark 2003). The imputation is done as follows (Van Ginkel & Van der Ark 2007: 2):

> Let PMi be the average of all observed scores of respondent i, let IMj be the average of all observed scores on item j, and let OM be the average of all observed scores on all items and all persons. The missing value of respondent i on item j is then based on Xij = PMi + IMj − OM.

Imputation was done for all cases with less than 60 per cent of the scale items missing. Those cases with more than 60 per cent of the values missing were deleted.

The language proficiency scale was constructed according to the same principle. The items are presented in Table A.5.

Table A.1   *Items measuring structural bonding social capital*

	Mokken Item H	Cronbach's alpha Alpha if item deleted
Received help from parent/child	0.53	0.70
Gave help to parent/child	0.52	0.70
Got advice from parent/child	0.39	0.71
Gave advice to parent/child	0.42	0.70
Saw parent/child in past 12 months	0.46	0.70
Had contact with parent/child in past 12 months	0.44	0.70
Scale coefficient	0.46	0.73

Source: SPVA 2002

Table A.2   *Items measuring cognitive bonding social capital*

	Mokken Item H	Cronbach's alpha Alpha if item deleted
Trust family more than trust friends	0.43	0.72
Rather discuss problems with family than friends	0.42	0.72
Family members should be there for each other	0.38	0.74
You can always count on your family	0.42	0.72
In case of worries the family should help	0.43	0.74
Family members keep each other informed	0.34	0.76
Scale coefficient	0.40	0.77

Source: SPVA 2002

Table A.3   *Items measuring structural bridging social capital*

	Mokken Item H	Cronbach's alpha Alpha if item deleted
Partner born in the Netherlands	0.44	0.71
More contact with native Dutch than own ethnic group	0.56	0.66
Has native Dutch friends or acquaintances	0.69	0.71
Receives visits from native Dutch friends or neighbours	0.63	0.62
Contact with native Dutch in personal life	0.70	0.59
Member of an association that has few or almost no members that have the same ethnicity as the respondent (Yes/No)	0.35	0.71
Scale coefficient	0.57	0.71

Source: SPVA 2002

Table A.4   *Items measuring cognitive bridging social capital*

	Mokken Item H	Cronbach's alpha Alpha if item deleted
Openness about sex is wrong	0.47	0.66
Contact between men and women is too liberal	0.46	0.66
It is best if children live at home until they marry	0.45	0.66
Unmarried men and women can live together (item reversed)	0.45	0.67
Scale coefficient	0.46	0.73

Source: SPVA 2002

Table A.5   *Items measuring language proficiency*

	Mokken Item H	Cronbach's alpha Alpha if item deleted
Problems reading Dutch	0.64	0.80
Frequency of using Dutch with partner	0.67	0.79
Frequency of using Dutch with children	0.68	0.76
Problems speaking Dutch	0.61	0.79
Scale coefficient	0.65	0.83

Source: SPVA 2002

Germany

Equally, several scales were developed for the measurement of social capital in the GSOEP. For the strength of family ties variable, the procedure followed was somewhat different to the one described for the Netherlands. Naturally, since people report only the strength of the relations of the family members they have, there are many missing values. For example, not everybody has grandchildren: some people (the older respondents) do have grandchildren while others (the younger respondents) do not; some people have parents (the younger part of the sample) while others (the oldest part of the sample) do not.

Since the Mokken scaling technique drops all cases with one or more missing values on the items to be included, this is problematic. One could impute all missing values with the technique as described above, but so many missing values does not yield a very reliable result. One could also recode all that are missing to zero, but this highly biases the scale values. It might be argued that this is not problematic and scaling techniques are unnecessary. Since the objective is to provide an average of the strength of the family relations of each respondent, one could simply calculate this average. However, despite the theoretical considerations, one would also like to know whether a scale of strength of family ties is indeed empirically coherent: do people that report a closer relation with some family members in general also report a stronger relation with other relatives?

Therefore, the scale is validated with reliability analysis. Since Cronbach's alpha compares pairs of items, it can handle missing values. This makes it possible to still calculate a scale coefficient if there are many missing values. For the final scale, since they were responded to differently, three items were not included: 'Previous spouse', 'Current spouse (if not living in the household)' and 'Grandparents'. In Table A.6, the coefficients of the final scale can be found both for 1996 and 2001. The Cronbach's alpha clearly indicates that these items can be seen as the measurement of a single construct; furthermore, the scales prove very similar for 1996 and 2001.

With respect to the strength of family ties, the final scale consists of the mean of all the items, in which missing items are not included when calculating the mean. The scale is thus the average relationship strength of the family members outside the household that a respondent reports to have. The measure of the number of family members outside the household is a normal count: it is the sum of all family members respondents indicate. I also tried to combine these measures by multiplying the number of family members by the strength of relationship (hence, number of brothers times the strength of the relationships indicated with the brothers). The result is a measure of the size of one's family network, weighted by the strength of the relations in this network. This was also included in the analyses, but did not yield different results. For reasons of parsimony, the two separate measures are presented.

Table A.6   *Scale bonding social capital: The strength of family ties*

Item: For those relatives that you do have, how close is your relationship?

	1996	2001
Mother	0.77	0.76
Father	0.78	0.78
Son/s	0.81	0.80
Daughter/s	0.81	0.80
Brother/s	0.79	0.78
Sister/s	0.79	0.78
Grandchild/grandchildren	0.80	0.79
Other relatives with whom you are in close contact (aunts, uncles, cousins, nephews, nieces)	0.84	0.82
Cronbach's alpha	0.82	0.81

Source: GSOEP 1996-2001

Table A.7   *Scale coefficients for visiting and receiving visits from native Germans*

Items: In the last 12 months, have you visited people of German origin at their home? (Yes/No)

In the last 12 months, have you receive a visit at your home from people of German origin? (Yes/No)

Survey year	Cronbach's alpha	Loevinger's H
1997	.86	.88
1999	.87	.85
2001	.80	.81
2003	.83	.84
2005	.83	.84
2007	.82	.81

Source: GSOEP 1999-2007

References

Agnitsch, K., J. Flora & V. Ryan (2006), 'Bonding and bridging social capital: The interactive effects on community action', *Journal of the Community Development Society* 37 (1): 36-51.

Aguilera, M. B. (2005), 'The impact of social capital on the earnings of Puerto Rican migrants', *The Sociological Quarterly* 46 (4): 569-592.

Aguilera, M. B. (2003), 'The impact of the worker: How social capital and human capital influence the job tenure of formerly undocumented Mexican immigrants', *Sociological Inquiry* 73 (1): 52-83.

Aguilera, M. B. (2002), 'The impact of social capital on labor force participation: Evidence from the 2000 social capital benchmark survey', *Social Science Quarterly* 83 (3): 854-874.

Aguilera, M. B. & D. S. Massey (2003), 'Social capital and the wages of Mexican migrants: New hypotheses and tests', *Social Forces* 82 (2): 671-701.

Alberts, H. C. (2005), 'Changes in ethnic solidarity in Cuban Miami', *Geographical Review* 95 (2): 231-249.

Alesina, A. & P. Giuliano (2007), 'The power of the family', Harvard Institute of Economic Research Discussion Paper No. 2132. Cambridge: Harvard University.

Alesina, A. & E. La Ferrara (2000), 'Participation in heterogeneous communities', *The Quarterly Journal of Economics* 115 (3): 847-858.

Allison, P. D. (1984), *Event history analysis: Regression for longitudinal event data*. Beverly Hills: Sage Publications.

Allport, G. W. (1979), *The nature of prejudice*. Cambridge: Perseus Books.

Arts, W. & J. Gelissen (2002), 'Three worlds of welfare capitalism or more? A state of the art report', *Journal of European Social Policy* 12 (2): 137-158.

Avci, G. (2008), 'Comparing integration policies and outcomes: Turks in the Netherlands and Germany', in R. Erzan & K. Kirisci (eds.), *Turkish immigrants in the European Union: Determinants of immigration and integration*, 63-80. London: Routledge.

Bade, K., M. Bommes & R. Münz (2004), *Migrationsrapport 2004: Fakten, Analysen, Perspectiven*. Frankfurt am Main: Campus.

Bakker, B., I. Sieben, P. Nieuwbeerta & H. Ganzeboom (1997), 'Maten voor prestige, sociaal-economische status en sociale klasse voor de standaard beroepenclassificatie 1992', *Sociale Wetenschappen* 40 (1): 1-22.

Bankston, C. L. & M. Zhou (2002), 'Social capital as a process: The meaning and problems of a theoretical metaphor', *Sociological Inquiry* 72 (2): 285-317.

Battu, H., P. Seaman & Y. Zenou (2004), 'Job contact networks and the ethnic minorities', Working Paper Series No. 628. Stockholm: Research Institute Industrial Economics.

Bauer, T. & K. F. Zimmermann (1999), 'Occupational mobility of ethnic Germans', IZA Discussion Paper No. 58. Bonn: IZA.

Becker, G. S. (1971), *The economics of discrimination*. Chicago: University of Chicago.

Becker, G. S. (1964), *Human capital: A theoretical and empirical analysis, with special reference to education*. New York: Columbia University Press.

Beugelsdijk, S. & S. Smulders (2003), 'Bridging and bonding social capital: Which type is good for economic growth?', in W. Arts, J. Hagenaars & L. Halman (eds.), *The cultural diversity of European unity, findings, explanations and reflections from the European values study*, 147-184. Leiden: Koninklijke Brill.

Beugelsdijk, S. & T. van Schaik (2003), 'Participation in civil society and European regional economic growth', in W. Arts, J. Hagenaars & L. Halman (eds.), *The cultural diversity of European unity, findings, explanations and reflections from the European values study*, 119-145. Leiden: Koninklijke Brill.

Bevelander, P. & J. Veenman (2006), 'Naturalisation and socio-economic integration: The case of the Netherlands', IZA Discussion Paper No. 2153. Bonn: IZA.

Bevelander, P. & J. Veenman (2004), 'Variation in perspective: The employment success of ethnic minority males in the Netherlands, 1988-2002', *International Migration* 42 (4): 35-64.

Bijl, R. V., A. Zorlu, A. S. van Rijn, R. P. W. Jenissen & M. Blom (2005), *Integratiekaart 2005: De maatschappelijke integratie van migranten in de tijd gevolgd: trend- en cohortanalyses*. The Hague: Statistics Netherlands.

Blossfeld, H.-P., K. Golsch & G. Rohwer (2007), *Event history analysis with Stata*. London: Lawrence Erlbaum Associates.

Bommes, M. & H. Kolb (2004), 'Economic integration, work, entrepeneurship', IMISCOE Cluster B4 state of the art report. Osnabrück: University of Osnabrück.

Borjas, G. J. (1994), 'The economics of integration', *Journal of Economic Literature* 32 (4): 1667-1717.

Bosch-Domenech, A. (1991), 'Economies of scale, location, age, and sex discrimination in household demand', *European Economic Review* 34: 1589-1595.

Bourdieu, P. (1986), 'The forms of capital', in J. G. Richardson (ed.), *Handbook of theory and research for the sociology of education*, 241-258. New York: Greenwood.

Boxman, E. A. W., P. M. de Graaf & H. D. Flap (1991), 'The impact of social and human capital on the income attainment of Dutch managers', *Social Networks* 13 (1): 51-73.

Bretell, C. B. (2005), 'Voluntary organizations, social capital, and the social incorporation of Asian Indian immigrants in the Dallas-Fort Worth Metroplex', *Anthropological Quarterly* 78 (4): 853-884.

Brisson, D. S. & C. L. Usher (2007), 'The effects of informal neighborhood bonding social capital and neighborhood context on homeownership for families living in poverty', *Journal of Urban Affairs* 29 (1): 65-75.

Brisson, D. S. & C. L. Usher (2005), 'Bonding social capital in low-income neighborhoods', *Family Relations* 54 (5): 644-653.

Bubolz, M. M. (2001), 'Family as source, user, and builder of social capital', *Journal of Socio-Economics* 30: 129-131.

Büchel, F. & J. R. Frick (2005), 'Immigrants' economic performance across Europe: Does immigration policy matter?', *Population Research and Policy Review* 24 (2): 175-212.

Burt, R. S. (2005), *Brokerage and closure: An introduction to social capital*. Oxford: Oxford University Press.

Burt, R. S. (2004), 'Structural holes and good ideas', *American Journal of Sociology* 110 (2): 349-399.

Burt, R. S. (2002), 'Bridge decay', *Social Networks* 24 (4): 333-363.

Burt, R. S. (2001), 'Structural holes versus network closure as social capital', in N. Lin, K. Cook & R. S. Burt (eds.), *Social capital: Theory and research*, 31-56. New York: Aldine de Gruyter.

Burt, R. S. (2000), 'The network structure of social capital', in R. I. Sutton & B. M. Staw (eds.), *Research in organizational behavior*, 345-423. Greenwich: JAI Press.

Burt, R. S. (1992), *Structural holes: The social structure of competition*. Cambridge: Harvard University Press.

Chandra, K. (2006), 'What is ethnic identity and does it matter?', *Annual Review of Political Science* 9: 397-424.

Chiswick, B. R. & P. W. Miller (2002), 'Immigrant earnings: Language skills, linguistic concentrations and the business cycle', *Journal of Population Economics* 15 (1): 31-57.

Chiswick, B. R. & P. W. Miller (1996), 'Ethnic networks and language proficiency', *Journal of Population Studies* 9 (1): 19-35.

Coleman, J. S. (1990), *Foundations of social theory*. Cambridge: Belknapp Press.

Coleman, J. S. (1988), 'Social capital in the creation of human capital', *American Journal of Sociology* 94 (supplement): S95-S120.

Constant, A. & D. S. Massey (2005), 'Labor market segmentation and the earnings of German guestworkers', *Population Research and Policy Review* 24 (5): 489-512.

Constant, A. & Y. Schachmurove (2003), 'Entrepreneurial ventures and wage differentials between Germans and immigrants', IZA Discussion Paper No. 879. Bonn: IZA.

Cox, D. R. (1972), 'Regression models and life-tables', *Journal of the Royal Statistical Society, Series B (Methodological)* 34 (2): 187-220.

Crul, M. & J. Schneider (2005), 'Integration of Turkish second-generation men and women in Germany and the Netherlands: The impact of differences in vocational and academic tracking systems', paper presented at the SSRC Working Group on Education and Migration Conference, London, 11-12 February 2005.

Cyrus, N. & D. Vogel (2007), 'Germany', in A. Triandafyllidou & R. Gropas (eds.), *European immigration: A sourcebook*, 127-140. Aldershot: Ashgate.

Dagevos, J. (2001), 'Perspectief op integratie: Over de social-culturele en structurele integratie van ethnische minderheden in Nederland', Werkdocumenten No. 121. The Hague: Wetenschappeljke Raad voor het Regeringsbeleid.

De Graaf, P. M. & H. Flap (1988), 'With a little help from my friends: Social resources as an explanation of occupational status and income in the Netherlands, the United States and West Germany', *Social Forces* 67 (2): 453-472.

Die Beauftragte der Bundesregierung für Migration Flüchtlinge und Integration (2007), *Bericht der Beauftragten der Bundesregierung*. Berlin: Die Beauftragte der Bundesregierung für Migration, Flüchtlinge und Integration.

Doomernik, J. (1998), 'The effectiveness of integration policies towards immigrants and their descendants in France, Germany and the Netherlands', International Migration Papers No. 2. Geneva: ILO.

Doomernik, J. & M. Jandl (eds.) (2008), *Modes of migration regulation and control in Europe*. IMISCOE Reports Series. Amsterdam: Amsterdam University Press.

Drever, A. I. & O. Hoffmeister (2008), 'Immigrants and social networks in a job-scarce environment: The case of Germany', *International Migration Review* 42 (2): 425-448.

Dronkers, J. & R. A. Wanner (2006), 'Waarom verdienen immigranten minder? Effecten van immigratiebeleid en arbeidsmarktkenmerken', *Tijdschrift voor Arbeidsvraagstukken* 22: 379-394.

Duleep, H. & M. C. Regets (1999), 'Immigrants and human capital investment', *American Economic Review* 89 (2): 186-190.

Dustmann, C. & A. van Soest (2002), 'Language and the earnings of immigrants', *Industrial and Labor Relations Review* 55 (3): 473-492.

Elliott, J. R. (2001), 'Referral hiring and ethnically homogenous jobs: How prevalent is the connection and for whom?', *Social Science Research* 30: 401-425.

Elliott, J. R. (1999), 'Social isolation and labor market insulation: Network and neighborhood effects on less-educated urban workers', *The Sociological Quarterly* 40 (2): 199-216.

Entzinger, H. (2001), 'Towards a model of incorporation: The case of the Netherlands', in K. Phalet & A. Orkeny (eds.), *Ethnic minorities and inter-ethnic relations in context*, 321-347. Aldershot: Ashgate.

Erickson, R. & J. H. Goldthorpe (2002), 'Intergenerational inequality: A sociological perspective', *Journal of Economic Perspectives* 16 (3): 31-44.

Esping-Andersen, G. (1990), *The three worlds of welfare capitalism*. Cambridge: Polity Press.

Euwals, R., J. Dagevos, M. Gijsberts & H. Roodenburg (2007), 'The labour market position of Turkish immigrants in Germany and the Netherlands: Reasons for migration, naturalisation and language proficiency', CPB Discussion Paper No. 79. The Hague: Centraal Planbureau.

Euwals, R., J. Dagevos, M. Gijsberts & H. Roodenburg (2006), 'Immigration, integration and the labor market: Turkish immigrants in Germany and the Netherlands', CPB Discussion Paper No. 75. The Hague: Centraal Planbureau.

Faist, T. (1995), 'Ethnicization and racialization of welfare state politics in Germany and the United States', *Ethnic and Racial Studies* 18 (2): 219-250.

Faist, T. (ed.) (2007), *Dual citizenship in Europe: From nationhood to societal integration*. Ashgate: Aldershot.

Falcon, L. & E. Melendez (2001), 'The social context of job searching for racial groups in urban centers', in T. O'Connor & L. D. Bobo (eds.), *Urban inequality: Evidence from four cities*. New York: Sage.

Fennema, M. (2004), 'The concept and measurement of ethnic community', *Journal of Ethnic and Migration Studies* 30 (3): 429-447.

Fennema, M. & J. Tillie (2001), 'Civic community, political participation and political trust of ethnic groups', *Connections* 24 (1): 26-41.

Fennema, M. & J. Tillie (1999), 'Political participation and political trust in Amsterdam: Civic communities and ethnic networks', *Journal of Ethnic and Migration Studies* 25 (4): 703-726.

Fernandez, R. & D. Harris (1992), 'Social isolation and the underclass', in A. Harell & G. Peterson (eds.), *Drugs, crime and social isolation: Barriers to urban opportunity*. Washington, D.C.: Urban Institute Press.

Fernandeze-Kelly, M. P. (1995), 'Social and cultural capital in the urban ghetto: Implications for the economic sociology of immigration', in A. Portes (ed.), *The economic sociology of immigration: Essays on networks, ethnicity and entrepreneurship*, 213-247. New York: Russell Sage Foundation.

Flap, H. D. (2002), 'No man is an island: The research program of a social capital theory', in O. Favereau & E. Lazega (eds.), *Conventions and structures in economic organization: Markets, networks and hierarchies*. Cheltenham: Edward Elgar.

Flap, H. & E. A. W. Boxman (2001), 'Getting started: The influence of social capital at the start of a career', in N. Lin, K. Cook & R. S. Burt (eds.), *Social capital: Theory and research*. New York: Adine de Gruyter.

Flap, H. D. & B. Völker (2004), *Creation and returns of social capital*. London: Routledge.

Forrest, J. & R. Johnston (2000), 'The occupational attainment of immigrant groups in Australia', *International Migration* 38 (2): 269-296.

Franzen, A. & D. Hangartner (2006), 'Social networks and labor market outcomes: The nonmonetary benefits of social capital', *European Sociological Review* 22 (4): 353-368.

Friedberg, R. M. (2000), 'You can't take it with you? Immigrant assimilation and the portability of human capital', *Journal of Labor Economics* 18 (2): 221-251.

Fukuyama, F. (2001), 'Differing disciplinary perspectives on the origins of trust', *Boston University Law Review* 81 (3): 479-494.

Fukuyama, F. (1995), *Trust: The social virtues and the creation of prosperity.* New York: The Free Press.

Gambetta, D. (1988), *Trust: Making and breaking cooperative relations.* Oxford: Blackwell.

Ganzeboom, H. & D. J. Treiman (2003), 'Three internationally standardised measures for comparative research on occupational status', in J. Hoffmeyer-Zlotnik & C. Wolf (eds.), *Advances in cross-national comparison: A European working book for demographic and socio-economic variables,* 159-193. New York: Kluwer Academic Press.

Ganzeboom, H. & D. J. Treiman (1996), 'Internationally comparable measures of occupational status for the 1988 international standard classification of occupations', *Social Science Research* 25 (3): 201-239.

Ganzeboom, H., P. M. de Graaf & D. J. Treiman (1992), 'A standard international socio-economic index of occupational status', *Social Science Research* 21 (1): 1-56.

Garcia, C. (2005), 'Buscando trabajo: Social networking among immigrants from Mexico to the United States', *Hispanic Journal of Behavioral Sciences* 27 (1): 3-22.

Georgas, J. (2006), 'Families and family change', in J. Georgas, J. W. Berry, F. J. R. van de Vijver, C. Kagitcibasi & Y. H. Poortinga (eds.), *Families across cultures,* 3-50. Cambridge: Cambridge University Press.

Gitell, R. & A. Vidal (1998), *Community organizing: Building social capital as a development strategy.* Thousand Oaks: Sage.

Goldthorpe, J. H. (1992), *Revised class schema.* London: Social and Community Planning Research.

Goldthorpe, J. H. (1987), *Social mobility and class structure in modern Britain.* Oxford: Clarendon Press.

Goldthorpe, J. H. & K. Hope (1972), 'Occupational grading and occupational prestige', in K. Hope (ed.), *The analysis of social mobility: Methods and approaches,* 19-80. Oxford: Clarendon Press.

Gonzen, K. N., D. A. Gerber, E. Morawska, G. E. Pozzetta & R. J. Vecoli (1992), 'The invention of ethnicity: A perspective from the U.S.A.', *Journal of American Ethnic History* 12 (1): 3-41.

Granato, N. & F. Kalter (2001), 'Die Persistenz ethnischer Ungleichheit auf dem deutschen Arbeitsmarkt', *Kölner Zeitschrift für Soziologie und Sozialpsychologie* 53: 497-520.

Granovetter, M. (1995), *Getting a job: A study of contacts and careers,* 2nd ed. Chicago: University of Chicago Press.

Granovetter, M. (1973), 'The strength of weak ties', *American Journal of Sociology* 78 (6): 1360-1380.

Green, G. P., L. M. Tigges & D. Diaz (1999), 'Racial and ethnic differences in job-search strategies in Atlanta, Boston and Los Angeles', *Social Science Quarterly* 80 (2): 263-278.

Green, S. (2004), *The politics of exclusion: Institutions and immigration policy in contemporary Germany.* Manchester: Manchester University Press.

Grenier, G. J. & A. Stepick (1992), *Miami now! Immigration, ethnicity, and social change.* Gainesville: University Press of Florida.

Greve, A. & J. W. Salaff (2005), 'Social network approach to understand the ethnic economy: A theoretical discourse', *GeoJournal* 64 (1): 7-16.

Groeneveld, S. & Y. Weyers-Martens (2003), *Minderheden in beeld, SPVA-02.* Rotterdam: Instituut voor Sociologisch-Economisch Onderzoek (ISEO).

Grootaert, C. (2002), 'Does social capital help the poor? A synthesis of findings from the local level institutions in Bolivia, Burkina Faso and Indonesia', Local Levels Institutions Working Papers No. 10. Washington, D.C.: World Bank.

Grusky, D. B. (ed.) (2001), *Social stratification: Class, race and gender in sociological perspective,* 2nd ed. Boulder: Westview Press.

Guiraudon, V., K. Phalet & J. ter Wal (2005), 'Monitoring ethnic minorities in the Netherlands', *International Social Science Journal* 57 (1): 75-88.

Hagan, J. M. (1998), 'Social networks, gender, and immigrant incorporation', *American Sociological Review* 63: 55-67.

Halaby, C. N. (2004), 'Panel models in sociological research', *Annual Review of Sociology* 30: 507-544.

Hartung, A. & K. Neels (2009), 'Destination manual worker or clerk? Ethnic differences in the transition from school to work', *Schmollers Jahrbuch* 129 (2): 343-356.

Haug, S. (2007), 'Soziales Kapital als Resource im Kontext von Migration und Integration', in J. Lüdicke & M. Diewald (eds.), *Soziale Netzwerke und soziale Ungleichheit: Zur Rolle von Sozialkapital in modernen Gesellschaften*, 85-112. Wiesbaden: VS Verlag für Sozialwissenschaften.

Haug, S. (2008), 'Migration networks and migration decision-making', *Journal of Ethnic and Migration Studies* 34 (4): 585-605.

Haug, S. (2003), 'Interethnische Freundschaftsbeziehungen und soziale Integration: Unterschiede in der Ausstattung mit sozialem Kapital bei jungen Deutschen und Immigranten', *Kölner Zeitschrift für Soziologie und Sozialpsychologie* 55 (4): 716-736.

Heath, A. & S. Y. Cheung (eds.) (2007), *Unequal chances: Ethnic minorities in western labour markets*. Oxford: Oxford University Press.

Heath, A., C. Rothon & E. Kilpi (2008), 'The second generation in Western Europe: Education, unemployment, and occupational attainment', *Annual Review of Sociology* 34: 211-235.

Heath, A. & S. Yu (2005), 'Explaining ethnic minority disadvantage', in A. Heath, J. Ermish & D. Gallie (eds.), *Understanding social change*, 187-224. Oxford: Oxford University Press.

Hollstein, B. (2001), *Grenzen sozialer Integration: Zur Konzeption informeller Beziehungen und Netzwerke*. Opladen: leske+budrich.

Hondagneu-Sotelo, P. (1994), *Gendered transitions: Mexican experiences of immigration*. Berkeley: University of California Press.

Hughes, P., J. Bellamy & A. Black (1999), 'Building social trust through education', in I. Winter (ed.), *Social Capital and Public Policy in Australia*, 225-249. Melbourne: Australian Institute of Family Studies.

Ireland, P. (2004), *Becoming Europe: Immigration, integration and the welfare state*. Pittsburgh: University of Pittsburgh Press.

Jacobs, D., K. Phalet & M. Swyngedouw (2004), 'Associational membership and political involvement among ethnic minority groups in Brussels', *Journal of Ethnic and Migration Studies* 30 (3): 543-559.

Janjuha-Jivraj, S. (2003), 'The sustainability of social capital within ethnic networks', *Journal of Business Ethics* 47 (1): 31-43.

Joppke, C. (1999), *Immigration and the nation-state: The United States, Germany and Great Britain*. Oxford: Oxford University Press.

Kääriäinen, J. & H. Lehtonen (2006), 'The variety of social capital in welfare state regimes: A comparative study of 21 countries', *European Societies* 8 (1): 27-57.

Kadushin, C. (2004), 'Too much investment in social capital?', *Social Networks* 26: 75-90.

Kahanec, M. & M. Mendola (2007), 'Social determinants of labor market status of ethnic minorities in Britain', IZA Discussion Paper No. 3146. Bonn: IZA.

Kalter, F. (2006), 'Auf der Suche nach einer Erklärung für die spezifischen Arbeitsmarktnachteile von Jugendlichen türkischer Herkunft. Zugleich eine Replik auf den

Beitrag von Holger Seibert und Heike Solga: "Gleiche Chancen dank einer abgeschlosse-nen Ausbildung?"', *Zeitschrift für Soziologie* 35: 144-160.

Kalter, F. & N. Granato (2007), 'Educational hurdles on the way to structural assimilation in Germany', in A. Heath & S. Y. Chueng (eds.), *Unequal chances: Ethnic minorities in western labour markets*, 271-319. Oxford: Oxford University Press.

Kalter, F. & N. Granato (2002), 'Demographic change, educational expansion and structural assimilation of immigrants: The case of Germany', *European Sociological Review* 18 (2): 199-216.

Kanas, A. & F. van Tubergen (2009), 'The impact of origin and host country schooling on the economic performance of immigrants', *Social Forces* 88 (2): 893-916.

Kanas, A., F. van Tubergen & T. van der Lippe (2009), 'Immigrant self-employment: Testing hypotheses about the role of origin- and host-country human capital and bonding and bridging social capital', *Work and Occupations* 36 (3): 181-208.

Karoly, L. A. & G. Burtless (1995), 'Demographic change, rising earnings inequality, and the distribution of personal well-being, 1959-1989', *Demography* 32 (3): 379-405.

Kazemipur, A. (2006), 'The market value of friendship: Social networks of immigrants', *Canadian Ethnic Studies Journal* 38 (2): 47-71.

Kim, D., S. V. Subramanian & I. Kawachi (2006), 'Bonding versus bridging social capital and their associations with self rated health: A multilevel analysis of 40 US communities', *Journal of Epidemical Community Health* 60: 116-122.

Kloosterman, R. & J. Rath (2001), 'Immigrant entrepreneurs in advanced economies: Mixed embeddedness further explored', *Journal of Ethnic and Migration Studies* 27 (2): 189-201.

Kloosterman, R., J. van der Leun & J. Rath (1999), 'Mixed embeddedness: (In)formal economic activities and immigrant business in the Netherlands', *International Journal of Urban & Regional Research* 23 (2).

Kogan, I. (2007a), 'A study of immigrants' employment careers in West Germany using the sequence analysis technique', *Social Science Research* 36 (2): 491-511.

Kogan, I. (2007b), *Working through barriers: Host country institutions and immigrant labour market performance in Europe*. Dordrecht: Springer.

Kogan, I. (2004), 'Last hired, first fired? The unemployment dynamics of male immigrants in Germany', *European Sociological Review* 20 (5): 445-461.

Kohli, M. (2000), 'The battlegrounds of European identity', *European Societies* 2 (2): 113-137.

Koopmans, R. (2010), 'Trade-offs between equality and difference: Immigrant integration, multiculturalism and the welfare state in cross-national perspective', *Journal of Ethnic and Migration Studies* 36 (1): 1-26.

Koopmans, R. (2003), 'Good intentions sometimes make bad policy: A comparison of Dutch and German integration policies', in R. Cuperus, K. A. Duffek & J. Kande (eds.), *The challenge of diversity. European social democracy facing migration, integration, and multiculturalism,* 163-168. Innsbruck: StudienVerlag.

Koopmans, R., P. Statham, M. Giugni & E. Passey (2005), *Contested citizenship: Immigration and cultural diversity in Europe*. Minneapolis: University of Minnesota Press.

Kossoudji, S. A. (1988), 'English language ability and the labour market opportunities of Hispanic and East Asian immigrant men', *Journal of Labor Economics* 6 (2): 205-228.

Lancee, B. (2011), 'The economic returns of bonding and bridging social capital for immigrant men in Germany', *Ethnic and Racial Studies* DOI:10.1080/01419870.2011.591405.

Lancee, B. (2010), 'The economic returns of immigrants' bonding and bridging social capital: The case of the Netherlands', *International Migration Review* 44 (1): 202-226.

Lancee, B. & J. Dronkers (2011), 'Ethnic, religious and economic diversity in Dutch neigh-
      bourhoods: Explaining quality of contact with neighbours, trust in the neighbourhood and
      inter-ethnic trust', *Journal of Ethnic and Migration Studies* 37 (4): 597-618.
Lancee, B. & A. Hartung (2012), 'Turkish migrants and native Germans compared: The effect
      of inter-ethnic and intra-ethnic friendships on the transition from unemployment to work',
      International Migration 51 (1): 39-54.
Lautenbach, H. & F. Otten (2007), 'Inkomen allochtonen blijft achter door lage opleiding',
      Sociaaleconomische trends No. 2e kwartaal. Voorburg: CBS.
Leonard, R. & J. Onyx (2003), 'Networking through loose and strong ties: an Australian qua-
      litative study', *Voluntas: International Journal of Voluntary and Non-Profit Organizations*
      14 (2): 189-203.
Li, P. S. (2004), 'Social capital and economic outcomes for immigrants and ethnic minorities',
      Journal of International Migration and Integration 59 (2): 171-190.
Liebig, T. (2007), 'The labour market integration of immigrants in Germany', OECD Social
      Employment and Migration Working Papers No. 47. Paris: OECD.
Light, I. & S. J. Gold (2000), *Ethnic economies*. San Diego: Academic Press.
Light, I., G. Sabagh, M. Bozorgmehr & C. Der-Martirosian (1995), 'Internal ethnicity in the
      ethnic economy', *Ethnic and Racial Studies* 16 (4): 581-597.
Lin, N. (2008), 'A network theory of social capital', in J. Deth, D. Castiglione & G. Wolleb
      (eds.), *The handbook of social capital*, 50-69. Oxford: Oxford
Lin, N. (2004), 'Job search in urban China', in B. Volker & H. Flap (eds.), *Creation and re-
      turns of social capital*, 145-171. London: Routledge.
Lin, N. (2001a), 'Building a network theory of social capital', in N. Lin, K. Cook & R. S.
      Burt (eds.), *Social capital: Theory and research*, 3-30. New York: Aldine de Gruyter.
Lin, N. (2001b), *Social capital: A theory of social structures and action*. Cambridge:
      Cambridge University Press.
Lin, N. (1999), 'Social networks and status attainment', *Annual Review of Sociology* 25: 467-
      487.
Lin, N. & D. Ao (2008), 'The invisible hand of social capital', in N. Lin & B. H. Erickson
      (eds.), *Social capital: An international research program*, 107-133. Oxford: Oxford
      University Press.
Lin, N., W. M. Ensel & J. C. Vaughn (1981), 'Social resources and strength of ties: Structural
      factors in occupational attainment', *American Sociological Review* 46 (4): 393-405.
Lindbeck, A. & D. J. Snower (1988), *The insider outsider theory of employment and un-
      employment*. Cambridge: The MIT Press.
Livingston, G. (2006), 'Gender, job searching, and employment outcomes among Mexican im-
      migrants', *Population Research and Policy Review* 25: 43-66.

Marsden, P. V. (1990), 'Network data and measurement', *Annual Review of Sociology* 16:
      435-463.
Martens, E. P. (1999), *Minderheden in beeld, SPVA-98*. Rotterdam: Instituut voor
      Sociologisch-Econmisch Onderzoek (ISEO).
Massey, D. S., R. Alarcon, J. Durand & H. Gonzalez (1987), *Return to Aztlan: The social pro-
      cess of international migration from Western Mexico*. Berkeley: University of California
      Press.
Massey, D. S. & K. E. Espinosa (1997), 'What's driving Mexico-U.S. migration? A theoreti-
      cal, empirical, and policy analysis', *American Journal of Sociology* 102: 939-999.
McPherson, M., L. Smith-Lovin & J. M. Cook (2001), 'Birds of a feather: Homophily in so-
      cial networks', *Annual Review of Sociology* 27: 415-444.
Menjivar, C. (2000), *Fragmented ties: Salvadoran immigrant networks in America*. Berkeley:
      University of California Press.

Menjivar, C. (1997), 'Immigrant kinship networks: Vietnamese, Salvadoreans and Mexicans in comparative perspective', *Journal of Comparative Family Studies* 28 (1): 1-24.

Mokken, R. J. (1996), 'Nonparametric models for dichotomous responses', in W. J. van der Linden & R. K. Hambleton (eds.), *Handbook of modern item response theory*, 351-367. New York: Springer.

Molenaar, I. W. & K. Sijtsma (2000), *User's manual MSP5 for windows: A program for Mokken scale analysis for polytomous items.* Groningen: ProGAMMA.

Morgan, L., D. B. Grusky & G. S. Fields (eds.) (2006), *Mobility and inequality.* Stanford: Stanford University Press.

Morris, L. (2002), *Managing migration: Civic stratification and migrants' rights.* London: Routledge.

Mouw, T. (2006), 'Estimating the causal effect of social capital: A review of recent research', *Annual Review of Sociology* 32: 79-102.

Mouw, T. (2003), 'Social capital and finding a job: do contacts matter?', *American Sociological Review* 68 (6): 868-898.

Mouw, T. (2002), 'Racial differences in the effects of job contacts: Conflicting evidence from cross-sectional and longitudinal data', *Social Science Research* 31 (4): 511-538.

Münz, R. (2002), 'Ethnos or demos? Migration and citizenship in Germany', in D. Levy & Y. Weiss (eds.), *Challenging ethnic citizenship: German and Israeli perspectives on immigration*, 15-35. New York: Berghahn.

Musterd, S. (2005), 'Social and ethnic segregation in Europe: Levels, causes, and effects', *Journal of Urban Affairs* 27 (3): 331-348.

Nannestad, P., G. L. H. Svendsen & G. T. Svendsen (2008), 'Bridge over troubled water? Migration and social capital', *Journal of Ethnic and Migration Studies* 34 (4): 607-631.

Narayan, D. (1999), 'Bonds and bridges: Social capital and poverty', Policy Research Working Paper Series No. 2167. Washington, D.C.: World Bank.

Nauck, B. (2001), 'Social capital, intergenerational transmission and intercultural contact in immigrant families', *Journal of Comparative Family Studies* 32 (4): 465-488.

Nee, V. & J. Sanders (2001a), 'Trust in ethnic ties: social capital and immigrants', in K. S. Cook (ed.), *Trust in society*, 374-392. New York: Russell Sage Foundation.

Nee, V. & J. Sanders (2001b), 'Understanding the diversity of immigrant incorporation: A forms-of-capital model', *Ethnic and Racial Studies* 24 (3): 386-411.

Newton, K. (1997), 'Social capital and democracy', *American Behavioral Scientist* 40 (5): 575-586.

Niessen, J., T. Huddleston & L. Citron (2007), *Migrant integration policy index.* Brussels: British Council and Migration Policy Group.

Nooteboom, B. (2007), 'Social capital, institutions and trust', *Review of Social Economy* 65 (1): 29-53.

Ode, A. & J. Veenman (2003), 'The ethno-cultural and socio-economic position of ethnic minority groups in the Netherlands', in L. Hagendoorn, J. Veenman & W. Vollebergh (eds.), *Integrating immigrants in the Netherlands: Cultural versus socio-economic integration*, 2nd ed., 173-198. Aldershot: Ashgate.

OECD (2004), 'Employment protection legislation and labour market performance', in OECD (ed.), *Employment outlook*, 61-125. Paris: OECD.

Offe, C. & S. Fuchs (2004), 'A decline of social capital? The German case', in R. D. Putnam (ed.), *Democracies in flux*, 189-244. New York: Oxford University Press.

Onyx, J. & P. Bullen (2000), 'Measuring social capital in five communities', *Journal of Applied Behavioral Science* 36 (1): 23-42.

Parkin, F. (1974), 'Strategies of social closure in class formation', in F. Parkin (ed.), *The social analysis of class structure*, 1-18. London: Tavistock.

Parkin, R. & L. Stone (2004), 'General introduction', in R. Parkin & R. Stone (eds.), *Kinship and family: An anthropological reader*, 1-25. Oxford: Blackwell.

Patacchini, E. & Y. Zenou (2008), 'Ethnic networks and employment outcomes', IZA Discussion Paper No. DP 3331. Bonn: IZA.

Patulny, R. V. & G. L. H. Svendsen (2007), 'Exploring the social capital grid: Bonding, bridging, qualitative, quantitative', *International Journal of Sociology and Social Policy* 27 (1/2): 32-51.

Petermann, S. (2002), *Persönliche Netzwerke in Stadt und Land: Siedlungsstruktur und soziale Unterstützungsnetzwerke im Raum Halle/Saale*. Wiesbaden: Westdeutscher Verlag.

Pettigrew, T. (1998), 'Intergroup contact theory', *Annual Review of Psychology* 49: 65-85.

Phalet, K. & A. Heath (2006), 'From ethnic boundaries to ethnic penalties: The Turkish second generation in a European metropolis', paper presented at the Construction of Boundaries in Contemporary Europe Conference, Florence, 26-27 May 2006.

Pichler, E. (1997), *Migration, Community-Formierung und ethnische Ökonomie: Die Italienschen Gewerbetreibenden in Berlin*. Berlin: Edition Parabolis.

Pichler, F. & C. Wallace (2009), 'Social capital and social class in Europe: The role of social networks in stratification', *European Sociological Review* 25 (3): 319-332.

Pichler, F. & C. Wallace (2007), 'Patterns of formal and informal social capital in Europe', *European Sociological Review* 23 (4): 423-435.

Poortinga, W. (2006), 'Social relations or social capital? Individual and community health effects of bonding social capital', *Social Science & Medicine* 63: 255-270.

Portes, A. (2000), 'The two meanings of social capital', *Sociological Forums* 15 (1): 1-12.

Portes, A. (1998), 'Social capital: Its origins and applications in modern sociology', *Annual Review of Sociology* 24 (1): 1-24.

Portes, A. (1995a), 'Children of immigrants: segmented assimilation and its determinants', in A. Portes (ed.), *The economic sociology of immigration. Essays on networks, ethnicity and entrepreneurship*, 248-279. New York: Russell Sage Foundation.

Portes, A. (1995b), 'Economic sociology and the sociology of immigration: A conceptual overview', in A. Portes (ed.), *The economic sociology of immigration: Essays on networks, ethnicity, and entrepreneurship*, 1-41. New York: Russell Sage Foundation.

Portes, A. & J. Sensenbrenner (1993), 'Embeddedness and immigration: Notes on the social determinants of economic action', *American Journal of Sociology* 98 (6): 1320-1350.

Portes, A. & M. Zhou (1993), 'The new second generation: Segmented assimilation and its variants among post 1965 immigrant youth', *Annals of the American Academy of Political and Social Science* 530: 74-96.

Putnam, R. D. (2000), *Bowling alone: The collapse and revival of American community*. New York: Simon and Schuster.

Putnam, R. D. (1993), *Making democracy work: Civic traditions in modern Italy*. Princeton: Princeton University Press.

Rabe-Hesketh, S. & A. Skrondal (2008), *Multilevel and longitudinal modeling using Stata*, 2nd ed. College Station: Stata Press.

Reitz, J. G. (2002), 'Host societies and the reception of immigrants: Research, themes, emerging theories and methodological issues', *International Migration Review* 35 (4): 1005-1019.

Reitz, J. G. (1998), *Warmth of the welcome*. Boulder: Westview Press.

Reitz, J. G. & S. M. Sklar (1997), 'Culture, race, and the economic assimilation of immigrants', *Sociological Forum* 12 (2): 233-277.

Riphahn, R. T. (2003), 'Cohort effects in the educational attainment of second generation immigrants in Germany: An analysis of census data', *Journal of Population Economics* 16 (4): 711-737.

Sabatini, F. (2006), 'The role of social capital in economic development', paper presented at the Social Capital, Sustainability and Socio-Economic Cohesion Conference, London School of Economics, 29-30 June 2006, London.

Sabatini, F. (2005), 'An inquiry into the empirics of social capital and economic development', unpublished PhD dissertation. University of Rome La Sapienza, Rome.

Sainsbury, D. (2006), 'Immigrants' social rights in comparative perspective: Welfare regimes, forms of immigration and immigration policy regimes', *Journal of European Social Policy* 16 (3): 229-244.

Sanders, J. (2002), 'Ethnic boundaries and identity in plural societies', *Annual Review of Sociology* 28: 327-357.

Sanders, J. & V. Nee (1996), 'Immigrant self-employment: The family as social capital and the value of human capital', *American Sociological Review* 61 (2): 231-249.

Sanders, J. & V. Nee (1987), 'Limits of ethnic solidarity in the enclave economy', *American Sociological Review* 52 (6): 745-773.

Sanders, J., V. Nee & S. Sernau (2002), 'Asian immigrants' reliance on social ties in a multi-ethnic labor market', *Social Forces* 81 (1): 281-314.

Schuller, T. (2007), 'Reflections on the use of social capital', *Review of Social Economy* 65 (1): 11-28.

Scruggs, L. (2006), 'The generosity of social insurance', *Oxford Review of Economic Policy* 22 (2): 349-363.

Sijtsma, K. & I. W. Molenaar (2002), *Introduction to nonparametric item response theory.* Thousand Oaks: Sage Publications.

Sijtsma, K. & L. A. van der Ark (2003), 'Investigation and treatment of missing item scores in test and questionnaire data', *Multivariate Behavioral Research* 38 (4): 505-528.

Singer, J. D. & J. B. Willett (2003), *Applied longitudinal data analysis: Modeling change and event occurrence.* New York: Oxford University Press.

Smith, S. S. (2000), 'Mobilizing social resources: Race, ethnic and gender differences in social capital and persisting wage inequalities', *The Sociological Quarterly* 41 (4): 509-537.

Snijders, T. A. B. (1999), 'Prologue to the measurement of social capital', *La Revue Tocqueville* 20 (1): 27-44.

Sollors, W. (ed.) (1996), *Theories of ethnicity. A classical reader.* New York: New York University Press.

Solon, G. (2002), 'Cross-country differences in intergenerational mobility', *Journal of Economic Perspectives* 16 (3): 59-66.

Sorensen, B. (2001), 'The basic concepts of stratification research: Class, status, and power', in D. B. Grusky (ed.), *Social stratification: Class, race and gender in sociological perspective*, 2nd ed., 287-300.

Soysal, Y. N. (1994), *Limits of citizenship: Migrants and postnational membership in Europe.* Chicago: University of Chicago Press.

Stainback, K. (2008), 'Social contacts and race/ethnic job matching', *Social Forces* 87 (4): 857-886.

Statistics Netherlands (2008), *Jaarrapport integratie 2008.* The Hague: Statistics Netherlands.

Statistisches Bundesamt (2009), 'Bevölkerung und Erwerbstätigkeit. Bevölkerung mit Migrationshintergrund: Ergebnisse des Mikrozensus 2007', Fachserie 1 Reihe 2.2. Wiesbaden: Statistisches Bundesamt.

Stolle, D. (2001), 'Getting to trust: An analysis of the importance of institutions, families, personal experiences and group membership', in P. Dekker & E. M. Uslander (eds.), *Social capital and participation in everyday life*, 118-133. London: Routledge.

Szreter, S. & M. Woolcock (2004), 'Health by association? Social capital, social theory, and the political economy of public health', *International Journal of Epidemiology* 33 (4): 650-676.

Takle, M. (2007), *German policy on immigration: From ethnos to demos?* Frankfurt: Peter Lang.
Ter Wal, J. (2007), 'The Netherlands', in A. Triandafyllidou & R. Gropas (eds.), *European integration: A sourcebook*, 249-262. Aldershot: Ashgate.
Tesser, P. & J. Dronkers (2007), 'Equal opportunities or social closure in the Netherlands?', *Proceedings of the British Academy* 137: 359-401.
Thränhardt, D. (2000), 'Conflict, consensus and policy outcomes: immigration and integration in Germany and the Netherlands', in R. Koopmans & P. Statham (eds.), *Challenging immigration and ethnic relations politics*, 162-186. Oxford: Oxford University Press.
Treiman, D. (1977), *Occupational prestige in comparative perspective*. New York: Academic Press.

Uhlendorff, A. & K. F. Zimmerman (2006), 'Unemployment dynamics among migrants and natives', IZA Discussion Paper No. 5872. Bonn: IZA.
UNESCO (1997), *International Standard Classification of Education (ISCED)*. Paris: UNESCO.
Uunk, W. (2002), *Concentratie en achterstand: Over de samenhang tussen etnische concentratie en de sociaal-economische positie onder allochtonen en autochtonen*. Assen: Koninklijke Van Gorcum.
Uunk, W. (2003), 'The cultural integration of immigrants in the Netherlands: A description and exploration of modern attitudes of Turks, Moroccans, Surinamese, Antilleans and the indigenous population', in L. Hagendoorn, J. Veenman & W. Vollebergh (eds.), *Integrating immigrants in the Netherlands: Cultural versus socio-economic integration*, 199-234. Aldershot: Ashgate.

Van Alphen, S. & B. Lancee (2008), 'Compensating early school leave in Germany: The influence of social capital', paper presented at the 8th SOEP Users Conference, Berlin, July 9-11 2008.
Van der Gaag, M. P. J. (2005), 'Measurement of individual social capital', unpublished PhD dissertation. Groningen: University of Groningen.
Van der Gaag, M. P. J. & T. A. B. Snijders (2004), 'Proposals for the measurement of individual social capital', in H. Flap & B. Völker (eds.), *Creation and returns of social capital*, 199-218. London: Routledge.
Van der Meer, T., P. Scheepers & M. te Grotenhuis (2009), 'States as molders of informal relations? A multilevel test on social participation in 20 Western countries', *European Societies* 11 (2): 233-255.
Van Deth, J. (2008), 'Measuring social capital', in D. Castiglione, J. van Deth & G. Wolleb (eds.), *The handbook of social capital*, 150-176. Oxford: Oxford University Press.
Van Ginkel, J. R. & L. A. van der Ark (2007), 'SPSS syntax for two-way imputation of missing test data', http://www.uvt.nl/faculteiten/fsw/organisatie/departementen/mto/software2.html; accessed 13 September 2007.
Van Oorschot, W. & E. Finsveen (2009), 'The welfare state and social capital inequality', *European Societies* 11 (2): 189-210.
Van Ours, J. C. & J. Veenman (2003), 'The educational attainment of second generation immigrants in the Netherlands', *Journal of Population Economics* 16 (4): 739-754.
Van Schuur, W. H. (2003), 'Mokken scale analysis: Between the Guttman scale and parametric item response theory', *Political Analysis* 11 (2): 139-163.

Van Schuur, W. H. & H. A. L. Kiers (2004), 'Why factor analysis often is the incorrect model for analyzing bipolar concepts and what model to use instead', *Applied Psychological Measurement* 18 (2): 97-110.

Van Suntum, U. & D. Schlotböller (2002), *Arbeitsmarktintegration von Zuwanderern: Einfluss-faktoren, internationale Erfahrungen und Handlungsempfehlungen*. Gütersloh: Bertelsmann Stiftung.

Van Tubergen, F. (2004), 'The integration of immigrants in cross-national perspective: Origin, destination, and community effects', unpublished PhD dissertation. Utrecht: Utrecht University.

Van Tubergen, F. & I. Maas (eds.) (2006), *Allochtonen in Nederland in internationaal perspectief*. Amsterdam: Amsterdam University Press.

Van Tubergen, F., I. Maas & H. D. Flap (2004), 'The economic incorporation of immigrants in 18 western societies: Origin, destination and community effects', *American Sociological Review* 69 (5): 704-727.

Veenstra, G. (2002), 'Explicating social capital: Trust and participation in the civil space', *Canadian Journal of Sociology* 27 (4): 547-573.

Velling, J. (1993), 'Immigration to Germany in the seventies and eighties: The role of family reunification', Labour Economics and Human Resources Series Discussion Paper No. 93-18. Mannheim: Zentrum für Europaische Wirtschaftsforchung.

Vermeulen, F. V. (2008), *Diversiteit in uitvoering: Lokaal beleid voor werkloze migrantenjongeren in Amsterdam en Berlijn*. The Hague: NICIS.

Vermeulen, F. V. (2005a), 'Organisational patterns: Surinamese and Turkish associations in Amsterdam, 1960-1990', *Journal of Ethnic and Migration Studies* 31 (5): 951-973.

Vermeulen, F. V. (2005b), *The immigrant organising process: Turkish organisations in Amsterdam and Berlin and Surinamese organisations in Amsterdam, 1960-2000*. IMISCOE Dissertations Series. Amsterdam: Amsterdam University Press.

Voges, W., J. Frick & F. Büchel (1998), 'The integration into West German society: The impact of social assistance', in H. Kurthen, J. Fijalkowski & G. G. Wagner (eds.), *Immigration, citizenship, and the welfare state in Germany and the United States: Welfare policies and immigrant's citizenship*. Stanford: JAI Press.

Völker, B. & H. Flap (2004), 'Social networks and performance at work: A study of the returns of social capital in doing one's job', in H. Flap & B. Völker (eds.), *Creation and returns of social capital*, 172-196. London: Routledge.

Völker, B. & H. Flap (1995), 'The effects of institutional transformation on personal networks: East Germany, four years later', *The Netherlands' Journal of Social Science* 31 (2): 87-110.

Wagner, G. G., R. Burkhauser & F. Behringer (1993), 'The English language public use file of the German Socio-Economic Panel', *Journal of Human Resources* 28 (2): 429-433.

Waldinger, R. (2005), 'Networks and niches: The continuing significance of ethnic connections', in G. C. Loury, T. Modood & S. M. Teles (eds.), *Ethnicity, social mobility and public policy*, 342-362. Cambridge: Cambridge University Press.

Waldinger, R. (1995), 'The "other side" of embeddedness: A case-study of the interplay of economy and ethnicity', *Ethnic and Racial Studies* 18 (3): 555-580.

Waldinger, R. (1994), 'The making of an immigrant niche', *International Migration Review* 28 (1): 3-30.

Wiliams, C. C. (2005), 'Book review: The creation and destruction of social capital', *Journal of Rural Studies* 21 (3): 260-261.

Wilson, K. & A. Portes (1980), 'Immigrant enclaves: An analysis of the labor market experiences of Cubans in Miami', *American Journal of Sociology* 86: 295-317.

Wilson, W. J. (1987), *The truly disadvantaged*. Chicago: University of Chicago Press.

Woolcock, M. (1998), 'Social capital and economic development: Toward a theoretical synth-
    esis and policy framework', *Theory and Society* 27 (2): 151-208.
Woolcock, M. & D. Narayan (2000), 'Social capital: Implications for development theory, re-
    search and policy', *World Bank Research Observer* 15 (2): 225-249.
World Bank (2001), *World Development Report 2000/2001: Attacking poverty.* Oxford:
    Oxford University Press.
Wuthnow, R. (2002), 'Religious involvement and status-bridging social capital', *Journal for
    the Scientific Study of Religion* 41 (4): 669-684.

Zeng, Z. & Y. Xie (2004), 'Asian-Americans' earnings disadvantage reexamined: The role of
    place of education', *American Journal of Sociology* 109 (5): 1075-1108.
Zhou, M. (1992), *Chinatown: The socioeconomic potential of an urban enclave.* Philadelphia:
    Temple University Press.
Zhou, M. & C. L. Bankston (1998), *Growing up American: How Vietnamese children adapt
    to life in the United States.* New York: Russell Sage Foundation.
Zhou, M. & C. L. Bankston (1994), 'Social capital and the adaptation of the second genera-
    tion: The case of Vietnamese youth in New Orleans', *International Migration Review* 28
    (4): 821-845.
Zimmerman, K. F., H. Bonin, R. Fahr & H. Hinte (2007), *Immigration policy and the labor
    market.* Berlin: Springer.

Other IMISCOE titles

IMISCOE Research

Rinus Penninx, Maria Berger, Karen Kraal, Eds.
The Dynamics of International Migration and Settlement in Europe: A State of the Art
2006 (ISBN 978 90 5356 866 8)
(originally appearing in IMISCOE Joint Studies)

Leo Lucassen, David Feldman, Jochen Oltmer, Eds.
Paths of Integration: Migrants in Western Europe (1880-2004)
2006 (ISBN 978 90 5356 883 5)

Rainer Bauböck, Eva Ersbøll, Kees Groenendijk, Harald Waldrauch, Eds.
Acquisition and Loss of Nationality: Policies and Trends in 15 European Countries, Volume 1: Comparative Analyses
2006 (ISBN 978 90 5356 920 7)

Rainer Bauböck, Eva Ersbøll, Kees Groenendijk, Harald Waldrauch, Eds.
Acquisition and Loss of Nationality: Policies and Trends in 15 European Countries, Volume 2: Country Analyses
2006 (ISBN 978 90 5356 921 4)

Rainer Bauböck, Bernhard Perchinig, Wiebke Sievers, Eds.
Citizenship Policies in the New Europe
2007 (ISBN 978 90 5356 922 1)

Veit Bader
Secularism or Democracy? Associational Governance of Religious Diversity
2007 (ISBN 978 90 5356 999 3)

Holger Kolb, Henrik Egbert, Eds.
Migrants and Markets: Perspectives from Economics and the Other Social Sciences
2008 (ISNB 978 90 5356 684 8)

Ralph Grillo, Ed.
The Family in Question: Immigrant and Ethnic Minorities in Multicultural Europe
2008 (ISBN 978 90 5356 869 9)

Corrado Bonifazi, Marek Okólski, Jeannette Schoorl, Patrick Simon, Eds.
International Migration in Europe: New Trends and New Methods of Analysis
2008 (ISBN 978 90 5356 894 1)

Maurice Crul, Liesbeth Heering, Eds.
The Position of the Turkish and Moroccan Second Generation in Amsterdam and Rotterdam: The TIES Study in the Netherlands
2008 (ISBN 978 90 8964 061 1)

Marlou Schrover, Joanne van der Leun, Leo Lucassen, Chris Quispel, Eds.
Illegal Migration and Gender in a Global and Historical Perspective
2008 (ISBN 978 90 8964 047 5)

Gianluca P. Parolin
Citizenship in the Arab World: Kin, Religion and Nation-State
2009 (ISBN 978 90 8964 045 1)

Rainer Bauböck, Bernhard Perchinig, Wiebke Sievers, Eds.
Citizenship Policies in the New Europe: Expanded and Updated Edition
2009 (ISBN 978 90 8964 108 3)

Cédric Audebert, Mohamed Kamel Doraï, Eds.
Migration in a Globalised World: New Research Issues and Prospects
2010 (ISBN 978 90 8964 1571)

Richard Black, Godfried Engbersen, Marek Okólski, Cristina Pantîru, Eds.
A Continent Moving West? EU Enlargement and Labour Migration from Central and Eastern Europe
2010 (ISBN 978 90 8964 156 4)

Charles Westin, José Bastos, Janine Dahinden, Pedro Góis, Eds.
Identity Processes and Dynamics in Multi-Ethnic Europe
2010 (ISBN 978 90 8964 046 8)

Rainer Bauböck, Thomas Faist, Eds.
Diaspora and Transnationalism: Concepts, Theories and Methods
2010 (ISBN 978 90 8964 238 7)

Liza Mügge
Beyond Dutch Borders: Transnational Politics among Colonial Migrants, Guest Workers and the Second Generation
2010 (ISBN 978 90 8964 244 8)
Peter Scholten

Framing Immigrant Integration: Dutch Research-Policy Dialogues in Comparative Perspective
2011 (ISBN 978 90 8964 284 4)

Blanca Garcés-Mascareñas
State Regulation of Labour Migration in Malaysia and Spain: Markets, Citizenship and Rights
2011 (ISBN 978 90 8964 286 8)

Albert Kraler, Eleonore Kofman, Martin Kohli, Camille Schmoll, Eds.
Gender, Generations and the Family in International Migration
2011 (ISBN 978 90 8964 285 1)

Michael Bommes, Giuseppe Sciortino, Eds.
Foggy Social Structures: Irregular Migration, European Labour Markets and the Welfare State
2011 (ISBN 978 90 8964 341 4)

Giovanna Zincone, Rinus Penninx, Maren Borkert, Eds.
Migration Policymaking in Europe: The Dynamics of Actors and Contexts in Past and Present
2011 (ISBN 978 90 8964 370 4)

Julie Vullnetari
Albania on the Move: Links between Internal and International Migration
2011 (978 90 8964 355 1)

Marek Okólski, Ed.
European Immigrations: Trends, Structures and Policy Implications
2012, forthcoming

Ulbe Bosma, Ed.
Post-Colonial Immigrants and Identity Formations in the Netherlands
2012, forthcoming

IMISCOE Reports

Rainer Bauböck, Ed.
Migration and Citizenship: Legal Status, Rights and Political Participation
2006 (ISBN 978 90 5356 888 0)

Michael Jandl, Ed.
Innovative Concepts for Alternative Migration Policies: Ten Innovative Approaches to the Challenges of Migration in the 21st Century
2007 (ISBN 978 90 5356 990 0)

Jeroen Doomernik, Michael Jandl, Eds.
Modes of Migration Regulation and Control in Europe
2008 (ISBN 978 90 5356 689 3)

Michael Jandl, Christina Hollomey, Sandra Gendera, Anna Stepien, Veronika Bilger
Migration and Irregular Work In Austria: A Case Study of the Structure and Dynamics of Irregular Foreign Employment in Europe at the Beginning of the 21st Century
2008 (ISBN 978 90 8964 053 6)

Heinz Fassmann, Ursula Reeger, Wiebke Sievers, Eds.
Statistics and Reality: Concepts and Measurements of Migration in Europe
2009 (ISBN 978 90 8964 052 9)

Karen Kraal, Judith Roosblad, John Wrench, Eds.
Equal Opportunities and Ethnic Inequality in European Labour Markets: Discrimination, Gender and Policies of Diversity
2009 (ISBN 978 90 8964 126 7)

Tiziana Caponio, Maren Borkert, Eds.
The Local Dimension of Migration Policymaking
2010 (ISBN 978 90 8964 232 5)

Raivo Vetik, Jelena Helemäe, Eds.
The Russian Second Generation in Tallinn and Kohtla-Järve: The TIES Study in Estonia
2010 (ISBN 978 90 8964 250 9)

IMISCOE Dissertations

Panos Arion Hatziprokopiou
Globalisation, Migration and Socio-Economic Change in Contemporary Greece: Processes of Social Incorporation of Balkan Immigrants in Thessaloniki
2006 (ISBN 978 90 5356 873 6)

Floris Vermeulen
*The Immigrant Organising Process: Turkish Organisations in Amsterdam
and Berlin and Surinamese Organisations in Amsterdam, 1960-2000*
2006 (ISBN 978 90 5356 875 0)

Anastasia Christou
*Narratives of Place, Culture and Identity: Second-Generation
Greek-Americans Return 'Home'*
2006 (ISBN 978 90 5356 878 1)

Katja Rušinović
*Dynamic Entrepreneurship: First and Second-Generation Immigrant
Entrepreneurs in Dutch Cities*
2006 (ISBN 978 90 5356 972 6)

Ilse van Liempt
*Navigating Borders: Inside Perspectives on the Process of Human
Smuggling into the Netherlands*
2007 (ISBN 978 90 5356 930 6)

Myriam Cherti
*Paradoxes of Social Capital: A Multi-Generational Study of Moroccans
in London*
2008 (ISBN 978 90 5356 032 7)

Marc Helbling
*Practising Citizenship and Heterogeneous Nationhood: Naturalisations
in Swiss Municipalities*
2008 (ISBN 978 90 8964 034 5)

Jérôme Jamin
*L'imaginaire du complot: Discours d'extrême droite en France et
aux Etats-Unis*
2009 (ISBN 978 90 8964 048 2)

Inge Van Nieuwenhuyze
*Getting by in Europe's Urban Labour Markets: Senegambian Migrants'
Strategies for Survival, Documentation and Mobility*
2009 (ISBN 978 90 8964 050 5)

Nayla Moukarbel
*Sri Lankan Housemaids in Lebanon: A Case of 'Symbolic Violence' and
'Every Day Forms of Resistance'*
2009 (ISBN 978 90 8964 051 2)

John Davies
'My Name Is Not Natasha': How Albanian Women in France Use
Trafficking to Overcome Social Exclusion (1998-2001)
2009 (ISBN 978 90 5356 707 4)

Dennis Broeders
Breaking Down Anonymity: Digital Surveillance of Irregular Migrants
in Germany and the Netherlands
2009 (ISBN 978 90 8964 159 5)

Arjen Leerkes
Illegal Residence and Public Safety in the Netherlands
2009 (ISBN 978 90 8964 049 9)

Jennifer Leigh McGarrigle
Understanding Processes of Ethnic Concentration and Dispersal:
South Asian Residential Preferences in Glasgow
2009 (ISBN 978 90 5356 671 8)

João Sardinha
Immigrant Associations, Integration and Identity: Angolan, Brazilian
and Eastern European Communities in Portugal
2009 (ISBN 978 90 8964 036 9)

Elaine Bauer
The Creolisation of London Kinship: Mixed African-Caribbean and White
British Extended Families, 1950-2003
2010 (ISBN 978 90 8964 235 6)

Nahikari Irastorza
Born Entrepreneurs? Immigrant Self-Employment in Spain
2010 (ISBN 978 90 8964 243 1)

Marta Kindler
A Risky Business? Ukrainian Migrant Women in Warsaw's Domestic Work
Sector
2011 (ISBN 978 90 8964 3278)

IMISCOE Textbooks

Marco Martiniello, Jan Rath, Eds.
Selected Studies in International Migration and Immigrant Incorporation
2010 (ISBN 978 90 8964 1601)